GETTING IN!

The **Zinch® Guide** to College Admissions and Financial Aid in the Digital Age

By Steve Cohen, Anne Dwane, Paulo de Oliveira, Michael Muska

Wiley Publishing, Inc.

For general information on our other products and services or to obtain technical support please contact our Customer Care Department within the U.S. at (877) 762-2974, outside the U.S. at (317) 572-3993 or fax (317) 572-4002.

Wiley also publishes its books in a variety of electronic formats. Some content that appears in print may not be available in electronic books. For more information about Wiley products, please visit our web site at www.wiley.com.

Library of Congress Control Number: 2011922779
ISBN 978-1-118-00597-2 (pbk)
ISBN 978-1-118-04856-6 (ebk)

Printed in the United States of America

10 9 8 7 6 5 4 3 2 1

Book design and composition by Kristine Mudd
Cover design by José Almaguer

Table of Contents

4 Choosing the Right (vs. "Best") Colleges   77

5 Your Application Strategy   119

6 The Hook: Putting It All Together   161

7 Athletic Recruiting and College Admission   187

Foreword

There really was a fat envelope. And after getting a series of skinny-letter rejections, my anticipation was tempered by the improbability of this particular package. That's because it was from Princeton University. With my family gathered around, I tore it open like it was a present on Christmas morning. I fumbled through the papers nervously. And then I found it.

"Congratulations. You've been accepted to the Princeton University."

I couldn't believe it. It was the beginning of a new chapter of my life; a chapter that would transform my life.

I was a public school kid from a small town in Utah. And although I had worked hard and had a pretty good GPA and extracurricular activities, my standardized test scores were . . . well, unremarkable. They were so "average" that I never got a single brochure from an Ivy League or other top-tier college. I just wasn't on their radar screen. In fact, I was told repeatedly that not only wasn't I going to get "recruited" by a top school, but my ACT scores were probably going to keep me out entirely.

Despite this discouraging advice, I threw myself into the college admission process with gusto. I put together a portfolio to showcase my basketball achievements, computer science awards, and photography. I was convinced that if the colleges got to know the real me, they would surely be impressed. My tagline was "I am more than a test score."

And yes, it worked. Later, once on the Princeton campus, one of the admissions officers approached me and said, "I remember you." I asked how he could possibly remember me from all the tens of thousands of applications. He replied, "How could anyone forget?" He went on to say that the entire admissions office was impressed with what I had sent in; it put me on the map.

I spent much of my freshman year at Princeton thinking about how the digital revolution that was changing education and society had been totally ignored by the college admission process. Colleges were stuck in the stone age, sending direct mail brochures to kids based largely on their standardized test scores. It didn't make sense to me. In an age of digital and social media, there had to be a better way.

I started Zinch in my dorm room at Princeton, convinced there was a more effective way to allow students to express their talents and interests, and for colleges to discover and connect with kids who would do well on their particular campuses.

Along the way, I met Steve. His story about how he created *Getting In*—which he wrote with Paulo, his classmate and former Brown admission officer—more than 25 years ago sounded remarkably similar to my own. Steve had recently been through the admissions process with his two sons and saw the things that had changed—and not changed—since his own college applications. Finally, Steve introduced us all to Mike, one of the most experienced and respected admission professionals in the country. It was a "perfect storm" for an admissions revolution.

College can be an extraordinary experience. But that very much depends on finding the right college—not just the "best" college—getting in, figuring out how to pay for it, and then making the most of it.

This book—and Zinch—are dedicated to helping you do just that.

Now, let's get going!

—Mick Hagen
Founder, Zinch

Acknowledgments

Enormous thanks to our agent-extraordinaire, Lisa Leshne; our editor Kristi Hart, who really knows how to edit and add value; our supporters and friends Ronnie and Bob Bailin, Monica Wambold, Stephen Rudin, and Chris Michel, and our designer Kristine Mudd.

We also want to thank the truly professional colleagues who inspired and supported us through the years: Ted McLaughlin, Ken O'Brien, Mel Rosen, Bob and Anne Rothenberg, Carl Bewig, Alice Purington, Susan Case, Chuck Duncan, Mike Goldberger, Eric Widmer, Debra Chermonte, Paul Marthers, Chris Ajemian, Sally McGinty, Nancy Meislahn, Tom Parker and our friends and colleagues at Poly Prep: Susan Beiles, Amy Kohn, Jackie Kornblum, Pam Pratt-Galik, John Rearick, and especially Headmaster David Harman, who really understands this process. Plus David Blake, Sean Castillo, Angela Chang, Christopher Girgenti, Nathaniel Hancock, Michael J. Levinthal, Thomas Melcher, and Ashley Sherwin.

For their help on this book, we particularly want to thank Scott Farber at A-List Education, Sonia Arora at Chicago, John Birney at Johns Hopkins, Alyssa Ellowitch at Muhlenberg, Jami Silver at Wesleyan, Lee Coffin, Karen Richardson, David Kochman, and the students from Tufts who shared their essays with us; the many students and parents we have worked with over the years who have helped us learn; and Sharon Cuseo at Harvard-Westlake and the Los Angeles Area Independent School Case Studies Program, who developed the case studies used in the book.

Personally, we want to thank our parents, who have inspired us, and our life partners, spouses, and kids who get us through each day, a bit happier, excited and ready to face the next: Evan, Elizabeth, Isabel Ian, Sarah, Peter, and Jacob.

About the Authors

Steve Cohen Steve has been a publishing entrepreneur, author, and teacher for more than 25 years. A former marketing executive and publisher at Time and Scholastic, he is the founder and CEO of Brainquest.com, Multimedicus—created with Harvard and Dartmouth Medical Schools—and iCollegeBound. He has been an adjunct faculty member at NYU, Fordham, and at the Stanford Publishing Course. In addition, he has lectured at Dartmouth, Brown, and Columbia Business School. Steve cochaired the Clinton White House literacy task force Prescription for Reading Partnership. He is a Director Emeritus of the pediatric literacy initiative, Reach Out and Read, and the United States Naval Institute. Steve attended the United States Naval Academy, received his AB from Brown, attended the University of California at Berkeley for graduate school, and is currently a candidate for a Juris Doctor at New York Law School.

Anne Dwane Anne is President and CEO of Zinch, the network connecting 3 million students globally with colleges, scholarships, and graduate schools. As an entrepreneur, she is passionate about applying technology to education and college access, and enhancing career opportunities. In 1999, Anne cofounded Military.com to connect service members and veterans to their benefits, including GI Bill and tuition assistance. Military.com now serves over 10 million members and was acquired by Monster Worldwide in 2004. At Monster, Anne led several businesses as General Manager, Affinity Networks. Previously, she was in business development at Paul Allen's Interval Research Corporation in Silicon Valley, and in brand management for Nabisco's Planters Peanuts. Anne holds a bachelors degree in Marketing and International Management from Georgetown University and an MBA from the Harvard Business School. She is a member of the 2010 class of Henry Crown Fellows at the Aspen Institute.

Paulo de Oliveira After graduating from Brown University, Paulo began his working life as an admission officer and Assistant Director of Admission there. He went on to a 25-year career as a television programming executive and producer, working at companies including HBO, The Disney Channel, Universal Television, and NBC-Universal and developing shows such as *Monk, Battlestar Galactica,* and *Eureka.* He now lives in the San Francisco Bay Area, where he is cofounder of an Internet startup and is a consultant on content development to traditional TV and Web 2.0 companies.

Michael Muska Mike is currently completing his first decade as Dean of College Relations at Poly Prep Country Day School in Brooklyn, New York. He previously worked in college counseling at Phillips Andover and Milton Academy in Massachusetts. Mike spent six years at Brown University in Admissions and Athletics and in a similar capacity at Oberlin College in Ohio. His early career in athletics was highlighted by twice being named the Southeastern Conference Coach of the Year in cross country while at Auburn University, and once as the Big Ten Coach of the Year at Northwestern University. During those years, he coached more than 20 Division I All-Americans. As an openly gay male, Mike became a national spokesman for gay student-athletes while serving as Oberlin College's athletic director, and he continues to lecture across the country on creating safe opportunities for all student-athletes. Having worked in so many arenas of admission, college counseling and athletics, Mike is respected by college professionals and counseling colleagues and has served on numerous panels at both the NACAC and College Board Meetings. He graduated with honors in history from the University of Connecticut and earned his master's degree in Sports Studies and Administration from the University of Massachusetts. He resides in Brooklyn with his partner, Evan Sweet.

Introduction

"War is hell!"
(For extra credit, who said that?)*

Many people think college admission falls into that category. More kids are applying to more colleges than ever before. Plus, there is a significant influx of foreign students seeking admission to American colleges and universities. As a result, the odds of being admitted to most good schools are getting tougher and tougher.

Stress over which college to attend—and then how to get in—gets pretty intense for many families. Arguments abound; deadlines loom; nagging over essays is common; and anxiety about how to pay for it is the norm.

So our goal is to help reduce the anxiety. We do that by making you smarter about your choices and about the admission and financial aid process. We can't guarantee admission to the college of your choice—no one can! (And you should beware of anyone who tries to make that promise, whether consultants, coaches, or congressmen!) But we can help you improve your odds of making better college choices, getting in, and securing the money to pay for your college education.

Why This Book

The first edition of this book was published way back in 1983, literally a generation ago. At the time, one of us was still marveling over the fact that we had been admitted to—and graduated from—an Ivy League university. Steve was convinced that

his acceptance at Brown was an act of providence, proof-positive that miracles never cease.

Paulo, Steve's classmate and friend at Brown, had just finished a five-year stint as an admission officer at Brown

---

*William Tecumseh Sherman, in a letter to the Mayor and City Council of Atlanta—before he marched on, and burned the city.

and was moving on to a successful career as a television producer. Mike, who had just been named an NCAA Southeastern Conference (SEC) Coach of the Year for his work with the track team at Auburn, was about to transition into admissions work. And Anne—well, Anne was just a kid at the time, and Georgetown and Harvard Business School weren't even on her radar screen.

Back in 1983 *Getting In!* caused a bit of a revolution in the admissions world and became a best-seller. At the time there were several books offering admissions advice. Most were pretty good. But *Getting In!* struck a responsive chord among students, parents, and college counselors. Sales soared and we (Paulo and Steve) appeared in dozens of newspapers and magazines as well as on television and radio. (Not only was there no Internet, but there were hardly any personal computers and no cell phones at all.)

Exactly why *Getting In!* connected with folks is open to debate. Yes, we explained the admissions process candidly. True, we introduced the concepts of "packaging and positioning." Our case studies—putting the reader in the admission officer's chair having to make tough decisions—were a first. The book's appealing design helped make the information come off the page. No doubt all of those factors contributed to its success.

And none of that is sufficient to do the job today.

The admissions process is still pretty much the same today as it was when we wrote the first edition. Applicants still submit applications and write essays. Counselors and teachers still write recommendations. And admission committees still deliberate over whom to admit—though it has become much more competitive at all selective schools.

What has changed is the world. And a big part of that is how we now do things via technology. Our perspectives and our experiences also expanded. Steve helped his kids go through the college search and admissions process three times in five years. Paulo continued to advise and assess prospective Brown students through the alumni interview program. Mike went on to help run admissions at some of the top colleges in the country, and then to counsel students as Dean of College Counseling as several of the most prestigious private schools in the country. And Anne became CEO of the most revolutionary social networking Internet site for college-bound students. It was this "perfect storm" of family needs and professional experience that led us to team up and write this completely new book.

The Best Way to Use This Book

To take best advantage of this book, you should follow these six moderately easy steps.

1. Read it.

You should really read the book from beginning to end at least once. Don't worry about details or specific recommendations, or how to apply them to your own situation. Reading the book from cover to cover—even very quickly—will give you an overview of the admission process, and what we mean by "packaging" and "positioning" yourself. This will prove invaluable when you get down to specifics.

A Note on the Editorial "We"

In order to make sure the advice we offer is as clearly stated as possible, we decided to employ the "editorial we" as our voice of choice. (Now don't think that wasn't a mouthful!) It is a collective "we;" our combined experiences and advice. That said, however, we occasionally depart from it, mentioning one of the authors by name or including sidebars signed by the individual author. Sometimes those are personal stories or even dissenting opinions.

We also use a broad "you." Generally, the "you" refers to you the student. This book is written first for students; college choice is your decision; the application yours. But we also know that parents can be heavily invested in the process. And influential. So we also assume parents are reading this—sometimes more carefully than students. When there is some part of the process specifically affecting parents, we say so. And we suspect some college counselors and admission folks will read this too.

2. Ask your parents to read it.

Most parents know very little about the college admission process or know it from 20-plus years ago—things have changed. It's important that all of you be liberated from the myths that surround college admissions.

3. Start early.

Optimally you should read this book, and begin your college search, no later than the middle of your junior year. It may help to start earlier, but until your junior year you won't have a proper grasp of the record—grades and SATs/ACTs—you'll be presenting to the colleges. If you start later than that, you will be scrambling.

4. Role play.

The case studies in Appendix A are designed to give you a feel for what various admission committees think of a particular applicant. Put yourself in the role of admission officer and evaluate each one. Ask your parents to role play as admission officers as well. By doing this, you'll be better prepared to evaluate your own application. The actual decisions made in each case, as well as explanations of those decisions, are provided. But don't peek at the "answers" until you've actually played admission officer. We purposely placed them at the end so you might have an overview of the process before you role play.

5. Reread the appropriate chapter.

Your first reading should have given you real insight into the admission process. As you create your application, return to the relevant chapter and prepare. Prepare for the interview; prepare for the essay; prepare for the campus visit. The chapters on these subjects contain specific recommendations that should make the whole process less bewildering and alienating—and more manageable. The information they provide can make a difference.

6. Work smarter, not harder.

If you are serious about getting into a good school, you are probably already putting in a lot of effort. This book should not make you work harder at being admitted. Instead, it is designed to enable you to work smarter. Doing well in your courses, preparing for the SATs/ACTs, and excelling at extracurricular activities must remain your principal objectives. Your college application efforts should not interfere with them. This book provides you with the information and tools to enable you to make the most of what you've got without taking too much of your time.

How to Improve Your Odds

The purpose of this book is three-fold and quite simple:

1. To help you figure out what you *may* want to do in college and identify which colleges and universities might be right for you.

2. To demystify college admissions and improve your chances of getting into those *right* schools.

3. To help you and your family understand the financial options available to you and put together the necessary funding.

Note that we say what you *may* want to do in college. You may think that you absolutely positively know what you want to major in while in college. And perhaps you even know what you want to do when you graduate. We applaud you and encourage you. But even you folks who are absolutely certain you know what you want to major in, what type of graduate program you intend to pursue, and which career paths have your name stamped in gold-leaf along that path, may just change your mind. Here's a fact: fully 79% of students said they "definitely knew" or were "pretty sure" what they wanted to major in. But according to a study by Penn State, 70% of students change their major at least once while in college, and 20% change it two or more times. So be prepared for the possibility of changing your mind. We address this in depth in later chapters.

In Chapter 5 we focus on tools to help you choose the "right" college, and we make a very clear distinction between the right college and the so-called "best" college. This distinction is one of the most critical you need to understand. Because, odds are, there are lots of "prestigious" colleges where you might be able to get admitted—and then be incredibly unhappy. So our first goal is to help you really figure out which colleges might be right for you and then help you get into those places.

Finally, you—and probably your family—have to figure out how to pay for the colleges that might be right for you. And yes, asking for financial aid can affect your chances of admission at some colleges. So we'll address the strategic and tactical issues accompanying what is known as **need-aware admissions.**

Here is the overview of how this book helps you maximize your chances of admission at the college of your choice:

1. It explains what colleges are looking for in prospective students. You will learn how admission policy reflects institutional needs—needs for football players, for alumni offspring whose parents can help build a new library, for cellists for the university orchestra, for classicists or chemists or aspiring historians to keep academic departments happy, for "nice kids" to maintain the school's social life. Once you can identify and analyze these needs, you'll better understand what they mean in terms of your admission.

2. It demystifies the admission process: what the information in the application means, how it is evaluated, and how a decision is finally made. Most people—be they students, parents, or teachers—simply do not understand the realities of college admissions.

3. It discusses ways to improve the quality of the information in your application and how to communicate—or "package"— that information. Your interview, your essay, your selection of an intended major, and a dozen other factors can make a difference. We will show you how to provide more useful information to the admission committee.

4. It explains how to set yourself apart from the thousands of other applicants with whom you'll be competing—to "position" yourself so that you stand out from the crowd and to package yourself in the most effective way. Having that special "hook"—the one thing that an admission officer will remember and peg your acceptance on—is a key element of your strategy.

5. It clarifies the financial aspects of paying for college, applying for financial aid, and making sense of recent changes in the college aid system. By understanding how aid is distributed, how to complete appropriate forms like the FAFSA and Profile, and how to navigate the college loan process, you'll be able to put together the most suitable package for yourself.

While the purpose of this book is to enhance your chances of getting into the college of your choice, we will not claim—and you should not deceive yourself—that there is any instant formula for admission. College admission is a complex business. There are no secret answers that will trigger an automatic acceptance. What we do offer you, however, are tools: tools to understand schools, their applications, and their admission committees.

CHAPTER 1

The Truth About College Admissions

1

Hype, buzz, terror, and misconception. That pretty much sums up the world of college admission. It's hard not to be intimidated by the process or the prospects.

Given the level of alarm about the competition for slots at America's best colleges, it's not surprising that a slew of myths about the process have gained credence. Just looking at the sheer number of applicants in recent years, the prospect of applying can seem incredibly daunting and intimidating. You might even conclude that Thomas Jefferson wouldn't be able to get into the University of Virginia today.

But when you begin to look under the surface—and actually analyze both statistics and the conventional wisdom about how the system really works—you'll find that much of it is misleading. And a lot of it is outright wrong! What is routinely thought to be "the word" really isn't true at all. And, more importantly, there are very real ways to counter the competitiveness of the process—and better your odds.

First, we address some of the most popular misconceptions about the admission sweepstakes. We're going to burst a few bubbles and tell you the truth about each one. This chapter is an overview to get you started, and we'll go into more detail on each point later in the book. That's where we reveal the really good stuff: how to figure out which colleges are right for you, how to improve your odds of admission at those places, and how to pay for your education.

We also let you in on some important "trade secrets" that colleges would rather you didn't know. Then as a savvy consumer, you'll be better able to read (and listen) between the lines as you do your research. And you can better judge what each school has to offer—and how it compares to the other schools you're interested in.

The Top 10 Myths of College Admissions

1. The top colleges are looking for well-rounded applicants.

The top colleges *aren't* looking for well-rounded kids. They're looking for a well-rounded **class.** Every school has institutional needs it must fulfill. That means they need scholars for every academic department, athletes for each team, performers for every arts group, and even some "really nice" kids to organize hall-hockey.

So what does that mean for you? You have assets; you have something the college wants to make up that well-rounded class. How you identify those assets—in the context of the school's needs—is what we refer to as **positioning.** How you communicate your positioning becomes your **packaging.**

Importantly, positioning and packaging become as important to the harried admission officer as they are to you. Giving that hard-working person an easy "handle" or "hook" and showcasing your strengths helps the college and helps you.

2. The more extracurriculars, the better.

Once you understand that top colleges are looking for the well-rounded class rather than kid, you'll recognize that admission officers don't really care about a student having a laundry list of extracurricular activities. They would much rather see a student who excelled at one or two activities and who attained a leadership position in just one. And even better, admission officers love kids who did surprisingly well in those pursuits. Find your passion and let the admission officer find it in you as well.

3. Great extracurriculars and talents are the keys to getting in.

FUHGETABOUTIT! What really count are your grades and SAT/ACT scores. Only after you qualify on those two measures—grades and test scores—does everything else come into play. Extracurricular activities, athletic skill, musical, artistic, or theatrical talent, background, overcoming unusual hardship, personality, and the institutional needs of the college in a given year all come into play. But to make it into the admissions sweepstakes you've got to have an academic "ticket."

4. Admission officers secretly enjoy rejecting all those applicants.

No, they really don't. Most admission officers are aware that a majority of candidates are qualified to be at their college, and they don't relish denying that opportunity to good kids. But every selective college has more qualified applicants than it can possibly admit—and thus admission folks will be looking for reasons to deny applicants as well as accept them. So, they quickly dismiss applications that don't pass muster. The easiest to reject are

- Those with stupid mistakes on their application: misspellings, essay questions answered thoughtlessly or not at all, or pieces of the application left blank or missing altogether.

- Those in which applicants come across as arrogant, grade-obsessed, or narrow preprofessionals.

- Applicants who fail to show genuine interest in that college.

Aren't the Rules Different for Top Athletes?

Yes, the rules are different for the very top athletes. But 95% of you aren't world-class top athletes. You may be absolutely capable of competing at the collegiate varsity level, and you may even get recruited or win an athletic scholarship. But you're still not at that level where academics are less significant. For 95% of college athletes, grades and SAT/ACT scores really do count. We devote a whole chapter—Chapter 8—to this subject.

5. By the time I apply, the die is cast—and there's not a lot I can do to improve my chances.

It is difficult to overcome a weak or spotty academic record. But if you are in the academically acceptable (but not strong) zone, there are things you can do to better your odds. The fact is that most applicants fall into a middle group of qualified—but not "killer"—applicants. This means that in committee sessions, the admission officers like having a clear hook or positioning for each student. It helps to categorize, assess, and justify accepting or denying an applicant: "Another grade-obsessed pre-med from a high-powered suburban New Jersey high school." Or, "Interesting, bright Mendocino, California, flower-child home-schooled by organic farmer parents." (Who would you rather hang out with at college?)

So, while not having a solid academic record will make your chances of admission to a good school more difficult, it won't make it impossible.

6. Get as many recommendations and letters of reference as possible.

There is an expression in the admissions world: "The thicker the folder, the thicker the kid."

Many parents think they should secure extra recommendations for their student from business leaders, politicians, or people with connections to the college. Bad idea! Unless the recommender really knows the applicant—preferably through a work or academic experience—don't do it. A vague or uninformed reference is worse than no reference at all. An application folder stuffed with letters of recommendation from "high-powered" references is not appreciated by any admission officer. They are often vague and quickly recognized as favors being done for the applicant's parents. And they backfire with an admission officer burning the midnight oil in order to get through her nightly quota of applications.

This is also true for your teacher, counselor, and employer references as well. Make sure they come from people who know you well and who can write something thoughtful and meaningful about you. You don't want recommendations that are well-meaning but vague or filled with generalizations—because you really didn't take a course from, or work for, that person.

7. Send lots of stuff to the admission office to prove how interested you are.

Just as you shouldn't inundate the admission office with extraneous recommendations, think long and hard if you are submitting examples of your work to the admission committee. Whatever you send them (special projects, art, photos, awards, etc.) better be pretty impressive or unique.

In one illustrative case, a young man sent the admission office an Excel spreadsheet listing all the movies he had ever seen—complete with each movie's director, actors, and notable crew members. He was trying to prove how interested he was in the entertainment industry. But, rather than being impressive, it contributed to a picture of the applicant as a grind. This became especially apparent as he made no effort to get involved with the drama club or an independent filmmaking project, or even to volunteer at a local film festival.

As an alternative, think of how to use technology to your benefit. Providing a link to your website, a YouTube video, or a well-produced short DVD gives an interested admission officer an opportunity to investigate you further without weighing down your file.

8. It's getting harder than ever to get admitted to a top college.

Many educators and journalists said that 2010 was the toughest ever to get into a top college. This was the result of three factors: the largest high school graduating class in history, seniors submitting more applications to more colleges, and a larger number of international kids interested in top name colleges. Fortunately, the number of kids in the senior class will now decline for each of the next few years. Add to that the weak economy and families deciding on less-expensive state and community colleges, and the combination may ease the severe admissions pressure just a bit. But don't expect the competition for getting into a top college to change dramatically. The value proposition of "name" schools will keep admissions formidable for years to come.

But believe it or not, it's still a buyer's market—if you are willing to do some research and not just focus on the obvious popular choices

What Your College Investment "Buys"

The "value proposition" of college is often described as the second-largest expenditure a family will ever make—after one's home. As with any significant investment, one expects a return on that investment. That return may be in the quality of the education, the enjoyment of the experience, the marketability of the degree, or all of those things. Everyone derives value—in different degrees and in different measures—from going to a college. You should think seriously about what that value proposition is for you.

in "top" colleges. For all the hype and stress of college admissions, far more schools accept more applicants than they reject—even some of the name schools.

That doesn't mean the competition isn't tough; it is. But once you get beyond the top 50 or so colleges and universities, the acceptance rate is typically above 50%. Admission is still a daunting prospect, but smart targeting and a good application should give you a fighting chance of getting in.

9. Admission statistics don't lie.

As Mark Twain once wrote, "There are three types of lies: lies, damn lies, and statistics." Admission statistics don't lie—too much. But they can be misleading.

For example, what's the number-one most selective institution of higher learning in the country? Did you guess Harvard? Stanford? Princeton? Sorry, you're wrong. The answer is the Curtis Institute of Music. In the fall of 2007, Curtis had the lowest acceptance rate in the country—only 4.8%. That is far more selective than Harvard's 7%, Stanford's 8%, or Princeton's 10%. Why? Because Curtis is a small specialty school that attracts many of the nation's top musicians—those who are looking for music-oriented education. So kids self-select, and admission is very competitive.

The raw numbers of admission are useful—up to a point. Believe it or not, more than a few colleges try to encourage applications from students who don't really have a chance of getting in—in order to reject them. Why? Because a college's selectivity rate improves its standing in the *U.S. News & World Report* "Best Colleges" rankings. It's a little sick, but it's a fact.

Throughout this book we'll focus on various statistics—SAT/ACT scores in the mid-percentile ranks, yield numbers, early admission acceptance rates versus regular admission, legacy admissions. We'll explain each one in the appropriate context.

But just remember: the numbers don't lie, but they don't necessarily tell the whole truth either.

10. Kids from private, prep, or high-powered public schools always do better in the admission sweepstakes.

Not necessarily. Schools like Harvard, Stanford, Yale, Brown, and the like see scores of applicants from good public school systems. They also receive lots of applications from notable private and boarding schools nationwide. In fact, applying from one of those "name" places can actually be a disadvantage. That's because so many applicants come every year from these high-powered towns and schools that it makes each candidate seem less unique.

For example, it's always refreshing to admission gatekeepers to see applicants from rural areas. In fact, all other things being equal, a kid from a small-town school no one has ever heard of will have a better chance of getting in than a kid from a well-known high school. That well-known or high-powered school may routinely have 10 or more kids all applying to the same college. So not only are they vying for acceptance against the national applicant pool, they're competing against their classmates! There is one downside to the small, unfamiliar, rural applicant's high school: the admission officer may not know much about the rural school's rigor or grading policy but is well aware of the well-known school's standards.

Now, there's not a lot you can do about where you go to school— unless you are reading this early in your high school career and are ready to move to Montana—so you may as well avoid obsessing about things you can't control. Instead, focus on how to improve your chances with the factors you *can* control. That's what we discuss throughout the book. And if you are applying from a high school that's never before sent anyone to the college of your dreams, we'll tell you how to turn that into an asset as well.

The Truth About "Best College" Rankings

Every year, like clockwork, a half-dozen magazines and newspapers publish their rankings of the "best" colleges. Some are insightful; others are fun; a few are meaningless. The real question is how can they help you?

The granddaddy of all college rankings is the *U.S. News & World Report* annual rankings of "America's Best Colleges." It's been around since 1983. The *Princeton Review* has been surveying college students for years to generate top-10 lists of characteristics that often mean more to students—such as quality of life, political activism, and sex-drugs-and rock-and-roll. (My favorite is Dodgeball Targets.) And, of course, there is *Playboy's* annual pronouncement of the best party schools.

Whether they like to admit it or not, college administrators jump through hoops to improve their ranking every year.

Why? The answer is simple: money and bragging rights. Colleges that rank higher attract more applicants. That, in turn, means less pressure to control tuition increases. It is simple supply and demand. But an equally significant reason colleges make substantive changes, tweak their statistics, and sometimes lie outright in order to improve their ranking is that a higher ranking means better bragging rights. And inasmuch as most colleges and universities are not-for-profit organizations, bragging rights are the equivalent of . . . well, something.

Be forewarned: many thoughtful people—those without an axe to grind or a place on the list to explain or defend—think the rankings are just plain wrong. Edward Fiske, the long-time Education Editor of the *New York Times* and creator of the best-selling *Fiske Guide to Colleges* probably makes the clearest case. He says, "There are two fundamental problems with the rankings. First, they lead parents and students to ask the wrong question. Instead of asking, 'What's the best college?' students and parents should be asking, 'What's the best college for me?' Second, the rankings are compiled based solely on inputs; really they are just a measurement of institutional wealth. And this works against the entire public sector. Although *U.S. News & World Report* separates public from private colleges, you would never get the sense from their rankings that the

University of Michigan or Berkeley were among the great universities of the world. And that's a disservice."

So, should these rankings make a difference to where you go? Or at least to what schools you consider?

The honest answer is: probably. And there are two reasons for this. First, some of the rankings—the *Princeton Review's,* for example—give a pretty good insight, from the students' perspective, of what a place is really like. These subjective assessments and candid comments can be useful.

Second, you will be paying a lot of money for college. No, modify that: you're not just paying, you're investing a lot. And, after four years, you will want a return on your investment. Part of that "ROI" will be a function of what you put into your college experience: how hard you work, what courses you take, what experiences you take advantage of, and what friendships and connections you make. But part of it is also "brand equity." When, after graduation, you say, "I went to X College," does that statement elicit recognition or a blank look?

Here's the not-so-secret "dirty little secret": some colleges do open more doors—at least initially—than do others. If you don't think that having a Harvard-Yale-Princeton-Stanford-or-other-"prestigious"-college degree makes a difference, you are being naïve. More doors are opened more quickly, but they don't guarantee anyone a job. And not having a degree from one of these "top" schools certainly doesn't reduce your chances of a successful, fulfilling career. As a first step along the career path, though, they can provide a bit of a head start.

Brand recognition should not be the determining factor in where you choose to go to college, but we'd be fibbing if we suggested it shouldn't—or won't—be a factor.

One important reminder: do not get hung up on whether a particular school is number 17 versus its crosstown rival which is number 14. Don't get into the minutiae; try to keep a big-picture perspective. Rankings differ from list to list and year to year. And they are largely subjective!

10 Things Colleges Don't Want You to Know

Most colleges are nonprofit institutions. Most also have a lofty sense of mission. But that doesn't mean they aren't managed like businesses—particularly those schools that must work harder to get applicants and enrollees. Administrators and admission officers have their trade secrets just like executives in other businesses. And the angst and perceived secrecy surrounding the admission process help create a mystique for their schools. That mystique (or mystification) is, if not encouraged, at least not discouraged by the colleges' gatekeepers.

We're here to tell you that there's nothing sacrosanct or sacred about what admission officers do. Their decisions grow largely out of institutional needs such as achieving full enrollment; keeping the faculty and alumni happy; maintaining athletic programs; keeping student groups and other campus activities vibrant; having a well-balanced class; and preserving the image and legacy of the school. This is not a cynical observation, but rather one that acknowledges the best of what colleges do: educate and socialize young people.

You should enter into the process with eyes open and be neither overawed nor overconfident. To that end, here are 10 things that admission officers would prefer that you not know.

1. It is a buyer's market.

Believe it or not, you are in a better position than you realize. That doesn't mean you can play Yale against Princeton, unless you are a phenomenal applicant; or USC against UCLA, if you are a very good one. But only about 65 colleges nationwide reject more applicants than they accept. Among the remainder, there are still many excellent and well-regarded institutions. And this is the group you want to focus on in terms of your core school choices (vs. your reaches).

2. Attracting good applicants is a competitive business— for the colleges.

Get on a college's radar screen early and enable them to come after you. There are a number of ways to accomplish that—such as connecting with a particular professor about her work and *demonstrating* your own interest and abilities in the area. The easiest way is to utilize Zinch. (Yes, this is a plug for Zinch; we partnered with them because we think what they're doing is smart and effective.)

3. More than a few colleges cook the books to achieve a better "ranking."

The U.S. News & World Report "Best Colleges" rankings drive university administrators nuts. As a result, more than a few have been known to misrepresent the data that they provide to the magazine for its calculations. (The most recent involved a well-known university in South Carolina. They fudged the number of small classes offered by the university. The result pushed them from a ranking of 38 to 22.) If the rankings are important to you, make sure you do a

---

Use Social Media to Get on the Radar of Your Dream Schools

Social media can be a way for you to get on the radar of your dream schools. This is important because 76% of colleges said that demonstrated interest played at least some role in admissions decisions. And 20% of colleges now place considerable importance on demonstrated interest when making admissions decisions. College campus visits and information requests also get you on the radar.

On the flip side, including a link to your social media profile, blog, video, or website can help you put your best foot forward—and to show the admission officer what differentiates you "at a glance." Many schools list their optional application elements, and we discuss that in Chapter 6.

Most colleges monitor social media sites where they maintain a presence. "Liking," commenting on, or otherwise engaging with a college's social media site can start a conversation or get you noticed.

Google search to see if there have been any negative stories suggesting less-than-kosher behavior by the colleges you're interested in.

4. Don't get snookered by the rankings.

First, the magazine rankings are often very misleading. They reflect a formula that purports to be objective. But objective criteria like class size, student-faculty ratio, alumni giving, and the number of volumes in the library can't capture the subtle but more important factors that determine just a how good a college really is: the quality of the faculty, the school's location, its physical attributes, and, probably most important—and elusive—the happiness of the student body. Second, there are lots of sub-lists that allow colleges to tout their rankings. By now all colleges know how to spin their numbers to make things sound better. Third, you should ask yourself what value the rankings have *to you?* If it is simply "brand" recognition, that's OK; but recognize it for what it is. The important thing is to be sure to take any of the rankings with healthy doses of salt.

5. Colleges have personalities.

No one would ever confuse Brown with Princeton. Or Georgetown with Wesleyan. Rankings don't reflect personality, and personality is often far more important to a student ultimately being happy on a campus. Where you're happy, you'll excel—academically and otherwise. So do your research. And after you get your fat envelopes, don't enroll at a "name" college that doesn't really excite you. You're probably better off at a school that has less cache but fits you better.

6. Stereotypes are sometimes true.

Often the rumors about a college campus are indeed on target. One well-known Ivy is known as "the gay Ivy." A major Midwest state college is reputed to be populated largely by kids from Long Island. How accurate are these stereotypes? Often more on target than a school wants to admit. If you are concerned that these stories paint a picture of a place where you may not be happy, it is worth your

Colleges' Biggest Secret: Why Colleges Market Themselves

Every college markets itself. Yes, even Harvard, Yale, Stanford, the Naval Academy—you name it—they all sell themselves to students. While their methods may be more subtle and low key than that of diploma mills, even the top colleges know they have to pitch themselves to students.

Although the most prestigious schools promote themselves only to a limited, highly desirable group of students—the very top academic prospects, musicians, athletes, etc.—it is still marketing. Not surprisingly, a school like Harvard is competing against Yale, Princeton, Stanford, and a handful of other extremely selective schools.

Now, follow the model to the next level. Highly selective liberal arts colleges—let's say Middlebury, Bates, Bowdoin, Colby—are also competing for the best student candidates. These schools are competing against each other as well as against liberal arts schools in Pennsylvania and Ohio, and even against Pomona and Claremont-McKenna. Who is Duke competing against? How about USC? Or Syracuse? Or the University of Wisconsin? Every school has competition, and they all spend significant sums of money going after students, trying to lure them to apply to—and attend—their college rather than their cross-town or cross-country rival.

Colleges market to students—and sometimes to parents—in a variety of ways. It starts with college fairs and proceeds to the direct-mail brochures you often receive after taking the SATs/ACTs. (Colleges will buy lists of students who score above certain thresholds—that's why you high scorers get all that mail from schools you've never heard of!) Marketing then extends to their website, the admission office orientation you typically sit through when you visit a college, and the student-led campus tour. It might also include application fee waivers and even use of the Common App. Each is designed to make your life a little easier and thus encourage you to submit an application.

For those of you who aren't yet familiar with the Common App, it is a free online application used by more than 400 colleges. We discuss it in Chapter 5.

time and effort to track down their veracity. After all, West Point and Annapolis offer great educations—but they are certainly not for everyone.

7. Colleges play up what you "think" is important.

For example, colleges always talk about their terrific student-faculty ratio. Unfortunately, that number is largely misleading. So are measurements of the percentage of classes with fewer than 20 students. Both of these measures are typically included in various guidebooks and rankings, and both are good examples of how colleges "cook the books."

At most schools, you'll probably have to take some large lecture classes—and you shouldn't worry too much about them in your freshman year. They are part of the college experience. More important are questions like these: How many upper-level undergraduate courses are taught by full professors? (One very prestigious Ivy is known for elusive faculty who tend to stick to research and grad students.) Are they available to all undergraduates or reserved for students in a particular major? Similarly, how accessible are small seminar courses to undergrads? The point? Don't get snookered by—or hung up on—college-reported statistics.

8. Every school has weird traditions.

Some are cute; others are a bit bizarre. Painting "A" mountain before the first football game at Arizona State is a big tradition at ASU. Unfortunately, students do it in the 110-degree heat of late August. Alternatively, at Bennington, there is a tradition of scheduling "cross-dressing night" on the first evening of Parents' Weekend. The students seem to love it, but more than a few visiting parents are in shock. Be sure to explore some of these more quaint traditions, and think about whether you'd be comfortable participating in them.

9. Colleges are businesses.

As we said earlier, most colleges are nonprofit institutions, but they do operate on a profit-and-loss basis. And in tough economic cycles, it is very useful to see what a particular college has cut back on—or what fees they've increased. Those choices will often give you an insight into what the school considers most valuable.

10. Colleges are political institutions.

They have powerful constituencies that must be attended to—the faculty, the alumni, the surrounding community, sometimes the state legislature, and occasionally the church, among others. When you look at a college, keep these constituencies in mind, and think about how they influence the college.

Schools Are Eager to Make You Think You're Wanted!

You're probably already receiving mailings from colleges. Colleges often buy student names after the PSAT/SAT/ACT tests have been taken. Schools are increasingly eager to get their mailings opened the University of Dayton didn't pay for overnight postage, but they did pay for the right to use the "overnight" for eample, express envelopes from UPS and DHL in the hopes of getting attention.

2

CHAPTER 2

Before You Ever Apply

Most of you reading this book are in your junior or senior year of high school. That's perfectly appropriate. It also means there is only so much you can do to change your overall high school record before actually applying to college. But there are some things you still can do. And at the very least, you should understand how these earlier elements may affect your chances of admission.

Course Selection

Few colleges will deny that the most important piece of the application is a student's transcript. It is a tale of their journey through high school, their likes and dislikes, their successes and their failures. Most colleges also believe—quite reverentially—that it is a window into their future. How a student has done in high school is not determinative of how they will do in college. But it is one pretty good predictor. And for most colleges, the high school transcript—the courses you've chosen and what grades you've achieved—is where they start the evaluation process.

Students are expected to "major" in college but not in high school. Consequently, the high school transcript should reflect this, with a challenging and wide array of courses. The colleges expect the high school experience to cover five academic core areas: English, mathematics, science, foreign language, and history/social sciences. (A quick note: for students who hope to study in England, particularly at Oxford or Cambridge—not as an exchange student, but for the full four years—it is different. These universities expect you to *really focus* on one or two subjects.)

Individual states may mandate particular courses of study in order to graduate from high school—for example, this normally involves four years of English and one year of U.S. history. Individual high schools then impose their own graduation requirements, typically involving math, science, and probably a foreign language. Then, as you'll see, every college spells out its requirements for admission. And, finally, student-athletes hoping to compete in NCAA

Division I and II athletics must fulfill the NCAA core requirements while in high school.

Confusing? Contradictory? Don't worry, not really. Today, college websites are full of advice about which courses a student should pursue in high school, and most of them really are pretty similar. Harvard defines their "ideal" candidate as a student with:

- Four years of English— along with "extensive practice in writing"
- Four years of mathematics
- Four years of science with advanced work in one of the three science disciplines: biology, chemistry, or physics
- Four years of one foreign language
- Three years of history— including American and European

Although they say "ideal," exceptions abound. But take note that the "unhooked" academic candidate (see Chapter 6) will be in competition with thousands of candidates whose transcripts mirror the above description. And most of those applicants will have completed advanced work in almost every area.

The Brown website paints a similar picture, with a bit more flexibility. Brown requires:

- Four years of English
- Three years of mathematics—but *"preferably"* four
- Three years of a foreign language—but *"preferably"* four
- Three years of science— including two years of laboratory science
- Two years of social studies

They also *"encourage"* study in music and art. Finally they add: "Students who stretch themselves with advanced courses in one or more academic areas may stand out among applicants who choose a less demanding route. After all, we are looking for students who are exceptionally eager to learn and willing to accept academic challenges." In admission speak, academic challenges means the transcript better be loaded with the advanced placement and honors work that your high school offers. We also highlighted "preferably" and "encourage" as buzz words that one *better* follow.

For those who can't get started early enough, the University of Michigan website is particularly useful. It describes a student's path from 8th through 11th grades, and what courses are of particular value to them. Michigan is more forgiving in foreign language, requiring only two years of the same language. If you're an out-of-state applicant, however, we'd advise a year or two more in that discipline if you really want to be a viable candidate in their extremely competitive pool.

We hope you're starting to get the picture of how important course selection is in the admission process. And one of the first things anyone even remotely interested in applying to a selective college should do is compare your likely course selection to the requirements of the colleges you might be interested in. You don't want to reach senior year and suddenly realize you're missing a course required by your dream college.

The High School Profile

Just as you will present yourself to a college, so will your high school. Colleges typically assign an admission officer to a particular geographic region. This geographic responsibility and focus allows the admission officer to become familiar with the high schools in his or her area. She'll get to know which ones are academic powerhouses and which ones inflate grades. She'll know which require real community service and which allow minimal activity to qualify. And she'll figure out which schools have cut-throat environments and which are more laid back or collaborative. Each of these insights will help the admission office put an applicant's transcript in perspective.

Any high school doing even the minimum job in college counseling will produce what is known as a **school profile** for use by the college admission offices. That profile contains the school's mission statement and philosophy, the requirements for graduation, the advanced courses it offers, and the grade distribution among the most recent graduating class. It might also include where recent graduates of the school went to college. Among other uses, the college admission officer will use the profile to judge how a student has challenged himself during high school. For example, have you taken AP or other "high-level" courses? Or were such courses not offered in your high school? Ask your high school counselor to see a copy of what your school submits to colleges. Before you even begin the application process, it's useful to know how your high school is positioning itself to the college admission offices.

Although many high schools no longer rank individual students, the profile often contains a grade distribution for individual subject classes offered by the school. The distribution helps a college establish where you stand vis-à-vis your peers if several of you apply to the same college. It can also help put into context grade inflation at a particular school. And it can help your counselor explain a B in an advanced placement class or show where a particular teacher gives few or even no As.

Most kids and parents have heard that the junior year is the most important to admission officers. That is true. It is also a pivotal year in the college process. An ascending record in a strong-curriculum junior year can often sway an admission committee in your favor. When a high school doesn't rank students or even compute a grade point average (GPA), most colleges will calculate their own GPA for a student. It will be based on three years of high school work and is often weighted on the later years. This GPA may also often exclude courses outside the major disciplines. It is not unusual for a college admission officer to share with the high school counselor why they view one student as stronger than another from that same high school. The rationale is often based on the GPA the college has calculated and the weight they have given to each student's curriculum.

The Advanced Placement Class vs. the Regular Class

Perhaps the most frequently asked question of admission officers and college counselors is: "Is it better to get a B in an AP class or an A in the standard class in a particular subject?" The answer, disappointingly, rarely gets a laugh: "It is better to get an A in the AP class." It's easy for us to say, "Lighten up gang." But unfortunately, that is the reality of college admissions today.

Let's cut right to the bottom line. If you want to be competitive in a "selective college" application pool, you need to have a transcript that compares favorably with the majority of other people in the pool. And that means having As in AP classes.

Our rule of thumb about taking AP classes is first to know your academic strengths and weaknesses and then to use that candid self-assessment to take courses that will present your strongest profile. We'll talk more about presenting that profile—what we call positioning and packaging—in Chapter 5. But your choice of courses is one important element in your academic packaging.

The potential engineer with genuine strength in mathematics and science might start loading up her transcript in the 10th grade with advanced work in those areas. By senior year, then, she will have taken the most challenging courses her school offers in science and math. (Remember, the school profile is the school's "brag sheet" presenting its toughest, highest-level courses.) It is important, however, that she not abandon English, history, or a language, and we'd encourage her to try one or two AP or top-level courses in those subjects as well. The most competitive colleges like to see you stretch in those "weak side" subjects.

Similarly, the gifted linguist or future classicist might load up on AP English and history courses, along with advanced work in one or more foreign languages. And he would likewise be well advised to take tough courses in mathematics and the three core sciences.

Interestingly, we've found that many students who load up on

AP courses in their senior year are given the benefit of the doubt by admission officers—even though senior grades will typically have no bearing on the admission decision. So, while admission officers obviously put more emphasis on courses and grades in the sophomore and junior years, a strong senior-year course load doesn't hurt. And with the admission pools at selective colleges becoming more and more competitive, every small advantage helps.

It is also important to remember that AP, honors, or advanced classes are often the best preparation for SAT subject tests. We encourage students to look at their mathematics curriculum for a specific year and compare it to what is covered on the SAT subject-matter test. Typically, the syllabus covered during sophomore year best prepares you to take the Level I math subject test. Similarly, what you cover during the junior year pre-calculus course often prepares you well for the SAT Level II math exam. Likewise, a student studying a high-intensity science course as a sophomore is probably best suited to take the SAT science subject test while still a sophomore. Before you register for the tests, however, it is always advisable to consult your teacher. Ask her whether you are sufficiently prepared. Some schools "teach to the test" more than others, and your teacher should be able to give you the straight story.

Many schools are now debating the academic merits of AP classes. The issue centers around the tendency to "teach to the test," rather than providing a more free-flowing—and perhaps even more intellectually rigorous—exploration of the subject. (This non-test-focused approach is often more satisfying to the teacher and student alike.) Complicating this philosophical debate is the College Board's increasing rigidity in approving schools' AP curricula and syllabi. As a result, high schools are increasingly debating the cost-benefit trade-off of offering AP courses.

Colleges are attuned to this debate and won't penalize students if their high school doesn't offer AP courses—as long as there are higher-level and more rigorous courses that challenge students. There is one "compromise" circumstance that admission officers find interesting: students who voluntarily take an AP exam without having been in a formal AP course. This demonstrates an intellectual self-discipline and independence that colleges find appealing. And it is becoming particularly popular among foreign students—of whom there are increasing numbers—applying to American universities.

Many selective universities are discouraging—and even preventing—students with a significant number of AP credits from speeding through college. While students used to use AP work done in high school to graduate from college in three years, that is no longer the typical or preferred path. Keeping dorm beds filled and tuition revenue coming in may be part of the college's rationale, but the motivation is also educational and social. Many schools believe a student will have a fuller intellectual—and more meaningful social—experience by spending four years on campus. (Study abroad is considered an appropriate piece of that four-year experience.)

The trend today is to use AP work to enable the student to start at a higher level in a particular subject. But contrary to the old days, high school AP work does not count toward college credits needed for graduation. Exceptions to this policy/philosophy certainly still exist at many schools. So take the time to see how each school you eventually consider applying to treats AP credits, and what scores you need on the AP exams in order to take advantage of those benefits.

SAT vs. ACT

We're not sure whether "versus" is the right word when we address this topic. But in many families and school systems, it is the operative word. Parents, kids, and counselors typically ask which test a student should take and which test colleges prefer. Often, the best judge of which standardized test a particular student should take is an SAT/ACT test-prep tutor. (We discuss test-prep tutors more thoroughly later in this chapter.) A good tutor will understand a student's strengths and weaknesses:

what types of questions you are good at and which ones stump you. They should also be very familiar with the types of questions and subject matter each standardized test focuses on. As you'll read later on, using some sort of test-prep service is, almost always, a smart investment of time and money. And one of the first questions you should ask of a tutor is, "Which test is right for me?"

Many schools across the country have their students sit for the PSAT as early as sophomore year, and virtually all schools have their kids take the test in their junior year. That's because the PSAT serves as the National Merit qualifying exam. It is also excellent preparation for the SAT and serves as a terrific diagnostic tool to determine testing strengths and weaknesses.

A good rule of thumb about whether you should take the SAT or the ACT may well be geographical—where you live and what colleges you plan to apply to. The SAT has historically been the test of choice along the East Coast. (The College Board, which administers the SAT, is located in New Jersey.) The ACT (located in Iowa) is more common west

of the Mississippi. The SAT test is regularly given in most New York City, Boston and Washington, DC, high schools; but few of these same schools administer the ACT. Nothing weds you to these geographic traditions, but it is more convenient to take the test that is more broadly given in your area.

Another way to think about which test to take is more strategic: What is the traditional test that students at your high school take? Do you want to be the "odd duck"—test-wise—in your high school by not taking the popular choice? Importantly, it is not what your classmates might think if you don't take the same test as them. Rather, it is what the colleges might think. Let's say you and nine of your classmates all apply to a particular college. They all take the SAT, and you're the only one to submit ACT scores. In some college admission offices, that will raise a red flag. Though most colleges will say that is not so, we have heard, in private, from several highly selective East Coast universities who will admit that it does.

On the flip side, the University of Iowa, (remember, west of the Mississippi) certainly sees the ACT as its test of choice and will convert your SAT scores to an equivalent ACT score in the evaluation process. The ACT folks provide the following conversion chart, (which they refer to as "concordance" because it is not an exact one-for-score conversion).

Table 2-1 Converting SAT Scores to Equivalent ACT Scores (and Vice Versa)

SAT Writing (Score Range)	ACT English/ Writing Score	SAT CR+M (Score Range)	ACT Composite Score
800	36	1600	36
800	35	1540–1590	35
770–790	34	1490–1530	34
730–760	33	1440–1480	33
710–720	32	1400–1430	32
690–700	31	1360-1390	31
660–680	30	130–1350	30
640–650	29	1290–1320	29
620–630	28	1250–1280	28
610	27	1210–1240	27
590–600	26	1170–1200	26
570–580	25	1130–1160	25
550–560	24	1090–1120	24
530–540	23	1050–1080	23
510–520	22	1020–1040	22
480–500	21	980–1010	21
470	20	940–970	20
450–460	19	900–930	19
430–440	18	860–890	18
410–420	17	820–850	17
390–400	16	770–810	16
380	15	720–760	15
360–370	14	670–710	14
340–350	13	620–660	13
320–330	12	560–610	12
300–310	11	510–550	11

The Writing Section

When the College Board added the writing section to the traditional SAT several years ago, many colleges were not quite sure how to evaluate it. Some selective schools reduced their requirement for SAT subject tests from three to two. They saw the new writing section as a substitute for the former English Composition subject test. More recently, however, colleges are appreciating the value of the written essay and are requesting a copy of what a student wrote. In this era when applications are often reviewed by parents, teachers, and independent counselors—who too often just "polish" the essays—the SAT writing sample becomes solid evidence of the student's own ability to write an essay. There is no question that it is the student's own work. And many admission officers see it as a better approximation of actual college test-taking conditions.

Even the Ivy League has now incorporated the writing section of the SAT into their academic index (see Chapter 6). So pay careful attention to what you write and how you write it. And though the ACT allows you to take their test without the writing section, we strongly advise against that. Most colleges specifically state they require the ACT with the writing section, and you don't want to disqualify yourself from consideration simply because you were not in the mood to complete the writing section.

Score Choice

Score choice allows students who have taken the SAT more than once to decide which score they wish to submit to colleges. This recent decision by the College Board to reinstate score choice—it had been suspended for several years—creates a dilemma for both students and colleges.

The new policy allows students to choose which sitting(s) of a complete SAT 1 they wish to submit to the college. Students may not pick parts of different sections of the SAT 1 from different sittings. It also allows students to choose which particular subject tests—formerly known as achievement tests—to submit to a college for consideration in the admission process.

We say dilemma for several reasons. First and most importantly, several highly selective colleges (Yale,

Columbia, Cornell, and Georgetown come to mind), do not endorse score choice and require students to submit scores for all tests taken. You should consult each college you are applying to and find out their policy. Schools can change their policy from year to year, so devising a score-choice strategy too far in advance can be a dangerous practice. This is especially true for the student who thinks score choice is a good way to take the SAT or subject test as a "practice test," a strategy encouraged by many ill-informed tutors. Our best advice is to simply take the test when you are confident that you are ready to be successful.

One argument that might favor taking the ACT rather than the SAT is that many colleges allow a student to submit the ACT in lieu of SAT subject tests. The philosophy behind this is that the ACT is more subject-based—especially in science—than the SAT. But we would argue that the SAT subject tests are seen as more useful by most colleges, and many schools even use them for placement and advanced standing purposes.

Subject Test

Not all colleges require the submission of subject test scores. But most selective colleges do. The majority of colleges that require them ask that students submit scores from two different subject tests. And certain special programs, particularly in science or pre-medicine, often require additional or specific tests.

As a rule of thumb, someone applying to a science-based or engineering program will want to submit a subject test in math (preferably Level II) along with a science test. If you want to apply to highly selective schools, a third test—though not required—in a verbal discipline is a very good idea. It helps demonstrate your overall academic strength.

On the flip side, a humanities-oriented person might take SAT subject tests in English Literature, U.S. History, or their foreign language specialty. But we would still suggest submitting a strong math score. Remember that while most colleges only *require* two subject tests, submitting additional strong scores—just like high AP scores in multiple disciplines—can only enhance a candidacy. But as you plan your testing and application strategy, also remember that schools which do not honor score choice will expect to see all of your test results.

The "Test Optional" Debate

More and more colleges are eliminating the need to submit any standardized test scores. This, of course, makes the choice of which test to take—SAT vs. ACT—less significant. Obviously, not taking any standardized tests is both attractive and a risk. Not having to sit for hours on a "make-or-break" exam is very appealing. So is not having to take an SAT prep course. Just the thought of eliminating these activities reduces the stress level significantly.

The flip side is that you better have high grades. And you will be limiting your college choices to a small—though attractive—subset of all the colleges out there.

Relax: Tests A...

Georgetow... became the... schools to s... SAT subject ... prior to the 2010–11 admission cycle. In doing so, however, long-time Harvard Dean Bill Fitzsimmons continued to stress the value of the tests. He notes that the subject tests are "the second best predictor of success after high school grades." He also stresses that he still expects outstanding students to submit more than two scores in areas where they have achieved excellence. He recently explained that Harvard was comfortable with their decision to drop the third subject test requirement because of the added value of the writing section of the SAT 1.

What should you read into these comments by the Harvard Admissions Dean? It is pretty clear: as we've said before, selective colleges want more evidence that you have done—and can do—top-level work. And they look to the SAT subject tests and the writing section as very useful measures.

...ead, we believe ...nvestigate your ...ns: take the PSAT ...ee how you do. You ...ould also sit for subject tests where you've done well in class. And in the final analysis, discuss it with your guidance counselor. If the two of you believe you might present a stronger profile without test scores, by all means avoid the exams. The classic over-achiever in the classroom who does not do well in testing conditions might be a prime candidate for test avoidance. But remember to save some of your best written work in English or history because many schools will require a graded paper in lieu of scores.

When you finally apply to college, we suggest a two-pronged strategy. The first prong might include a set of test-optional schools along with several schools that require standardized testing but that place less emphasis on them. The second prong might include more traditional test-dependent colleges. Notice that we use the word "might" here. Of course you don't have to follow our recommendations blindly, slavishly, or at all. But our objective is to help you improve your odds. So ignore our "might" at your peril. And, as we discuss in more detail later, putting together a range of colleges where you think you really will be happy is probably the most important component of your application strategy.

We'll talk more about SAT/ACT tutors on page 41, but most we have worked with say that it is easier to raise SAT scores than ACT scores. A good tutor will administer both tests in a simulated practice setting. And if the scores for both tests are in the same general range, we would advise continuing with SAT preparation—and forget about the ACT. Given the incredible time demands you face with course work and extracurricular activities, it would make little sense to continue to prepare for both tests.

Both tests measure something, but no one is in complete agreement about exactly what. Some folks argue that it is academic aptitude. Others suggest it is really IQ. A few say it is reasoning ability, or socio-economic status, or just plain test-taking facility. Something—but what. The major difference is that the ACT has a science component not contained in the SAT. At the same time, it is not totally science based (i.e., what you know about biology, chemistry, and physics.) Rather, it purports to measure your ability to use scientific and reading skills to answer each question. If you are hoping to impress an admission committee with your science skills, you are probably better off submitting an SAT subject test in a specific science area rather than an ACT sub-score.

Extended Time

One of the more debated and controversial topics in testing has been the use of extended time for testing. There is no question that students who have certain **learning disabilities** (LDs) can significantly benefit from having extra time to take the SAT or ACT. Both the SAT and ACT have made it more difficult over the past few years to qualify for extended time. The SAT folks have made it particularly difficult to get extended time since they discontinued noting on the score report that a student had extended time.

The argument against extended time has often centered on equity. In short, it is a political debate. The battery of tests that a student must take in order to qualify for extended time is very expensive—often costing around $3,500. In the current economic climate, few school districts will pay for such testing. Similarly, most middle- and lower-income families are hard-pressed to afford the cost. Consequently, the extended time option is, more and more, a wealthy family–only option. And many observers think that is neither fair nor equitable.

So, assuming you can get the documentation necessary to qualify for extended time, the question is whether you should tell the college admissions office of your learning disability. Our rule of thumb on extended time—and LDs in general—is that it should be something that is well documented throughout the student's high school career. Colleges frown upon students who take advantage of extended time for the first time in anticipation of taking the SAT or ACT. They are much more sensitive to a student with a documented learning disability that has been supported throughout their school career.

"Admitting" a Learning Disability or Difference

Should you tell a college about your learning disability during the admission process? There are many schools with excellent support programs. (American University, Marist College, and the University of Arizona are three that immediately come to mind.) Schools which are proud of—and often boast about—their LD support services typically take into account an applicant's LD. And the admission committee factors this element—without negative bias—into the application.

Other schools may not be as understanding or even transparent about their approach to LDs. (*No* school is going to say that they discriminate against applicants with LDs, but colleges that lack any real support for LD students are being less than transparent.) We would advise families to learn what support services are in place at each college to assist the LD student. However, we also suggest that you *not* advertise or identify yourself when asking these questions. Unfortunately, in these days of incredible selectivity at certain schools, you can never be sure what is discussed behind closed committee doors, or whether a school wishes to take in very many students with LD needs.

On the other hand, for a student diagnosed with an LD after a difficult freshman year who then blossoms during the sophomore and junior years, sharing this history and LD diagnosis might be very helpful to an admission committee.

We talked about course selection earlier in this chapter. Many LD kids struggle with foreign language study, particularly romance languages such as French or Spanish. Also, LD kids are very often given a waiver from their high school, allowing them to drop a language after their freshman or sophomore year. Be forewarned that even though you may not want to highlight your LD or extended time, the absence of foreign language study in the latter years can be a red flag to admission offices.

On the foreign-language front, we've seen some fascinating work being done with LD kids by a tutoring-mentoring company called Individual U. They have found that many LD students who previously struggled with romance languages have enormous success learning Japanese. And in some cases, the student's high school has agreed to award academic credit to this private Japanese study, thereby negating the no-language red flag.

Test-Prep Courses and Tutors

Today's college admission scene has created a growing market for standardized test support. Large national companies like Princeton Review and Kaplan have flourished for years. Hundreds of smaller local and regional companies have emerged as well. In the last few years, many school systems have begun hiring private companies—sometimes the big national firms and sometimes these newer local companies—to run their SAT/ACT prep courses. Moreover, schools are dedicating time in the curriculum and in the school day to such courses. Others make these prep courses available to students for free on the weekend. It certainly conveys the importance that schools give to success on the SAT/ACT.

As in any type of study, your success in test-prep will vary with the time and energy you put into it. Failure to complete assignments between sessions will slow your progress, and perhaps incite the wrath of your tutor. There are two major types of test-prep courses—one is group based and the other is individually focused. We encourage you to think about how you learn best, whether in a group setting or on a one-on-one basis. Often a student may start with a group program and then realize that more specialized, individualized attention is needed. Rarely is the reverse true where a student goes from individualized support to a group course. The rub, of course, is cost. Individual test tutoring can cost thousands of dollars.

Most knowledgeable experts on the SAT expect your scores to come up at least 100 points—without tutoring—from modest PSAT scores. So don't let a tutor or program take credit for this "natural rise." If you're doing your job in school, another year of reading, writing, and mathematics will trigger the natural score increase on its own.

The best tutors will administer practice tests, analyze the results, and identify your weak areas—whether it is a certain type of question that trips you up or specific concepts. One of the worst-kept secrets in the testing world—and one adamantly denied by the College Board folks—is that you can significantly improve your test results simply by learning how to better take the test itself. Good tutors will help you learn how to better read the questions. (Our good friends at A-List Education, a terrific tutoring firm in New York, say that one of the most important skills they impart to students is the "RTFQ" rule: Read The F'ing Question! From personal experience, we know this is a surprisingly powerful tool!)

Other "tricks" tutors will impart are when to guess and when not to, how to eliminate obviously erroneous answers, when to leave an answer blank, and when not to second-guess yourself. So, understanding these insights, gaining familiarity with question types, reviewing subject areas, and simply exercising your brain all combine to frequently produce improved results. All you have to do is put in the time and effort, and the return on that investment can be considerable.

Independent Counselors

Another industry that has blossomed in the past decade is that of independent counselors. They range from great ones to mediocre ones. Some are former admission people, and others are parents of recent applicants who now think they are qualified because they went through the process once. Some independent counselors charge by the hour—typically running up charges of $2,500—and others

charge a flat rate that can exceed $25,000!

The reasons for this quickly growing mini-industry are understandable. Many public high schools have very few college counselors, and their caseloads are unreasonably huge—often in excess of 300 students per counselor. With that many students to help through the selection and application process, few seniors can get the guidance they need and deserve. Another reason is competitiveness. As many name colleges become more and more competitive, parents (and some students) believe they need every advantage they can put together in order to increase their odds of admission. Other families engage independent counselors in order to reduce the tension in the household. Parents would rather pay someone else to nag their kid about completing the myriad pieces of the application.

Fortunately the National Association of College Admissions Counselors (NACAC) and the independent counselors themselves (the IECA—Independent Educational Consultants Association) have started monitoring the profession. They've also issued ethical guidelines and approved standards of behavior.

It is essential to restate what we said earlier: *only* the college admission office can guarantee admission to a college! An independent counselor—or agent for those of you reading this in a country outside the United States—cannot. Just because "Ivy" is in a company name—and it is in about a dozen counseling company names—does not mean the company has any special relationship with anyone at any Ivy League university. It could mean that one of their counselors once worked at an Ivy League school—perhaps even in admissions—but even that doesn't mean they have any "special in." It just means that as marketers, they're not asleep at the wheel: many families who hire independent counselors have Ivy League ambitions.

The best independent counselors will work in concert with the high school counselor. They will support the school-based counselor's work and often communicate what their role will be in the process. Colleges, however, are much more likely to call the school counselor rather than the independent counselor—if there is a question about an application. So, even if your school counselor is overwhelmed—or you've heard or decided he is underwhelming—keep him in the loop.

Sometimes independent counselors can be very helpful. For example, a school counselor with little experience in the college athletic recruiting process might encourage a family to seek assistance from an independent counselor who really does know about recruited athletes.

The independent counselor who, however, creates an unrealistic level of expectation for a family is doing the student and his parents a real disservice. Some independent counselors do indeed have "back-channel connections." Do these counselors have clout? No, but they may have a personal relationship that gets their phone calls returned. Typically they have former colleagues still working in an admission office willing to take the independent counselor's phone call. Then in that phone call, the counselor might be able to ask the admission officer to take a second look at a candidate; or they may be able to convey something special or overlooked in the applicant's file. But can they guarantee admission? Absolutely not!

3

Behind the Scenes

Everyone has a story about a "name" college and admissions. Usually they are horror stories: tales of unbelievably qualified kids, whose parents attended the college—thus designating the kid as a double legacy—who then gets rejected. We hear them ceaselessly, from parents, siblings, friends, teachers, counselors, acquaintances, magazine articles, web blogs, television, newspapers, and films—even characters in novels. Occasionally, these stories are accurate. More often than not, they aren't.

These tales attest to our obsession with "prestige" institutions and a college's ranking.

One by-product of that obsession is an assumption that all those ivy-covered communities are basically alike. We tend to lump Harvard, Yale, Stanford, Brown, Dartmouth, and about two dozen others in one batch, and assume their students are basically interchangeable.

But selective colleges are like people. They come in a variety of shapes, sizes, colors, and dispositions, with differing philosophies and directions. Like people, they also share common characteristics. We'll take a look at some of those distinctions and similarities and then give you tools to better understand a school's character.

A Vast Field

There are more than 3,000 colleges and universities in the United States—about 2,200 of them four-year colleges. About 12% of that total—approximately 350 schools—are typically featured in the most popular college guide books. The exact number of colleges included in the popular guidebooks changes from year to year, and there is no black-line rule about

why schools are included or omitted. For example, the *Fiske Guide to Colleges* typically covers just over 300 schools. The 2011 edition of Princeton Review's guide profiles what they consider *The Best 371 Colleges*. (In the 2010 edition, it was 368.) And College Prowler includes over 300 schools in *The Big Book of Colleges 2011*. By contrast, *U.S. News & World Report* includes approximately 1,400 different colleges and universities among its various "Best" lists. In short, if you compare editions or lists, don't try to divine too much from why a particular school is included on one list or left off another. Often it simply because a college has refused to provide the guide's editors with data—or they missed a deadline.

What's so special about the numbers in these collections? Not much, except that some reasonably informed, usually opinionated people have decided that these are colleges "worthy" of inclusion in their guides. Edward Fiske, whom we've known and admired for 25 years, says that schools on his list are among "the best and most interesting four-year institutions in the country—in other words, those which students should know about." He's not wrong.

Zinch includes links to many of these subjective guides' online profiles—plus others.

Some of these institutions could hardly be called selective, as they accept over 90% of the applicants who send in an application. Still, all of them qualify by virtue of their name recognition, prestige, faculty reputation, academic standards, athletic prowess, or high-powered student body. They range in size from the tiny College of the Atlantic, with a total student population of 327, to Arizona State with more than 38,000 undergraduates (plus graduate students!).

They range in location from small rural towns (Amherst) to huge urban centers (NYU in NYC). They differ in size and orientation from small, undergraduate, liberal-arts institutions to huge megaliths. Some are educationally progressive; others have reinstated distribution requirements and offer few curricular options. And the field is split between state schools, with their legislative mandates to give preference to in-state residents, and private schools that can pretty much determine the kind of student body to admit.

Even institutions in the same general category, with Common Application procedures, aren't exactly alike. The Ivy League, for example, is actually an athletic conference that was founded in 1956. It was essentially a gentlemen's agreement limiting athletic recruitment and making financial aid available solely on the basis of need. Of course, it's no ordinary athletic conference since it counts in its ranks eight of the most selective colleges nationwide. Among its members (Brown, Columbia, Cornell, Dartmouth, Harvard, University of Pennsylvania, Princeton, and Yale), only seven are fully private. Cornell University is actually New York state's land-grant college; three of its colleges are actually state supported.

This alliance of highly selective colleges hardly agrees on admissions procedures. In 2009 Harvard admitted only 9.2% of the students pounding on its door. By comparison Cornell admitted 27% of those who applied. The institutions also differ in their ratio of undergraduate to graduate students. Brown, Yale, and Princeton are best known for their undergraduate population. Harvard and Columbia, by contrast, are world-class graduate factories. On these campuses, beleaguered undergraduates are outnumbered by those pursuing graduate and professional degrees.

Obviously, in any grouping of supposedly similar schools, there will always be distinctions. Still, the ways that these colleges cull and put together a freshman class can be quite similar.

The Myth of Selectivity

In evaluating selectivity, people tend to take a quick look at acceptance statistics and nothing else. The fewer people accepted, they think, the more competitive the admission process. This is true—but it can be misleading, and the acceptance percentage reveals only part of the story.

Selectivity works two ways. First, there is the college which flexes its selectivity muscles by only admitting a certain number of students from the total group applying. Second, there is student selectivity. Once those acceptance letters go out to students, the balance of power shifts, and the colleges are competing against their competitive set—Harvard against Yale, Princeton, Stanford, and sometimes Brown. Brown against Penn, Columbia, and

Dartmouth. Amherst against Williams and Georgetown. USC against UCLA, and so on. The percentage of kids who choose to attend a particular school—from the total who have been admitted—is known as yield.

Table 3.1 shows some recent numbers of applications, acceptances, and yields at a handful of popular colleges.

Table 3.1 Admissions Statistics for the Class of 2013 at Popular Colleges

College	Total Apps Received	Total Apps Accepted	Overall Acceptance Rate	Enrolled	Yield %
Amherst	7,667	1,158	15%	465	40%
Brown	24,988	2,708	11%	1,485	55%
Chicago	13,600	3,645	27%	1,330	36%
Columbia	25,428	2,496	10%	1,391	56%
Cornell	33,786	6,567	19%	3,150	48%
Dartmouth	18.130	2,184	12%	1.090	50%
Harvard	29,112	2,046	7%	1,655	81%
Northwestern	25,422	6,864	27%	2,182	32%
Penn	22,939	3,926	17%	2,400	61%
Pomona	6,149	965	16%	390	40%
Princeton	21,964	2,150	10%	1,300	60%
Stanford	30,428	2,300	8%	1,580	69%
Wesleyan	10,068	2,215	22%	700	32%
Yale	26,000	1,951	7.5%	1,327	68%
Totals	**295,681**	**41,175**	**15%**		

The Gatekeepers

In his 2002 book, The *Gatekeepers,* Jacques Steinberg of the *New York Times* gives an insightful look into the admission process at one such highly selective college, Wesleyan University in Middletown, Connecticut. He examines the process from start to finish, and we credit Wesleyan for being so honest and transparent with him. Despite that transparency, we read about difficult conversations between the admission staff about various cases, including discipline issues or students of color and the factoring of race in the decision process.

Steinberg coins the term "gatekeepers" to describe the people who make these difficult decisions. Whether led by a Vice President for Enrollment Management or Dean of Admissions, these gatekeepers set the tone for their community, deciding for whom the gates will be opened with offers of admission.

So who exactly are these gatekeepers? At many highly selective colleges (Amherst, Georgetown, Harvard, and Princeton to name a few), their leaders are highly respected, long-tenured experts in the field of admissions, oft quoted for their beliefs and goals for the process. This group of "lifers" are the real professionals, generally sensitive to the politics of their situation. Most admission directors will admit that their jobs are very politicized—there's usually someone complaining about a decision. Lifers know their school and tend to take fewer high-risk candidates (unless told to do so by their bosses). They are the backbone of any admission office, providing a context and a historical continuity of admission standards and administrative savvy. You'll find them most often at select private schools, often moving through the ranks—paying their dues—to achieve such a position and then staying there for years and often decades.

Another group of gatekeepers are the "young turks," often also called "green deans," who are new to the profession and often stopping there on the way to their next stop of their life journey. What they may lack in experience, they more than make up for in energy and enthusiasm. And in a profession with a high degree of burnout (extensive travel in the fall and spring, long hours of file reading and committee meetings in the winter), they are the keys in keeping the process fluid and moving forward. Often they are recent alumni of the school, who share their love for their alma mater with prospective students and their families, both on campus and on the road. They are excited to be shaping the next freshmen class and can be counted on to go out and beat the bushes trying to find the best prospects they can. They are also often most willing to burn the late-night oil as they evaluate folders during the selection crunch.

Often the young turks are selected for who they were on campus and will fight for like candidates in the decision process. They tend to be more liberal and less excited about candidates of affluence from traditional feeder or independent schools, and they may advocate for a more high-risk kid they interviewed or met on the road. While the lifers provide sage advice and historical perspective, the young turks provide passion and idealism, as well as a lot of energy.

While the lifers and turks may seem to different attitudes, th a love of working with Generally, every admission office represents a variety of academic backgrounds, personal histories, and personalities. As a result, admission decisions are balanced, with any individual prejudices tending to be cancelled out by others on the committee.

You'll often find lifers and young turks involved in various aspects of campus life, often teaching a class or serving as academic advisors or advisors to campus clubs or groups. This contact with students is important to them and also explains why so many people from admission move to the other side of the table as college counselors later in their careers. This enables them to share their valuable admission experiences and work more closely with students and their families to guide them through this process.

Occasionally, students sit on admission committees. When they do, students are much like the young turk professionals. They're more passionate, willing to take

are
ith
color
ed.
to
l-

nd young
have
ey share
ids.

...young turks, come to grips with the realities of the process. Sometimes students have a vote in the committee, but often they do not and are there in an advisory role.

The final group of gatekeepers might be less obvious but is just as important. At many schools, key faculty members will serve on the admission committee, and serve as a

type of academic gatekeeper. They often focus more on the academic credentials and potential of a student, making sure particular majors are represented, and upholding the academic integrity of the school. Test scores may be more important to them than extracurricular activities. After all, they will teach these students and want the most intellectually curious and capable in their classrooms.

In our next section, we talk more about some of those constituencies who impact the decisions of the gatekeepers.

Be Smart: They're Listening to You

A student visited Northwestern and was put off by her campus tour. She then posted her reaction to the experience on her Facebook page and compared it to her tour at Marquette.

The Northwestern admission officer found it and contacted the student, seeking feedback on the tour.

And They're Watching You!

A 2009 Kaplan survey of 320 admission officers from the nation's top colleges and universities revealed that one out of 10 admission officers has visited an applicant's social networking website as part of the admission decision-making process.

A quarter of the admission officers who reported viewing applicants' sites reported that these viewings generally had a positive impact on their evaluation. The bad news: a greater percentage (38%) reported that applicants' social networking sites have generally had a negative impact on their admissions evaluation.

While busy admission officers don't have time to view the profiles of all applicants, they may look if you include social media links in your application. Similarly, if you are in touch with them via social media, your online presence is mentioned to them by a reference or third party, or you are applying for a highly competitive program or scholarship, it is more likely they will check you out.

The goal is protecting the school from potential embarrassment. No school wants to announce the winner of a prestigious scholarship only to have compromising pictures be discovered on the Internet the next day.

Inappropriate activities or actions—online or offline—reflecting poorly on an applicant's character can certainly impact adm[...] years ago, [...] admission [...] posting ho[...] college officials on his LiveJournal (blog) account.

While its rapid adoption seems like a big change, social media is really more evolutionary than revolutionary. Students have always tried to share and compare information with older students, family members, and friends. Word of mouth has always been powerful, and personal interactions have been the basis of assessing fit—by both students and admission officers. Social media makes dialog possible. It's also easier to obtain more information and to get past the marketing brochures and viewbooks.

Further, although Facebook appears to be the most popular social media site in college admissions today (with YouTube a close second), the technology tools will likely change. If this book was written five years ago, the focus would have been on MySpace.

The key is simply to use available technology to find the right fit for you and to put your best foot forward. Later, you can use social media to decide between schools and get information to start (and stay) successful at college—right through graduation.

...er or not the school is ...eyan in Steinberg's book, ...hio Wesleyan University, which recently accepted 2,500 of 3,800 applicants, or Columbia, which accepted roughly the same number from an application pool seven times as large (26,000), admission offices exist to meet the needs of the institution. Colleges' institutional needs determine their goals, which in turn lead to their admission policy. Admission officers are then charged with fulfilling that policy.

How are those institutional needs determined? Largely by the administration's attention to various constituencies, both on and off campus, beginning with the following groups.

1. **The faculty.** First and foremost, professors need students to teach. If the faculty had its way, the job of the admission office would be only to attract the most academically able. Admission decisions would be made solely on the basis of SATs/ACTs and class rank. Although they comprise but one of a number of constituencies on campus, faculty members have tremendous

influence. Most colleges have an admission policy committee that guides the admission office in its decisions. And professors are important voices on these committees. The faculty also has constant contact with administrators. This means that not only are teachers highly influential, but highly vocal as well.

2. **The students.** Students also have something to say about admission policy, and administrators do listen to them. After all, they provide the bulk of operating revenues. No students, no college. Many of the liberalizing reforms of the 1960s grew out of student protests. Brown's "new curriculum"—a very big part of what has made Brown so popular—was a student-led initiative in 1968–69. Similarly, affirmative action programs for minority students came about in response to student demands (along with federal legislation). As a result of these reforms, students sometimes sit on admission policy committees as well. They rarely, however, sit on the actual selection committee. Their primary impact is in the recruitment and admission of the underprivileged, but they often serve as tour guides and even as campus interviewers.

3. The coaches. Athletic staffers at most colleges are in a special position. While most are not faculty members, many earn salaries equal to or better than their professorial peers. And top coaches in "big" sports can earn ten times what senior faculty members make. So, although coaches and athletic directors may teach no classes, their needs and goals are believed by college administrations to be almost as important as those of academic departments. A top-notch athletic program brings in revenues from happy alumni, who are more likely to donate if they read that "Old Swami" took the league title. And the growth of multi-million-dollar TV sports contracts has further reinforced the great importance of college sports in the admission process.

At some football schools with heavy television revenues, coaches are given virtual carte blanche to accept a limited number of very hot prospects. And even in the Ivy League, with its stress on "amateurism" in athletics, coaches provide detailed information to admission directors about their prospects, indicating on a "depth-chart" which players they need most to round out next year's team.

4. Alumni. This constituency used to be less important to state schools than to private colleges, but that has changed dramatically in recent years. State-supported universities still get a portion of their operating revenues from state budgets—typically about 20% from taxpayers. Twenty-five years ago, when we wrote the first edition of this book, the College of William & Mary received 43% of its budget from taxpayer money. Today it is only 18%.

The bulk of a school's annual budget comes from student tuition. As a result, alumni donations are an important part of the state university's financial strategy. And, not surprisingly, alumni support is essential to the privates. So keeping loyal graduates happy (and contributing) is an administrative priority.

How does the alumni connection play out in the admissions world? Delicately! When an alumni son or daughter— and occasionally even a nephew or niece, depending upon the alum's financial contributions—applies, the college's admission office takes notice of the family connection. If at all possible, the admission office will do its best to admit that applicant. But being a legacy—or even a "development prospect" (a potential major contributor)—does not guarantee admission, even for prospects with pretty strong credentials. We have seen far too many "double legacies" get rejected at numerous highly selective colleges.

The desire to admit the legacy is made both to keep the family tradition intact and—more importantly—to encourage future financial support. But keeping alumni happy is not just a matter of admitting their offspring, although that is often the most telling and controversial factor in alumni loyalty. Colleges have whole departments devoted to alumni affairs. Old graduates take a fervent interest in their alma maters. It is not uncommon to see scathing complaints in letters to the editor of alumni magazines. Often these gripes center on social or curricular changes that threaten their rosy memories of university life.

Although it now seems like ancient history, what happened at Princeton

University in the early 1970s is a good case in point. Following the admission of women in the early 1970s, the college was faced with a group of hoary old alumni who split off from the university-sponsored alumni organization. They formed their own alumni group to protest the new, "radical" policy. Today, Princeton's newest and most luxurious residential college is Whitman College—funded by and named after Meg Whitman, Class of '77, former CEO of eBay and candidate for governor of California in 2010.

So, does being a legacy really improve your odds of admission? Yes, but the degree of that impact can range from miniscule to significant. If your parent is an alum but hasn't really been involved in alum affairs or contributed regularly to the school's annual fund, your legacy "advantage" will be minimal. The connection will be noted on your application folder, but it probably won't make a difference. (At some colleges, legacies get an additional "read" from one more admission officer.)

How active or how large a financial contribution is required to make a difference?

Alumni interviewers, association officers, and grads of modest means who make small financial contributions *every* year are truly appreciated. But rarely do they have significant admissions clout—especially for a candidate with marginal credentials.

5. Development prospects.

We distinguish development prospects from the much broader constituency of alumni. That's because development prospects—those wealthy folks who have or can contribute significant sums to the university—are a very powerful constituency on most college campuses.

Development prospects are *cultivated*. We're talking *big* money here, often in the millions of dollars. Most development prospects come from the alumni ranks. But not all. Every year there are a few wealthy families who have kids applying to Old Swami. Some make their willingness to contribute known to the development office at the same time their kid is applying. Alternatively, a kid may be applying and trying to keep his family's wealth a secret. He is determined to get in on his own merits, not on his family's potential to fund a new endowed chair. In these cases, an astute development officer may ferret out the kid's pedigree and have it noted on the application folder.

Is this fair? We're not going to weigh in on the philosophical merits. But we will talk about the practical implications. The development constituency is an important one, and we address it more fully in Chapter 6.

6. The world outside.

The press, the community, government. Colleges are very concerned about how they appear to the world outside their cloisters. Most institutions have a vice president for "university relations," whose department is a combination press bureau and mini-diplomatic corps. It is responsible for interesting journalists in the college's accomplishments and activities and then pushing hard to make sure that the resulting press coverage is positive.

Another concern is the school's relationship with the surrounding community. Administrators are forever trying to improve relations between town and gown. In some cities, colleges will court local residents—often to lay the groundwork (or inoculate themselves) in anticipation of campus expansion. Both NYU and Columbia are in constant "negotiations" with their city neighbors. Similarly, Brown University has gone to great lengths to reassure residents of its surrounding Fox Point neighborhood (most of whom are working-class Portuguese) that it will continue to build on-campus student housing and control off-campus student living. That's because the townspeople are understandably concerned that the "rich" college kids will move into off-campus apartments in Fox Point, driving up rents and displacing long-time local residents.

There are college administrators who are responsible for government affairs. That means keeping abreast of—and influencing—local, state, and national legislation affecting education. For state colleges, this connection is direct. The actual cost of providing an undergraduate college education is virtually the same at public and private colleges. But the price to the consumer—the student and his family—is much different. The difference is the result of state subsidies that keep in-state tuition low. That balance between tuition, subsidies, and in-state admission preferences is an on-going battle.

What this means for admission policy is that state governments usually dictate standards for admission, enrollment, and the ratio of in-state residents to out-of-staters. By law, for instance, 83% of the undergraduates at the University of North Carolina at Chapel Hill must be in-state residents. At the University of Vermont, the in-state percentage is maintained at 72%.

The balance between providing a preference for in-state residents—who pay in-state taxes and who vote—and bringing in out-of-state tuitions fluctuates. Out-of-state kids typically pay tuition that is four times higher than their in-state classmates pay. And to complicate matters, more and more colleges have been using the lure of in-state tuition to attract the best out-of-state students.

So for families about to enter the admissions sweepstakes, it is well worth the effort to do some research about the latest balance of in-state/out-of-state students a school is seeking to achieve.

7. The high school crowd.
Students, parents, and educators. These interlocking constituencies are crucially important to colleges—both private and public. College admission staffs are usually pretty sensitive to how they're perceived among students looking at colleges. Indeed, colleges spend a small fortune marketing themselves to students—in the hope of attracting the best and brightest kids to their campus.

But it's not only the actual high school prospects who matter. Colleges need good on-going relationships with high school counselors and teachers as well. And finally, colleges are waking up to the fact that parents are still the single most important influencers when kids make college choices.

Admission officers know that if parents and students hear horror stories about a college or its admission policies, they won't put that school on their college list. The flip side is also true: dealing with perceived problems head-on can help a college's popularity. For example, the University of Southern California suffered

for years from its location in south-central L.A. Public perception of the college's proximity to "the hood" made USC a tough sale to parents and some kids. So USC did two things. First, it beefed up its private security force to patrol areas a mile or two from the center of campus. Many off-campus student apartments were concentrated in these neighborhoods, and the school took responsibility for ensuring greater safety. And second, it addressed the safety issue head-on in the admission information sessions. It was literally the first topic brought up by the admission officer in the group session that Steve attended with his older son.

If teachers and counselors are unhappy with admission decisions, they may discourage their top prospects from applying to the offending college. High school officials have long memories. More than one visiting college rep has gotten a hostile reception at secondary schools, finding himself forced to defend admission decisions of past years—often made long before the visiting rep even joined the admission office.

The Constituency Influence

Each year colleges examine their previous years' enrollment management performance, and then plot the next year's goals and needs. Above all, every school needs a certain level of tuition to balance its budget. And from that dollar goal it must enroll a certain number of tuition-paying bodies. This will be comprised of full-tuition payers, partial-scholarship kids, full-free-ride athletes, and financial-need students.

College administrators will make projections of budget, faculty, enrollment, sports, activities, and dozens of other factors. With these variables, university planners can then suggest various options. For example, the college's trustees may wish to keep the size of the student body fixed and increase the number of faculty members. To accomplish this, the school may have to raise tuition costs. Alternatively, the trustees may want to hold the tuition costs at current levels, and increase the number of freshmen admitted in order to bolster revenues.

These institutional needs and goals may translate into an admission policy that makes it (temporarily) easier to get into the school. Standards may not drop, but the number of students admitted may go up.

Yield: How Many Students MUST be Admitted?

To illustrate how yield works, let's consider a scenario that is typical of many colleges. The administrators at (fictitious) Mid-Penn College might say: "We'll need 600 incoming freshmen to reach our trustee-mandated size of 2,400 undergraduates. And we need to generate $15,000,000 in tuition and room-and-board fees from those 600 bodies." (For our example, that's approximately $25,000 per incoming freshman, a discount of $15,000 from the "rate card" cost of $40,000.) The rate card is the cost of tuition that is published in the brochures and on the website.

The actual revenue received from a student is known in admission circles as a **tuition rate discount.**

Last year, our yield was 25%. And our competitive position has not changed significantly—we didn't suffer from any front-page scandals, nor did we make to the March Madness Final Four. So, for planning purposes, we'll plan on a similar yield rate, which means we need to admit 2,400 qualified applicants in order to get 600 to choose Mid-Penn over our competitors.

Our historical patterns also suggest that we need to accept about another 400 students onto the waiting list. We'll wind up taking only about 20 from the waiting list at the last moment.

Now, assuming we want to maintain our relative selectivity—we accepted 40% of the kids who applied last year—we need to attract at least 6,000 qualified applicants. And to attract those applicants, we need to reach out and "touch" at least ten times that many prospects (60,000!).

In building the class, we'd like to shoot for some balance between the sexes.

Now, recently, Mid-Penn has grown to 55% female and 45% male, but the trustees want to re-jigger that balance to make it closer to 50-50. That means next year we'll want to enroll slightly more guys than gals. Fortunately, our yield was noticeably better for our male applicants than our females: 29% vs. 24%, but our acceptance rate for men was 2% lower than for women. Given these statistics, we can give pretty good targets to the admission staff based on sex.

Now we have to address faculty needs. The French Department is concerned that an unusually large contingent of French majors will be graduating in the spring. The Biology Department received a sizeable gift that is allowing them to hire an additional professor. And the trustees think the school should de-emphasize business majors.

Then come the more generalized requests from specific constituencies. The University Planning Committee and Mexican-American students think that more Mexican-Americans should be admitted. (Efforts will also be made to increase recruitment of these students.) The trustees are complaining that not enough "legacies" (alumni sons and daughters) were admitted last year. And some folks on the committee think we have too many Easterners in the student body. They're arguing we should go for a more national profile and recruit and admit more students from the South. Plus the Music Department says it hasn't enough talent to put together a good school orchestra.

The coaches are ready to revolt. Although we don't compete in Division 1 sports—we're Division III and thus don't offer athletic scholarships—we do want to be competitive in both men's and women's lacrosse. So, we need to allocate a few more slots so the coaches can be competitive when recruiting.

We assume you're gathering from this that being an admission director isn't an easy task. And you're right. Admission people can never please every lobby, but they must be sensitive to their needs. In fact, they seldom please any constituency fully. There just aren't enough places in the freshman class.

Once admission policy is outlined—sometimes in these general terms and at other times very specifically—it is then the admission office's duty to implement it. The admission director will usually give his opinion, make recommendations for change, protest unrealistic demands by the administration or constituencies, and warn about the inevitable limitations on his ability to deliver everything asked of him. The discussion will continue until goals are generally agreed upon and a detailed policy is carved out.

Financial Aid and Admissions

An important part of this process is financial aid. Its importance has increased over the past few years as the economy tanked and colleges continued to get more expensive—far out-stripping the rate of inflation. In order to attract a first-rate student body—and satisfy all the constituencies who have outlined their needs and desires—the university will have to provide enough funding for financial aid.

Financial aid is used both to attract desirable applicants and to help people afford attending. There is a slight distinction between the two. Financial aid is a marketing tool that colleges use to get the kids they want to attend to actually apply and show up. Some more cynical—but not wholly incorrect—observers note that financial aid is a form of discounting (remember the tuition rate discount). If you want to purchase that 52-inch flat-screen TV and one store is offering it for $1,800 and another store, not too far away, is discounting it by 25%, there is a good chance you'll travel those few extra miles for the better price. The same is true with financial aid offers to attractive applicants.

Some well endowed colleges completely separate admissions decisions from financial aid awards. Others, like Mid-Penn, do not. When admissions decisions are made independently of financial aid need, the process is called *need-blind admissions.*

Remember our mandate from the trustees? We need to bring in $15,000,000 in tuition and fees. Our overall discount can aggregate to 37.5%. But financial aid can be outright discounting in the form of scholarships or grants, or it can be a package of low-interest government loans. The former actually "costs" the college money—note how many colleges provide a merit scholarship as a tuition discount; the latter do not.

So we'll have to weigh each constituency's list of preferred prospects against their financial aid needs. And sometimes we'll only be able to offer someone admission if they can attend without taking any of our scholarship money. Loans will be available, but outright grants will go to more deserving or needy applicants.

Need-Blind Policies Change Year to Year

The policy about need-blind admission can change at a particular college from one year to the next. Be sure to find out what the school's policy is for the year you are applying! It will probably be on their website. If it isn't there, or isn't clear, ask! Depending on that year's policy, your family's financial situation, and your application credentials, you'll have to decide whether to apply for financial aid when submitting your application. We address whether or not you should apply for financial aid—and how it affects your chances of admission—in Chapter 8.

Last year 65% of our applicants applied for financial aid, but only 50% qualified based on family resources. We were able to meet 85% of the financial aid needs of qualified students. When we connected these families with other sources of loans, however, 100% of the kids who wanted to attend were able to come up with the funds before classes began. It may not have been pretty or easy, but we know we can find some sort of funding for just about anyone we admit to Mid-Penn.

With the admission policy in place and the target yield determined, the process now really kicks into gear. Kids start looking at colleges; parents devour guidebooks; and colleges set off to find kids who satisfy each constituency.

The Well-Rounded Class

Forget everything you've heard about the prestige schools wanting well-rounded students. As we said earlier, what they want is a well-rounded class. As an individual, being too well-rounded can actually hurt your chances for admission. Colleges do want bright, versatile, nice students. But in order to fulfill their goals, they must have a student body that satisfies the constituencies' needs and is diverse—religiously, ethnically, economically, and geographically. Plus, throw into the mix a desire to put together a class with different interests, outlooks, and special talents.

Yes this mosaic satisfies the demands of the constituencies. But it also creates a lively college community that will enhance students' learning and experience. A great part of the college experience happens outside lecture halls and seminar rooms. In fact, if you really take advantage of your undergraduate days, you'll find you learn as much out of class as in—through extracurriculars, late-night bull sessions, intellectual patter at dinner, and every other sort of shared activity.

In a sense, college is a rehearsal for life, providing the transition from childhood to the adult world. It weans students away from their families and gives them the social skills and open-mindedness necessary for success. And these objectives are as important to colleges as book-learning.

Of course, colleges view heterogeneity in many ways. One school's idea of diversity can be quite different from another's. Some places are more attuned to background and personal factors in their admission decisions. They seek out students who will contribute to the quality of campus life in little ways. Carleton, for instance, looks for applicants with that special "pizzazz." Brown values character and the potential to contribute to campus activities. And still other universities emphasize scholarliness to a greater degree, seeking intellectual seriousness as the driving personality trait.

State institutions, on the other hand, are usually less concerned with variety. Operating under strict guidelines to admit a certain percentage of in-state students, they have less latitude in choosing applicants. Like the private colleges, state schools have obvious constituencies, the most active of which may be athletes and minorities. But their primary constituency is the state legislature, to whom they have a legal obligation. Generally this obligation causes state colleges to use specific admission formulas, which may take background characteristics into account only marginally and extracurricular achievement not at all. But not all state schools use only academic credentials to make admission decisions. The key is to find out which ones use what criteria.

If you want to maximize your chances for admission, you must understand that not only is every admission process complex, but it differs from campus to campus. It is essential to your application strategy that you begin to recognize these differences and put them to use to your own advantage. It is also important that you look beyond the college's buzzwords—those catch-all phrases that describe what a college supposedly wants to see in an applicant—and try to understand what each *really* wants. We'll give you tools to help do this later on. But you need to look for recurring patterns on the schools' websites and in their admission materials. The ability recognize sometimes subtle differences will enable you to sharpen your application strategy.

The Three Facts of Admission Life

Three basic facts apply to every lucky kid who gets into the college of his or her choice. As a wise old college counselor once said—"there is always a reason."

1. The applicant falls into a category of students that the college needs or wants on campus.

2. The applicant has credentials as good as or better than other kids who fulfill those needs. Those credentials can be SATs/ACTs, grades, recommendations, essay, extracurriculars, or the interview, in various combinations, depending on the college. Whatever the factors considered, every applicant competes with those in his "category" and is admitted by presenting credentials equal to or better than those of others in that category. That's not to say that every applicant competes only in his category. Some people fall into more than one category of the admission pool, and the lines between categories of applicants are flexible. Someone may be admitted because she falls into more than one category, breaking stereotypes, or because she is very different from the norm.

3. The successful applicant who is generally "equal to" other applicants in one category is usually accepted because he communicates the information better than other students who are applying for the same admission place.

Categorizing the Applicants

Admission offices differentiate between applicants in two ways: background factors and personal achievement, be it scholastic or extracurricular. The differences between these two categories should be clear to you. Having an Irish surname or being born in Kansas is pure background— you had nothing to do with it. Having won your high school basketball team's MVP award or being made editor of the school paper is achievement. You had a lot to do with those.

In an ideal world, it might seem that colleges would only look at your personal achievement. But would that really be ideal? Would you want to wind up at a school composed exclusively of grinds who are incapable of speaking in public? Or where extracurricular activity consists of nothing more than moving from one library to another in order to study?

As we said earlier, colleges need balance to provide a good undergraduate experience. Consequently, they balance background factors, which contribute to campus diversity and satisfy constituents, and personal achievement, which contributes to both diversity and the quality of life on campus. First we'll discuss some of the background factors that influence admission decisions. These are factors over which you have no control as an applicant. They may, however, affect your choice of schools—if you can find schools that respond favorably to your particular background.

Background Factors

1. **Alumni parents or relatives.** At some selective institutions, the percentage of "legacies," or alumni offspring, admitted is twice as high as the overall acceptance rate. Of course, just having a parent who is an alumnus is rarely sufficient for admission, especially for a marginal candidate. But the more influence a parent has at the college— whether through donation of time or money, or because the parent lives reasonably close to the school—the better off the legacy applicant will be.

Having a brother or sister who is an alumnus or current undergraduate can also help. Colleges do want to keep the tradition in the family. The more recent an older brother's or sister's association with the school, the better. Individual professors, coaches, advisors, or even an admission officer may remember—hopefully favorably—your sibling. If that relative is still on campus, it usually can't hurt to have them make contact with an admission officer and reinforce your case. Having a grandparent, an uncle, or an aunt who is an alumnus barely qualifies as a school tie, unless of course the relative is especially loyal, generous, or powerful.

Having a parent on the faculty or staff of the college may also be an advantage.

Be aware, though, that a family tie can't overcome a weak set of credentials, no matter how powerful the alum may be. The admission office has to feel confident that the legacy won't be an embarrassment and that his or her interests will be served by being at a high-powered school.

2. Diversity. Almost every college wants a heterogeneous student body, unless the school is highly specialized or church-supported. Diversity does not simply mean black or Latino—though for many years colleges' diversity initiatives were little more than race-based affirmative-action programs. Today that is changing. To a small degree, economic and cultural diversity has taken hold, and "first-gen" kids—applicants who are the first in their family to attend college—are highly sought after.

If you're a city or suburban kid, rooming with a farmer

from Kansas will be an education in itself. And it will be an equally eye-opening experience for the farm-boy as well. For the college, when that farmer returns to his hometown and becomes a big fish in a small pond, he'll remember Old Swami and spread its fame far and wide on the prairies.

Geographic diversity is a also desirable factor for colleges. You may have a distinct advantage as a result of where you live. Let's say there are two students applying to the same prestigious private college. One is from an area that sends very few kids to the college. The other is from a high school that sends 20 applicants every year. Not surprisingly, the one from the unusual area will be in a better position. While there is rarely an overt outcry in the committee room saying, "Get me someone from South Dakota!" a strong South Dakotan applicant will stand out from the crowd.

You don't have to live thousands of miles away from a college to be considered a "geo" applicant. Distance alone does not make for geographic diversity. Rather, it has more to do with the frequency and number of applications from that area. Shaker Heights, Ohio, is quite a distance from either the West or East coasts. Yet it is not considered a geo area by most colleges because every year hundreds of its students throw their hats in the ring for Stanford—two thousand miles away—as well as Wellesley, Princeton, Williams, and Duke. A wealthy suburban community with a high percentage of professionals, Shaker Heights is not that different from Brookline, Massachusetts; Scarsdale, New York; Highland Park, Illinois; Beverly Hills, California; or Bloomfield Hills, Michigan. No geographic diversity there.

But just an hour by car from Shaker Heights is Hudson, Ohio, a small town built like a New England village, with clapboard homes surrounding a commons area covered with grass and trees. Hudson High sends perhaps one applicant a year to each of the selective schools. That's geo status!

Geos also come from local areas—the "boonies," as some admission folk call them. Applicants from rural areas of Rhode Island, for example, are seen as geos by Brown University.

The diversity category also includes cultural backgrounds that are exotic or rare in the applicant pool. Having lived abroad may qualify you for this group. Being the child of immigrant parents, while not as compelling to colleges as being a minority applicant, still carries some weight.

This is especially true if there is clear evidence in the application of cultural differences in background. For example, a kid who came to the United States from Italy at age eight probably has a perspective and history that is pretty different from a typical American teenager. And the admission office bias is that such a background will contribute to the mix on campus. Finally, the diversity category can also include social, religious, economic, or even sexual diversity. Notre Dame doesn't see many Jewish applicants, and women's colleges that have recently gone coed love male applicants.

3. "Feeder" schools and "school groups." Until the mid-1960s, certain preparatory schools were considered virtual feeders into nearby Ivy League colleges: Lawrenceville School for Princeton, Moses Brown for

Brown, Phillips-Andover for Harvard, St. Paul's for Dartmouth. Each year a good percentage of students from these schools who did not get into other selective institutions managed to make it into one of these sister colleges.

Today these ties still exist, but only as shadows of once flourishing relationships. Lawrenceville still sends many graduates to Princeton. Lots of Andover graduates still go on to Harvard. But the feeder school relationship is not as strong as it once was; marginal candidates from these schools have a much, much tougher time of getting in. In addition, colleges may look at where you fall in the "school group"— those applicants from your particular school and the various academic and personal reasons for picking one applicant over another.

Most colleges have become more sensitive to their obligations to all "locals," as they're called. Whether this is because proximity allows for the prospect of in-person complaints or because the college truly wants to serve the community really doesn't matter. The fact is that certain public schools send many of their graduates to nearby selective colleges.

In his autobiography, *In Search of History,* Theodore White noted that most of the "townies" at Harvard in the 1930s came from Boston Latin School, a public high school. Other schools that fit this category include Classical High School and Brown, Bronx High School of Science and Columbia, and Philadelphia's School for Girls and the University of Pennsylvania. Being a local isn't of massive significance to admission, but it can improve your chances.

4. Development. This category encompasses a handful of students every year—those whose families are wealthy enough to contribute significantly to the college. We're talking serious money here: the cost of an endowed professorship may run $2 million and a small building 10 times that much. There is an obvious lack of transparency in this category since no one is willing to announce how much a development prospect may eventually be expected to donate.

The process of being considered a development prospect is a delicate one. Every admission director has a story about being promised a substantial sum of money for the college by some wealthy parent if Junior is admitted. And if it seems like bragging, or the family has no history of generosity to either the college or some other nonprofit, the tactic is likely to be counterproductive.

If your parents are sincere in their intent and ability to contribute to Old Swami, your college counselor—or a family friend connected to Old Swami—should alert the development office. But be prepared: the development office won't simply accept a vague promise of some future donation; they will scrutinize every donation your family has ever made, especially those made to educational institutions And while it helps to have a development officer weigh in as an advocate on your behalf, there is still no guarantee of admission.

5. **Minority and disadvantaged.** Through affirmative action recruitment programs, colleges today have a fair number of minority students. The minority category includes federally recognized minorities such as Native Americans, African-Americans, Mexican-Americans, Asian-Americans, and Puerto Ricans.

Being identified as a member of one of these groups can have a very positive impact on admission.

Disadvantaged students may not be "official" minorities, but they may also receive favorable treatment in the admission process. While there is no federal initiative pushing for the admission of blue-collar or economically poorer students, admission officers themselves are often receptive to these sorts of applicants. Most selective colleges have primarily middle- or upper-middle-class student bodies. Thus, applicants from less affluent families are rare and sometimes seen as desirable for their contribution to the school's diversity.

Personal Achievement

Now that you know which background characteristics interest selective colleges, let's consider the categories of personal achievement that cause colleges to really sit up and take notice. These should be especially crucial to you as an applicant since you can't very well change your background. But you do have some influence over achievement.

1. Athletic talent. We've all heard about the prep school quarterback who made it into some elite college but wasn't skilled enough or interested enough to join the football squad. That's not the sort of athletic talent we're talking about. There is a major distinction in admission between recruited athletes and amateur or unrecruited players. We have listed recruited athletes at the top of the achievement categories because they are in a group by themselves. They have a very powerful lobby on campus—coaches.

Coaches can't be ignored because they are very vocal and know what sort of players they need for a successful season. And there are always alumni who keep tabs on the teams' performances and grumble if they perform poorer than expected. For a coach's top wide receiver, the issue is not whether his lower-than-average scores and grades are "outweighed" by his talent. The bottom line is whether the jock can survive academically and not embarrass himself or the university. Of course, the coach will present the admission committee with a number of wide receivers, in hopes of getting at least one admitted.

A certain amount of bargaining goes on as the admission office decides whether to admit the top man, who has questionable academic credentials, or another, less impressive player with a better academic record. Not all colleges give as much weight to coaches' recommendations as others. The extreme cases of great athletic sway are at the major football powers, like Michigan State. On the other end of the spectrum, the smaller "Little Ivies" athletic programs are sometimes just as oriented to "walk-ons" or amateurs as to recruited players.

2. Scholarly excellence. By this we mean unusually good scholastic ability, as evidenced by SAT scores in the 700s, very high grades, and teacher references that consistently extol curiosity and high intellectual acumen. The scholar is the classroom provocateur, goading others to think and work harder. He satisfies the faculty constituency which is looking for real intellectual star-power.

The true scholar is rare, but when he appears, most colleges will grab him—unless his personality is so nerdy or driven and intense that his presence might be wearing on his peers. Most colleges find that true scholarship is an increasingly rare commodity, but essential to maintaining academic standards.

3. Special talent. Colleges have bands and orchestras, studio art classes, theaters, dance groups, and a host of other extracurricular efforts and courses which require talent and a flow of participants to keep all these activities going. All sorts of kids have abilities that fall into this category. For example, the violinist who has won a state music competition is probably highly desirable by most colleges. (And remember, he doesn't have to say he intends to be a music major; that opens up a wholly different constituent category.) This soloist will be even better off if the school orchestra happens to need a first violinist and the faculty advisor takes notice of him. (How the faculty advisor learns about our musician is addressed in Chapter 6.) Art, music, athletics, debate, drama, and other fields of creative or physical endeavor all fall into this category.

4. Extracurricular depth and community service. Colleges also have a variety of out-of-class clubs, associations, and activities that have to be populated by students. These include newspapers, yearbooks, radio and TV stations, film societies, academic clubs, musical organizations, political groups, religious organizations, student government, and so on. Although many state colleges and some of the larger private institutions are unconcerned about attracting extracurricular whizzes, the smaller prestige schools are careful to admit a student body that will be "involved." Colleges recognize that extracurriculars not only round out a student's education, but also provide leadership opportunities, social and career skills, and a real dose of responsibility.

5. Leadership/entrepreneurial ability. We have all known a campus leader—the student who ran the student council on budget for the first time in a decade. Or the kid who organized an annual school picnic to bring together faculty and students. Or the founder of a business that does some sort of specialized computer software and now grosses $5 million a year.

These are the applicants who colleges expect will shake

things up on campus—perhaps even reorganize them. They have the combination of guts, charisma, and discipline to lead others and make things happen. Because campuses usually have a thousand or more students, real leaders are wanted to bring people together and provide a focus for student activity.

6. **Personality.** Some colleges look for a spark of humor or warmth or zest in their applicants. They want kids whose smile and verve will make the campus a special place. Part of this quality shows up in extracurricular activities and part in sheer character. It may not come up at all in the application. It is most clearly visible in the essay, teacher references, or interview. It is often elusive and hard to discern on campuses where interviews are not offered and recommendations are not requested. But on some campuses and in some admission committees, personality can have a major impact on admission decisions.

Student vs. Student

It's difficult to give you a blueprint showing exactly how students in each of the previous categories compete with each other or within the overall applicant pools of various colleges. One college admission support service that some high schools subscribe to is called Naviance. Among the tools that Naviance provides college counselors is a software program that enables the guidance counselors to plug in historical data about their kids' admissions success at various colleges. The software then plots each kid on a graph where one axis is grade-point average and the other is standardized test scores. The graph that is produced is called a scattergram, and it shows the pattern of successful applicants compared to those who were not admitted. It is far from a foolproof projection of your chances, but it does give you some idea of how kids from your specific high school fared at particular colleges. It is worth asking your guidance counselor whether your high school subscribes to Naviance.

We are developing our own database of scattergrams. You can access them at www.zinch.com/scattergrams.

That mix of background and achievement—SATs/ACTs, grades, recommendations, essays—will differ from school to school. Each college gives a slightly different weight to each factor. And each has a slightly different mechanism for selecting. To say that every applicant is categorized by admission offices and then competes only with others in his or her "category" is a grotesque oversimplification. Most admission offices don't have specific committees for athletes, minorities, leaders, locals, and so on. They consider the whole person. Besides, many applicants belong to more than one category. Yet thinking about admission categories is useful for two reasons.

First, it provides a handle for you to categorize your own application, enabling you to position yourself within the applicant pool. You have some say in choosing which category you think you're in, or even would like to be in. Then you can "package" your application—present a stronger argument for admission than others in that category.

Second, it stresses that admission procedures aren't just formulated out of thin air: they stem from the college's various constituencies. Those constituencies determine institutional needs, which in turn prompt institutional goals. The admission office is then called upon to fulfill these goals. Keeping this information in mind, you should begin thinking about how you can best fulfill their requirements to maximize your chances of admission.

Notes from the Road—Fall 2010

Every fall, hundreds of college admission officers go on the road. They each visit scores of high schools in their respective geographic territories. The admission officers meet with both students and high school guidance counselors and typically have three objectives on these trips. First, they are getting the word out about their college. This is often one of the most effective marketing strategies a college can employ. By sending knowledgeable, attractive, articulate representatives out on the road, the college is positioning itself to prospective applicants.

Second, the admission officers are meeting individual students. They often have short conversations with kids who later submit applications. The student might be remembered for a smart question asked during an information session, a special sparkle or charisma, or because the college counselor was trying to be a matchmaker. However it happens, that brief meeting can help the applicant.

The third objective is to get to know the high school itself better. Are courses particularly tough, or are teachers likely to inflate grades? Are the kids cut-throat or laid-back? Are these the sorts of kids who would fit in on their college campus?

This year, Mike asked admission officers who were visiting his school—Poly Prep in Brooklyn, New York—to share insights about their colleges and their respective admissions processes. He also asked them to provide some insight into what they are looking for in an applicant or what might catch their attention. Some of the visitors were happy to be named and quoted, while others preferred anonymity. For those, the names of the visitor and school have been omitted.

Alfred University
by Jessica Frawley

We have the area rep do the first read, followed by a second officer who recalculates the GPA and reviews the first read. The Director can then approve that decision. Another 25% will go to committee. It would be great if students told us more about themselves in their essay or explained any irregularities in their transcript. At Alfred we have a motto: Individuals Inspired. We try to help support students while educating them in their desired field with a focus on hands-on learning. If I have one regret, I wish that we admission officers could stay involved in the student's lives after they come to school here. I'm always curious to know what they are involved in on campus and how they turned out.

Amherst College
by Tom Parker

At least two people will read each file (area rep goes first)—we run a two-committee system simultaneously so that each candidate receives full and fair consideration. Approximately 25–30% of our applicants will make it to committee, and it takes more than just a majority for an admit. If I had to give a piece of advice, most attempts at humor in the essay fall flat. Just be yourself. I think what makes our process special is our depth of consideration to the arts supplement and our commitment to socioeconomic diversity as well as racial diversity. I wish there could be less angst and more perspective with the process, but good luck with that.

Connecticut College
by Scott Alexander

Every applicant gets at least two or three reads, begin-ning with the area rep, a second random reader from the staff, and then the Dean of Admission. Only the Dean can make a pre-committee decision. About 20–25% of our applicants go to com-mittee. It's important that students understand that admission is storytelling. We want to hear the student's story, their journey, and how

we might fit in. Rare is the applicant (and counselor) that approaches the application with that perspective. Our goal is to build a community through our holistic approach to the application process. I do wish, however, that we might push back the time frame of the application process so we might put more emphasis on the senior year.

Emory College
by Scott Allen

Typically we read in teams and as many as four or five officers may read a file. One hundred percent of applicants will be reviewed by a team, though an Associate Dean or Dean can make a decision too. We believe all students get a fair review, and no one is indexed based on GPA or test scores. Every file gets a full review regardless of those numbers—we want to hear their story. We wish students would share more about their personality and what's going on in their life. And don't talk about activities that are really not important to you. If it's not important to you, it's not important to us. Tell us what you're passionate about. I think we're unique in that we do read each application, which I think is rare for a major research university with a large applicant pool. If I could change one thing in the college process, I'd wish there was more counseling and less marketing.

George Washington University

by Douglas Pineda

The majority of our applicants will make it to committee, and we take that process very seriously. Only senior staff can make a final decision before committee after a first read and consultation with the area rep. It would be great if a student shared with us the most important lesson they ever learned—good essay topic. I think the process is as fair as it can be in this crazy, competitive market. If anything, I would try to make college more affordable and, in turn, more accessible. Three final thoughts—don't use those inappropriate email addresses, check your Facebook access, and really explain why a particular school resonates for you when a college asks—give real examples.

Editors' Note

Several private schools use the expression "random reader" in their committee process. What that means is someone who reads the file in the context of the entire pool of applicants. They have no attachment to that high school or region and can often put a file from New York in context with one from Virginia in the total applicant pool. The area rep is seen as the expert of both the region and schools in their region. They can truly set the context of a school group, the rigor of the school's curriculum, and historical relationships with the school (the old feeder concept).

It's also very evident that while the committee process is alive and well in many private schools, the increased number of applications are forcing these schools to streamline their process. In the public sector, however, it is apparent how test scores and GPAs remain the major factors in their decision-making process.

Johns Hopkins

by John Birney

We really don't use a committee approach. Files are read by the area representative, an academic representative, and perhaps a special-interest group. All readers can make a decision, but then we review our numbers as a staff and make adjustments. We believe we are unique in that we give a true holistic read of each file and that we give the regional reader the majority of the say in the decision-making process. Most regional decisions are upheld by senior officers. We wish students might tell us more about how involved they are in certain activities and share where they are true leaders on their campuses. We suspect many of our applicants are interested in pre-med, or want to become doctors, so tell us something else about you that makes you stand out in our pool. If I could change one thing in the admission process, I'd like to slow down the push to "apply early somewhere," especially when that school may not really be your top choice.

Juniata College

by Ryan Hollister

The area representative has the power to make a decision on our applicants. Only about 10–15% of files go on to committee. We trust that the regional rep knows their students best and is capable of making a well-informed decision. Juniata takes a very holistic approach to a student's file. Students are encouraged to communicate with their counselor personally so, if need be, they can speak on their behalf in committee. We encourage a student to be up front if they had a bad semester and not let it be a shock or surprise to us. If I had one piece of advice, be open to new schools and new places. There are hundreds of choices across the country, all unique in their own way—one of them may be the right fit for you.

Lafayette College
by Chuck Bachman

Our typical applicant is read by two or three readers, starting with the area representative, followed by a senior reader. We don't take a huge percentage of files to committee as the senior admission officer can make most decisions. We wish students would share more of their honest feelings in the application and not try to tell us what they think we want to hear. I think we try to stress fit and keeping the college search in perspective. If we could give any advice to students, it would be to relax—it will all end up just fine. They will have wonderful college experiences regardless of where they attend.

Macalester College
by Lorne Robinson

Fifteen to 20% of our applicants make it to committee after a screening process that normally includes three reads by the area rep, a random staff member, and either the Dean or Director. People might be surprised by how much time we spend analyzing and discussing curriculum. It gets frustrating for us when the majority in committee want to admit a student, but there is just no more room left in the class. We wish that more students might explain special circumstances that affected their record and that they wouldn't share as many personal details that we really don't need to know. If I had one dream for a better process, it might be more standardized grading across schools (an unrealistic hope I realize), but at least more complete information on grade distributions would better enable us to interpret transcripts.

Muhlenberg College
by Alyssa Ellowitch

Our second reader is the area rep, and they can make the decision if it is a clear-cut admit or deny. About one-third of our applicants go to committee. Students connected to alumni and private-school applicants go through a separate committee review where the area rep meets with the Dean of Admission to discuss school groups and special cases. Since we care so much about community service, we wish students might tell us more about what they've done in their community. Many students only brush the surface, and we'd like to know more about their commitment. Our process is personalized—we read everything in the file. With two people doing such in-depth reads, we really get to know and understand the applicant better. I wish students would focus more on being students. Enjoy school for school's sake—enjoy the things they are learning and doing and not focus so much on their grades and boosting their resume. It would be great if students weren't so consumed by the college admissions process.

Union College

by Ann Fleming Brown

Normally two to three officers will read a file, starting with the area rep, followed by the director, and then our vice president. Only about 30% of our files go to committee as we try to avoid voting for consensus, which can often quash the minority opinion. We wish students might tell us more about their meaningful interests or what books they have read for pleasure. We like to know how they think and what they care about. We'd prefer not to hear about personal conflicts,

or relationship issues with family or teachers and why that affected their performance. Don't make excuses. We believe at Union that we still pride ourselves in trying to make a good match with students. I only wish students didn't feel the pressure to make decisions based on a timetable of deadlines.

Wheaton College

by Mike Geller

Unlike many schools, 100% of our applicants go to committee after two reads by admission staff, with the area representative being the first reader. I think I have a perspective of the school these applicants are coming from as the first reader, and I can set the context of the file for the committee. If there is one thing I wish applicants might share more is what their intellectual passion is, not what they think they want to do in the future but why they want to study a particular subject. I think what's unique about our process is that 100% of our files go through committee, and we encourage students to share personal portfolios as part of our review. If I had to change something about the admission process, I'd eliminate college rankings and tell students to focus on fit.

A New England Ivy League Institution

The reality is that with the volumes of applications we now receive, we just can't take everyone to committee. We rely on a first reader and an area rep to thin down our numbers, and the most impressive students and the weakest ones are reviewed by a senior-level officer for a decision. That middle 50% who remain will make it to committee, where we run two nonstop sessions in the early spring, including weekends. The reality today is you better have a passion or a hook—after we fill our institutional needs, there are just not that many spaces left. We want that well-rounded class with outstanding individuals, not well-rounded individuals.

A Select Northeast State University

We just started using the Common Application last year and saw a spike in our admission numbers, so things might get tougher this year. Traditionally, we've looked for a minimum of a 3.4 GPA, scores in the 1200 range (old

system), and a writing sample. Most applicants with that from in-state are in pretty good shape. Most of our pool comes from in-state, so we don't have the issue of big out-of-state numbers; so someone just a bit stronger than our in-state group should make it. We don't use much of a committee system—our senior-level people will do a quick review of those who make our cutoffs. With our rolling policy, however, we'd encourage students to apply early enough so we can review them before we fill up.

A Select Private Southern University

Most files get a second read by the area rep after a first read by a random staff member. In early decision, almost 100% of our applicants make it to committee—somewhat less in regular decision. If you really want us, tell us by going early—just look at our admit rate for early versus regular. It would be great if students might tell us what is unique and special about their curriculum and why they took those courses. Students should also remember they don't need to tell us how well they've done in school or all about their extracurriculars—that should be in their application. I think it would be great if we could limit students to a maximum of six applications, but I know that is unrealistic. They will need to narrow down eventually. And for advice—take a deep breath—strong students will do well wherever they go.

A Select Southern State University

We really don't run a traditional committee process for both in-state and out-of-state applicants. For our in-state students, we feel an obligation to take the top students in each high school in the state, who at a minimum should be in the top 10% of their class and have GPAs in range of 3.7 and test scores in the 1200 range (old SAT model). With our limited number of spaces for an out-of-state applicant, those numbers are even tougher for them. So it's rare we would spend much time on many applicants below those standards unless there is a special reason to look at them. I hope in the future we can become more sensitive to varying high schools' degree of difficulty, especially in grading practices, but that may be difficult to implement as numbers continue to grow.

To Friend or Not To Friend

Eighty percent of admission officers report getting friend requests (Kaplan 2010 study), but most don't accept friend requests. In some cases, colleges are eager to engage in conversations online, and they have created social media accounts specifically to converse with students. These are visible on the fan pages at social media sites. (Admissions officer profiles at Zinch are created expressly to communicate with interested students.)

If you do friend or accept friend requests, managing privacy settings is up to you—and remember that there can be glitches. Privacy settings change, requiring you to keep up with the changes. There can be technical glitches, too. In May 2010, Facebook changes temporarily allowed users to see friends' allegedly private information, including private chats.

Gil Rogers, Associate Director of Admissions Recruitment and Enrollment Technology at the University of New Haven, reports that while he accepts friend requests, he limits his activity to responding to wall posts or messages.

4

Choosing the Right (vs. "Best") Colleges

Choosing the "right" school is different from identifying the "best" school or the "most prestigious" college you can get into. Figuring out what the right school is for you is far more important than worrying about getting into the "highest ranking" college. In fact, it is misleading to use the singular "school" because the plural "schools" is far more accurate and important. That's because there are probably dozens of colleges where you'll be happy and successful, and some of those schools may be "lower ranked" than schools that you can actually get into. So, at least to start, we ask both students and parents to be open to the distinctions between right and best. Don't ignore prestige. Don't forget about rankings. Just recognize that they are different from what may be right for *you.*

In this chapter we discuss ways—and give you tools— to figure out which colleges might be right for you. We explore how to get beneath the surface of the glossy brochure and slick websites or the not-so-slick websites of schools that might be a great fit. Next we suggest ways to balance the tension between "right" and "best" schools. (Trust us: we're not oblivious to the lure of prestige or the importance of return-on-investment resulting from a "brand-name" college.) Then, we suggest ways for a family to decide which schools are truly good fits for the student.

Finally, we show you a way to assess which colleges that might be receptive to your candidacy. And then we show you how to reconcile the two sets of schools, those which might be right for you and those which will hopefully want you.

Throughout this chapter and the next, we refer to various lists of colleges that you should be making. We think of the process of choosing which colleges to apply to in terms of a funnel and a filter. You'll pour a few colleges into the funnel to begin—just to get started—and then fill that funnel pretty quickly. But with the filter—your research and the criteria that the college will be using in its admission decisions—many of those colleges that you poured in will not make it out of the funnel.

We recommend using four steps—which comprise four lists of colleges that you'll make. All four are discussed in detail later in the chapter, but here's an overview for now:

1. Create a **starter list** of the first colleges you think of that you may be interested in.

2. Create a **master list**—the widest part of the funnel—of all the colleges you're going to do research on.

3. Create a **semifinal list** of colleges reflecting those which have survived your research.

4. Create a **final list** of colleges you are actually going to apply to (usually about 9 to 12 schools).

Is This a Family Decision?

No! The use of the word "family" was an intentional and provocative tease. Choosing where to go to college really has to be the student's decision. But the process of exploration and consideration is going to be a family event. And whether everyone involved—particularly the student—likes it or not, that's the reality of the process.

Exploring the Possibilities

Everyone is going to have an opinion about where you should go to college. (Yes, we're changing voice here, simply to reinforce whose decision this is truly is.) Some families have known that Pat was always destined for Yale, or Notre Dame, or . . . wherever. How nice for them. And if you are like Pat and have "always" wanted to go to a particular college, that is a good place to start. But it is only a starting point. For the rest of you, here's how you should begin your search.

A Word About Numbers

Zinch is smart about reminding all of you that you're more than a test score. Indeed you are. But if your grades and SAT/ACT scores are pretty mediocre—and you're not a world-class athlete, musician, entrepreneur, or faith healer—you're going to have a pretty tough time getting into Harvard or Stanford or some other top school. It is not impossible, just very, very difficult. So as you put together your college list, we're going to recommend that you put aside your "numbers" and explore college possibilities very broadly. We'll come back to your grades, SAT/ACT scores, and extracurricular activities later in this chapter, as well as show you how to juxtapose your credentials against what a particular college "typically" looks for in a student.

Compile a List

Part of getting through the college search and admissions process—with as little stress as possible—is to stay organized. Start by creating a starter list of potential colleges. Some people do it on paper; others like to create an Excel spreadsheet. We've included Worksheet 4-1 below—just as a suggested format—to help get you started. We also have an interactive tool at www. zinch.com/firstcollegelist if you prefer to work online.

Worksheet 4-1 Starter List of Potential Colleges

Colleges You've Dreamed About	Colleges Your Parents Think You Should Explore	Colleges Your Counselor Suggests	Colleges Your Favorite Teachers Recommend	Colleges a Respected Adult Recommends

Your worksheet lists shouldn't be limited to just four or five colleges. Some columns might inlcude 20 different schools, while others only a few. Add as many as you like.

What Colleges Have You Thought About?

Many students—while still in high school or even in middle school—have been intrigued by certain colleges. It might have been where a parent or relative went. Or it could have been a military academy. Or an art college. Or a place where you attended a sporting event or a summer course. Add all the colleges that have hit your radar screen—for whatever reason—to your starter list. Importantly, include schools that you were turned off by in addition to places that intrigued you. Even if your initial reaction to a place is that you hate it, add it to the list. (Part of your exploration process should involve *why* you hate a place.)

These lists shouldn't be limited to just four or five colleges. Some columns might include 20 different schools, while others only a few. Add as many as you like.

Ask Your Parents for Their Opinion

Yes, this is your decision. But your parents (usually) know you better than anyone else, and they will have opinions and ideas. (Sometimes, they will intentionally express no opinion at all, in an effort not to influence you.) Even if you're furious at your parents at the moment—or convinced they really don't understand you—ask them anyway. Ask them what colleges they think would be right for you. Ask them what schools they think you should at least explore. You should even ask them what schools they think you would be wrong for. And you should ask them why—for all the schools they mention, the good and the bad. Then we strongly recommend that you add the schools they recommend to your starter list.

Ask People You Respect

Ask a few teachers who know you well what colleges they think might be right for you. Do the same with any relatives or friends' parents whom you respect. Listen to what they say, and add these schools to your starter list as well.

(Remember, this list is *not* the final list of where you're going to apply; it is a first-cut to help sort your choices.)

Put All of These Colleges onto a "Master List"

After you put all of the colleges you've thought about or that people have recommended to you on the starter list, you'll probably see some patterns. Certain colleges will appear multiple times. Some may have certain basic characteristics in common: size, location, religious orientation, reputation. Several might be outliers—places that have little in common with the others, but which someone you respect thinks may be right for you. Explore them all! Spending an hour or two researching a college where you might spend four years—and more than $100,000—seems like a pretty reasonable investment of your time.

Put all of the colleges onto a master list to use as you do your research. Add columns so you can keep track of the information you gather. We recommend using your master list as a dashboard, not a scorecard: a quick visualization of lots of information. By adding numerical assessments

to particular questions or characteristics, you'll be able to evaluate places a bit more easily. You shouldn't simply add up individual scores. Rather, use the scores to help guide you. Just as you don't want colleges to evaluate you simply as a combination of your SAT/ACT score and grade-point average, you shouldn't make determinations about colleges solely on their "ranking" or some over-simplified scorecard.

Research Every School

You may have some perfectly valid impressions of or gut reactions to a college, even before you've ever set foot on the campus or picked up their brochure. We respect that—to a point. Now you have to do some research.

For every college on your master list, we recommend that you start your research with two sets of tools:

- Respected guides—in short, what others say about a particular college
- The college's own website—what they say about themselves

Special Needs, Special Interests

Are you gay? Very religious? Disabled? Do you have some special need or interest that makes you "different"? If so, you shouldn't worry. But the burden is on you to do a bit of extra research to make sure that your needs will be met, or to ensure that you won't feel like an outcast.

So it really is a good-news, bad-news situation: you are virtually guaranteed that you will find a campus with people who share your interests, needs, orientation, desires. The bad news is that it is solely up to you to find these schools.

The other piece of good news is that there is an enormous number of reliable resources out there to help you with your search and to make sense of the results. For example:

The *Fiske Guide to Colleges* includes lists of schools with:

- Strong support for students with learning disabilities
- Pre-professional programs

  Architecture
  Art/Design
  Business
  Communications/Journalism
  Engineering
  Environmental Studies
  Film/television
  International Studies
  Performing Arts—Dance
  Performing Arts—Drama
  Performing Arts—Music

Princeton Review's *The Best 373 Colleges* includes lists of colleges that have:

- The most conservative students
- The most liberal students
- The most politically active students
- A very diverse student body
- Very little diversity
- Racial interaction vs. little racial interaction
- Strong tolerance for gay students
- Little tolerance for gay students
- The most religious students

Our Favorite Guides

There are lots of college guides out there. Some are good and some are garbage. Some do rigorous research and collect opinions from knowledgeable, insightful people. Others collect a handful of student opinions, or use abstract, often meaningless data and craft them into a definitive ranking. Be picky about which sources you use and trust. Here are some of our favorites.

The Fiske Guide to Colleges is a terrific resource. Its profiles of colleges are well-researched, thoughtful, and clearly written. Again, a great place to start; and we emphasize *start*. Ultimately you should do way more research about the places where you may be applying and attending. But start by reading the *Fiske Guide* profiles of all the schools on your starter list. We've added a column on our online master list called "Post *Fiske Guide* Reaction: More or Less Interested?" Very simply,

it means that after reading the college's profile in the *Fiske Guide,* was your immediate reaction to be more or less interested in the place? Just add that reaction to the list.

The Princeton Review is our next favorite. (Who can fault lists like "Best Party School" or "Dodge-ball Victims"?) We also like *College Prowler.*

As we go to press in the winter of 2010/2011, we have been working with Forbes to create a new ranking/report card of some 400 good colleges. (Forbes already has a ranking system which we find pretty useful.) But check our website—www.Zinch.com/forbesrankings—for the latest update on the project.

Whichever guidebooks or sites you choose to use, keep a record on your master list of your initial reactions to the colleges after reading the review. (That's why we call it a "post" review reaction.) We've provided Worksheet 4-2 to get you started.

Worksheet 4-2 Initial Reactions to Potential Colleges

College	Post *Fiske Guide* Reaction	Post *Princeton Review* Reaction	Post *Forbes* Reaction	Other Guide (Your Choice)

The College's Own Materials

Start with the college's brochure. They work hard and spend lots of money producing those colorful materials. You'll probably notice pretty quickly that all the brochures—and sometimes even the colleges—start to look alike. They all show old buildings covered with ivy; modern buildings of striking architecture; and college greens and quadrangles with students sprawled under trees laughing, reading, or engaged in serous conversations with professors and fellow students.

Most will probably include a handful of photos and profiles of diverse, interesting students who talk about what their experience at WonderfulU has been like.

Take it all in and take it with a grain of salt. Most of what appears in the brochure is probably true and a pretty reasonable depiction of what the experience can be like. Your experience at WonderfulU will be different—sometimes better and sometimes worse.

The important thing is to see what the college is saying about itself, and how that is different from what TerrificU is saying about itself. There will be subtle differences, and the closer you read the brochures and employ "an effective crap detector"—thank you, Ernest Hemingway—the better able you will be to read between the lines and recognize the differences between schools.

Every college has a website—DUH. Visit it. But visit it with a critical eye. What turns you on about it? What turns you off? Now start to dig deeper into the site.

Let's illustrate what we mean by the need to get beneath the lofty—and appealing—phrases colleges use to describe themselves. Worksheet 4-3 lists the colleges, then the descriptions. We chose 11 college websites—don't ask why it wasn't 10 or a full dozen; we don't remember—and copied the most descriptive portion of their "About Us" tab. Place the letter of the description next to the college you think is a match. (Yes, we provide the correct answers.) Then you'll understand why it is important to dig deeper in your research.

Worksheet 4-3 Assess Your College Knowledge

The Colleges

☐ Bates College	☐ Rice University	☐ Vanderbilt University
☐ Bowdoin College	☐ University of Chicago	☐ Washington University
☐ Cornell University	☐ University of Illinois	☐ Williams College
☐ Dickinson College	☐ University of Wisconsin	

The Descriptions

"A" is widely regarded as one of the finest liberal arts colleges in the nation, is a welcoming community whose members care deeply about the rigorous, challenging, and rewarding life of ideas and principles, and value their exchange and examination.

A liberal arts education at "B" isn't about being small and safe—it's about having the support to take surprising risks. Students undertake this journey with faculty members who are scholars and artists of distinction who actively shape their fields. From their first-year seminar through their senior year, students are immersed in subjects with teachers who illuminate their learning with their own passion for their discipline. Faculty and students work together in small classes, in labs, in performance halls, and in the field where students are active participants in performing real-world research.

"C" is a highly selective, private residential liberal-arts college known for its innovative curriculum. Its mission is to offer students a useful education in the arts and sciences that will prepare them for lives as engaged citizens and leaders.

Here at "D" we focus on undergraduate education, and our students get the benefit of full faculty attention and direct access to tremendous resources.

We attract accomplished, motivated people who tend to ask tough questions and who enjoy thinking through them in an environment where people take their studies—but not themselves—quite seriously.

Once called "the first American university" by educational historian Frederick Rudolph, "E" represents a distinctive mix of eminent scholarship and democratic ideals. Adding practical subjects to the classics and admitting qualified students regardless of nationality, race, social circumstance, gender, or religion was quite a departure when it was founded.

continued

The Descriptions *(continued)*

Today's "E" reflects this heritage of egalitarian excellence. It is home to the nation's first colleges devoted to hotel administration, industrial and labor relations, and veterinary medicine.

"F" is a world-class university, nationally and internationally recognized for our academic excellence, incredible students, inspiring faculty, exceptional value, and an amazing campus and community.

"G" is uniquely positioned to contribute to, and draw from, the strength and diversity of this world-class metropolis. We have also made an indelible mark on the world at large.

Our faculty and students are pioneers, discoverers, teachers, scholars, and change agents. We ask tough questions, engage the world around us, and pursue knowledge with rigor because we believe in the transformative power of ideas.

"I" is a world leader in research, teaching, and public engagement. We are distinguished by the breadth of our programs, broad academic excellence, and internationally renowned faculty

"J" is highly regarded nationally and internationally for the quality of our teaching, our research, and our service to society. No matter what your interests, you can find a top-notch program in our undergraduate curriculum.

At "K" you will discover a place that is passionate about teaching, undergraduate research and leadership development. We are a diverse community and support a student body from all economic backgrounds.

"K" is a comprehensive research university that fosters diversity and an intellectual environment that produces leaders across the spectrum of human endeavor.

Consistently ranked among the best values in higher education, with a highly recognized and respected residential college system, "K" transforms outstanding students into global scholars who envision new possibilities and leave their imprint on the world.

Use Social Media in Your College Search

Social media can be a great way to learn more about the admissions process and, more importantly, life at school. "Liking," "following," or subscribing to the YouTube channel of the admissions office can ensure that you get communications from the school, such as updates on local recruiting events, online chats, webinars, and school life highlights. Other social media links from the school (e.g., athletics office, faculty, departments, clubs) can also clue you in about academic and social life on campus.

Naturally, you should be a savvy social media consumer. Don't believe everything you read. Ask the admissions office if you have questions about information (e.g., application requirements or deadlines) or concerns about what you've seen online. Social media gives you access to the good and the bad. Some complaints could be "loud" online but be only isolated events. Use your good judgment. If a student online complains about the weather at a particular campus and weather matters to you, do online research to understand the climate.

LOOK AT COURSE LISTS

You probably have some idea about the courses you'd like to take. More likely, you have some idea about what you don't want to study. (We talk about exploring a college's distribution requirements later in this chapter.) Check out various departments' course offerings in a given semester. Do they offer lots of courses that seem interesting to you? Or only a few? Does a department's offerings have a particular focus or political approach?

Here's a tip that may seem obvious (but is often a surprise to many students once they enroll at a college): large universities typically offer lots and lots of choices in a given department. (Sometimes they are in large lecture formats or open only to upperclassmen. But variety is typically the watchword.) Small colleges, however, may offer just a few courses in a particular department in a semester. The upside is that they may be smaller seminars. It is very important for you to look at the offerings in a given semester and ask yourself, "Are there enough choices here—at any one time—that really interest me?"

LOOK AT COURSE READING LISTS

Check out the reading lists for particular courses. Only by drilling down and really exploring how a course is structured and what is expected of you will you really know if a course has the potential to excite you. Do the readings seem too basic? Too advanced? Too esoteric for your taste?

READ THE COLLEGE NEWSPAPER

Are the topics they cover of interest to you? Or do they leave you cold? Does the paper focus on campus politics or more national/ state issues? What issues do you find worthy of a bull-session? Are the events they publicize appealing to you or of little interest? Would you be double-booking events or spending your weekend evenings alone in your room?

TALK TO PEOPLE

Contact students who have gone to your high school and are now at colleges that you might consider. Do they like the college? Is it a happy place? Are the students grinds? Cutthroats? Too busy partying to learn much? Get some reactions from people who know the place now, not from adults who attended 20 years ago.

The "College" Facebook Scam

For the last few years, marketing companies trying to identify incoming freshmen have created College-specific Facebook groups for the "Class of . . .," complete with the school's logo. Students unwittingly joined these pages—sharing information—thinking they were connecting with the actual colleges. They weren't. Instead, they were connecting with private companies masquerading as those colleges.

Naturally, the affected colleges were quite upset. They felt their brand had been hijacked. And many students were also upset: they thought these were official pages of the institution and that they had friended real people at the colleges. So before you friend a college or join an online group, take the time to really check out what or who you're connecting with. The best way to do this is to go to the college's admissions site—or to Zinch to find the link to the official social media sites. Be a savvy online consumer!

The good news is that social networks are making it easier to find the official "university" groups and not just "interest" groups. For example, Facebook, YouTube, and Twitter have instituted "verified accounts."

Social media accounts without a verified-account badge are not necessarily fake; they just haven't been verified. (Getting a site verified costs time and money, and some places just haven't done it yet.) So, the best way to make sure that the accounts you're connecting with are legitimate is to get to them from the official admissions page on the college's website.

Certainly, you may enjoy exploring the perspectives of other social media groups related to the college, such as those of clubs, teams, alumni groups, departments on campus.

Also, in April 2010, Facebook launched community pages, which exist today for many colleges. This page pulls in content from Wikipedia and includes feeds from and about the school, and you can also see what your friends and others are saying about the school. If you post something on Facebook about the school, it may end up on the community page (as well as in Google Alerts or other ways that colleges monitor "mentions" online.

If you have questions or concerns about what you see on a social media site regarding a university, contact the school's Admissions Office. Most colleges are responsive. If they aren't, this is a data point to remember when considering that particular college.

Assume You Are Going to Change Your Mind

This is tricky but true: according to a recent Penn State study, more than 70% of college students change their academic major after their freshman year. Some 20% change it more than twice. Which means, odds are, that you will too. So although you will probably make your college choices based in large part on what you think you want to study, that major or course of study is probably going to change. That is OK. You have to start somewhere. But are the colleges you are looking at appealing if and when you change your mind?

Consider the Cost

The cost of a college education is significant. It is often described as the second largest purchase a family will ever make (after a home). It is also an investment, not simply an expense. The range of college costs is wide: from great public universities like the University of Arizona that can cost just over $13,000 per year for in-state students to private colleges such as Sarah Lawrence, which costs over $53,000 per year.

So, the cost of a college, a family's ability to pay, and its appetite to take on student debt are all factors. We can't prescribe when finances should enter into a family's decision about college choices, but we do recommend having candid conversations between parent and child throughout the process. (We discuss how applying for financial aid affects one's chances of admission—and how to maximize aid packages— in later chapters.)

Get Answers for Less Obvious Questions

Ask one of your high school friends whether she prefers a small college or a large university; an urban environment or a suburban setting; large lectures or small seminars. After an initial shrug of the shoulders, you'll probably get some thoughtful responses.

And they're probably all half-wrong—or at least mostly uninformed.

Huh? Think about it: how can you ask someone who has spent the last few years of high school in classrooms of never more than 35 people to give an informed opinion about a class with 300 students? Odds are you've never experienced a lecture class with 300-plus students. Large lecture classes can be great, or they can be deadly.

In fact, one of us was recently asked to recall the very best classes we remember from our college experience. Two courses immediately came to mind: a senior seminar with 12 people and a lecture course with more than 400. The surprise, of course, was the lecture. The class was in American History, and the professor was a master at weaving together political, social, and economic/business events, peppered by the impact of "personalities" who affected them. He brought all these factors together seamlessly and made history come alive in a way that we had never experienced. And he was a great storyteller. It was a "life-changing" intellectual experience: for the very first time, a history course was riveting. As a result, history became one of our life-long interests. Who would have predicted that such a transforming event would have taken place in a giant lecture course?

So what questions should you be asking? Here are some suggestions:

1. **Distribution Requirements** How do you feel about distribution requirements? Some colleges have extensive distribution requirements or core curricula. Is there a language requirement? A lab science?

2. **Sex, Drugs, and Rock & Roll** Are drinking or drugs a considerable element of the social scene? Do you care? What is the dating scene like?

3. **Competition** Is the place academically cutthroat or competitive? Or is there a serious but laid-back, cooperative approach to academics?

4. **Location** Is the campus near or far from a large urban center? Do you care? Is the campus an idyllic oasis in the center of an urban nightmare or in the middle of nowhere?

5. **Distance from Home** Does distance from home really matter to you or your parents? Will you want to go home for an occasional weekend? Or just major holidays? Is a four-hour drive on country roads more difficult than a one-hour flight?

6. **Community** Do you want to be recognized by professors, most of the other students, and maybe even the college president as you walk across campus? Or are you more intrigued by the unknown, by finding new activities, classes, or friends throughout your four years? We have no particular bias for or against big or small schools. The question is for you to think about where are you going to be more comfortable.

7. Weather Does weather matter? Do you hate the cold? Or have you never experienced a really hot climate? After growing up in the east, one of our sons wanted a college in a warm climate, but he wanted dry heat as opposed to humidity. It made his search a little easier.

8. Internships Are there pre-professional activities, jobs, or internships you want to explore? Do you think you want to work in government? In healthcare? In the media? Does the college offer good opportunities in those areas?

9. Study Abroad Is foreign travel or an exchange program part of your dream? Does the college encourage a semester abroad, and do they have easy options for taking advantage of foreign study?

10. Greek Life Is fraternity/ sorority life something you think you will be attracted to? Or turned off by? How prevalent is Greek life to the social scene on that particular campus? You may be very surprised by the importance of fraternities and sororities on campus. How do you see yourself fitting in with the campus social climate?

11. Political Orientation Are you political? Do you identify with a particular political philosophy, orientation, or party? Are you looking for a campus where the kids share your political persuasion? Or would you prefer energetic debate?

12. Sexual Orientation Are you straight? Gay? Bi-sexual? Still trying to figure it out? Would you feel more comfortable on a campus with a large, active gay community? Or would you prefer a more conservative atmosphere?

13. Art/Music/Theater Scene Is your idea of the perfect college experience one where you have lots of different performances every weekend? Is participation in theater dominated by theater majors? Or are walk-ons and open auditions encouraged?

14. **Sports** Is it a sports-oriented campus? Do most people participate in intramural sports? Or is the sports scene dominated by the varsity athletes? Do you love to work out at odd hours, and are there facilities available to you? Do you look forward to attending major intercollegiate athletic contests?

Visiting Colleges

Nothing compares to a college visit to help you decide whether a place may be right for you. We are continually amazed by how quickly kids decide whether a particular school is a good fit for them, often simply by spending 10 minutes on a campus. Sometimes it is a gut feeling: a quick assessment of how the students who attend a particular school dress or walk or look. Sometimes that instant assessment is the result of a campus tour guide. Other times it is hearing a presentation from the admission representative. Often it is the physical look-and-feel of the campus itself. But kids seem to know pretty quickly whether a place is right for them.

We once visited a well-known California university that had been our high-school junior's first choice. We gathered in the admission office before setting off on a bus for the campus tour—that's right, a bus! As we were boarding, our junior said, "Do we have to go?" "This is your first choice," we reminded him. "We really don't have to go on," he said. "We'll be stuck on the tour for the next two hours." We boarded the bus and took the tour. At the end, we said to each other, "We hate this place." And our junior said, "I told you we didn't have to get on the bus." He knew.

It's OK to Be Gay in College Admissions

Times have certainly changed on LGBT issues, and the Internet can be a valuable tool to identify a gay-friendly campus. Today's students are now out and proud, and campus organizations that support gay students abound across the country. Gay Straight Alliances (GSA) are present on many high school campuses, and those students have no desire to go "back in the closet" in college.

Colleges recognize this and seek to inform gay students about the safety and support for them on their campus. You may be surprised by how many colleges—from all across the country—are represented at college fairs presented by Campus Pride (www.campuspride.org). "Obvious" gay-friendly colleges such as Brown, Mount Holyoke, Oberlin, Smith, Vassar, and Yale make up only a part of their list. Schools like American in DC, U. of Oregon, Penn State, San Diego State, Southern Cal, and Syracuse all receive the maximum five-star ratings on the Campus Pride scales.

Not all schools are as welcoming. There are a few key signals to look for in identifying a gay-friendly campus. Does the school's nondiscrimination clause include sexual orientation? Are partner benefits available to faculty and staff on campus? Is there a student support group and faculty advisor for gay issues? How about course offerings? Every gay-friendly school should have courses that touch on gay issues, gay authors, or gay history.

I remember visiting a school in Pennsylvania several years ago and asking the tour guide about gay life on campus. Without missing a beat, the tour guide said, "We really don't have any gay students on campus." Suffice it to say that after I met with the admission director later that day, the tour message had a new script. It's important to let schools know if they are sending out a mixed message about this issue.

We discuss the college essay in many places in this book. The days of the "coming out" essay where a student tells their struggle of coming to terms with their sexual orientation is no longer unique or new. Tell your story of activism—how you've moved forward on your high school campus or in your community, inspiring others, organizing a GSA at your school, volunteered for gay causes, or raised funds to help gay youth less fortunate than you. You'll get your reader's attention, and maybe even turn your gay activism into a hook.

—MM

Our advice is to visit as many schools as you possibly can. Even schools you may not think are quite right for you or you think you may not get into.

We also suggest that you keep notes or keep a journal. Trust us: all these schools will start to blur after a few campus visits. You will want to remember whether it was "X" college that had the such-and-such requirements or it was "Y" university where everyone had to move off campus by sophomore year. Keep a record of your reactions: what you liked and what you didn't. You will be amazed by how much your notes will help sort through your choices.

How to Visit Colleges Intelligently

Visiting colleges is an essential part of the college selection and admission experience. *Every* student should do it— even if you've been absolutely certain since birth that you were going to attend Family-AlmaMater U. You've got to see it for yourself. But there are smart ways to visit colleges and less smart—no, make that dumb—ways to do it.

When Should You Visit Campuses?

Most kids start to visit prospective colleges during the summer between junior and senior year. That is too late! If at all possible, you should start midway through your junior year. Many "more informed" families—typically families whose kids attend high schools with very strong, well-resourced college advising staffs—use junior-year spring break to visit schools.

The reason for this "early start" is pretty basic: an earlier start allows you to do better, less harried research. It allows you to compare more schools and make better informed choices. It also gives you a head start if you want to apply early decision or early action. Those deadlines creep up on you way too quickly senior year.

The best time to visit colleges is when there are actual college kids on campus. Makes sense, no? You want to see what the students at Possible U really look like—and, if possible, actually get a chance to talk with a few of them. But that is not always possible. College kids do take off for spring break and summer vacation, and you can't necessarily coordinate your trips with the college's calendar.

Don't worry. There are usually some kids on a college's campus year-round. Many colleges have far fewer kids on campuses during the summer. In fact, many colleges run profitable athletic and academic enrichment programs for high school students over the summer. But there will be some college kids on campus—obviously the kids walking backwards running your tours.

One real plus of summer visits is that some colleges conduct personal interviews only during the summer months. That's because admissions officers are usually on the road in the spring and fall visiting high schools and doing college fairs. So check ahead to see if the colleges you're considering will schedule an interview.

Plan Ahead

Visiting colleges can be costly and a logistical nightmare. There are typically four parts to most visits:

- An orientation talk by an admission officer
- A campus tour (with a backward-walking student guide)
- Exploration of the campus on your own
- Perhaps an interview

Each of these elements take time, often about an hour each. That means you typically can't fit in more than two colleges in a single day—even if they are in the same city.

Very often colleges will want you to register for the orientation and campus tour before you ever visit the campus. Make sure you check well in advance of your planned visit!

Personal interviews virtually always require advance registration.

Should the Visit Be a Family Experience?

Kids usually don't visit colleges on their own. According to a Zinch survey, about 20% of last year's high school seniors reported visiting colleges without their parents. But another 20% reported that their parents went on visits with them only occasionally.

Do you need your parents (or just one parent) to visit with you? For transportation or logistical reasons, maybe. For any substantive interaction with the college? No. For a respected second opinion? Almost always yes.

Two concerns however: first, you don't want the college visit to be a stressed-filled experience. If you and your parent(s) are going to argue the entire time, make it a solo trip.

Second, and this is directed to parents: this is your kid's choice; this will be his or her college experience, not yours! A few years ago we visited an Ivy League college with our brother, sister-in-law and niece. (Yes, it was the niece who was the applicant.) She had an interview scheduled with a coach who was quite interested in recruiting her. For some reason, we all sat down together with the coach; for some reason, we didn't leave the office when the interview began. The coach started talking to the potential recruit, and our brother— Dad—started answering and asking questions. Our poor niece shot me a glance, and I dragged my brother out of the office. He looked half pissed and half perplexed. But I had to remind him that this was his daughter's interview and his daughter's potential college—not his. (She wound up loving the coach and the school, and got recruited. Four years later, she graduated and loved every minute on the campus— although she did stop playing the sport after her sophomore year.)

Many schools will often have two tours going on simultaneously because of the large number of visitors. It might make sense to separate—you go with one tour guide, and send your parents off with the other. You can compare notes after the tours.

Should You Visit with a Friend?

No. While it seems like a fun idea to visit colleges with your BFF, don't do it. Your friend may hate a campus while you (secretly) love it. You may be inseparable, but each of you has different strengths, weaknesses, ambitions, and dreams. This is going to be your decision and your experience. You've perhaps made eternal promises to each other never to part. Odds are, you'll both be better off by making the college decision on your own. Your friendship may be temporarily shaken by different school choices, but in the end, if you are really good friends, your friendship will survive. Don't complicate it by visiting schools together.

Keep a Journal

Try to make entries into your journal as soon after the campus visit as reasonably possible. In fact, here is something for Mom or Dad to do: you should keep a journal too. Your impressions of a campus count for something. More importantly, though, if you keep an objective record of your son's or daughter's reaction, that can be really valuable later on.

Keep a Filing System

You will pick up brochures, financial aid hand-outs, bookmarks, business cards, and just plain stuff. Keep it organized. While most of what you'll ultimately need is probably online, you may want to refer to something you've collected on your college visits. Stay organized.

Bookmark Useful Websites

How often have you found a really useful or important website; and then not been able to find it again? If you read something online that you like, don't like, or just want to be able to refer to again, make sure you bookmark it or keep it in a "favorites" folder.

Since finding key information on college websites can sometimes be difficult, Zinch offers school profiles with stats about the school, profiles for current students, profiles for admissions counselors, and reviews. You can maintain a list of "liked" schools.

Attend the Information Session

Don't forego the admission office information session thinking you will get everything you need from the school's website. We have never sat through a session that wasn't valuable—and often surprising.

For example, when we sat through the Princeton session recently—which took place in the unbelievably impressive and historic Nassau Hall—we were shocked to learn that not only did every Princeton senior have to write a thesis, but there were gobs of money available for seniors to travel and do original research.

Similarly, when our information session began at USC, the very first topic brought up by the admissions representative was campus safety. He knew his audience was largely comprised of parents—many of them from out-of-state—who were concerned about USC's South-Central LA location (a very tough and often dangerous neighborhood). His willingness to take on—without prompting—the one difficult subject that was on the minds of most parents effectively disarmed everyone in the room.

Take the Campus Tour

Students report (in the Zinch survey) that the campus tour was the single most important part of the search experience. Yes, most of the backward-walking college students who conduct these tours have a canned spiel, but they are also usually quite knowledgeable and candid. You will hear

Campus Tours

Many colleges, such as University of California at Santa Barbara, have a downloadable scavenger hunt for visitors who want to really get to know campus. You can check that one out at www.admissions. ucsb.edu/ToursAndPresentations.asp. Other colleges have scavenger hunts run for iPhone, Android, or other mobile devices to make campus visits more fun. Zinch strings these together into Treks—common routes for campus visits at www.Zinch.com/collegevisits.

what questions are on other potential students' (and their parents') minds. Typically you will hear some questions that are wacko and others that are insightful. Plus you'll get to ask your own. Enjoy the experience!

One warning: Sometimes, the tour guide can absolutely turn you off to the school, a school that you and/or your guidance counselor thought would be a perfect match. Tour guides often convey their personal biases or agendas during the tour. Sometimes it is intentional; often it is not. But you'll hear comments that are anti-athletic or anti-arts; pro-Greek life and anti-frat.

We really want to stress this point: don't judge the school by the tour guide! Your first impression and gut instinct are important, but be careful not to be too influenced by the tour guide. Remember, they are only one of many on that campus. Always get a second opinion, or go back for a second visit.

Do an Interview— If Offered

Most colleges don't require (or even offer) "substantive" interviews that count toward the admission decision. Because so many applicants typically live far away, most schools don't *require* interviews. But if the college encourages an interview, do it and take it seriously! Many of the smaller liberal arts colleges strongly recommend them. Hamilton, Muhlenberg, Wellesley, Bennington, Colorado College, and Swarthmore are just a few of the places where we've heard back from kids that the interview made a real difference in their decision to apply and, they believe, in their acceptance. Connecticut College hires a group of rising seniors each summer for the sole purpose of conducting interviews. (See the sidebar titled "The Interview" on pages 105–108 for a list of practice questions and do's and don'ts.)

Too often students do the interview without adequate preparation. Since a campus interview can come early in the process—before you even know where you might apply, you still want to make a good impression—you don't get a second interview if you think you fared poorly on the first. We encourage you to find someone who knows the admission process and do a mock/practice interview with them. And also do your homework about the school. Asking obvious questions like "How is the food?" will fail to impress an admission officer—and you really to want to make a positive impression on that admission officer! One way to do that is to have done your research about specific programs unique to the school that are of interest to you.

These interviews can make a real difference in their admission decision. Most schools will have a written report from your interview placed in your admission file after you apply. Even your decision whether to take advantage of the interview sends a message to the college that you are treating the search and admission process seriously. For example, if you live close to a campus and don't interview, that sends a message. A school which might have been in your "safety" category may suddenly become more difficult to get into—because you're sending the school a message that you are not that interested in them.

If you want an interview, plan ahead. Reserve an interview appointment well in advance of your campus visit. Most interview slots get booked far in advance.

Some larger schools, particularly the Ivies and Georgetown, will offer you an alumni interview after you have applied. The same interview questions apply to these alumni interviews as well. Know, too, that the alumni interview report will become part of your admission file. They count! (This is discussed again in Chapter 5—but in the context of your overall strategy.)

Some other schools may offer "informational" interviews. These are opportunities for you to ask subjective or probing questions that are important to you, and will help you make a more informed decision. Be sure you don't ask questions that are obviously answered on the school's website or in its written material. Even though these interviews don't "count," you still don't want to come across as a dolt.

So whether the school offers group information sessions or one-on-one interviews with an admission officer or summer admission intern, we strongly suggest you take advantage of these opportunities. But go prepared! And make sure you sign in that you were there—colleges really do keep track of that.

Send a Thank-You Note

Sending a thank-you note is good manners, and you want them to remember you positively. Also, most likely, that note will find its way to your admission file later in the process.

The Interview

You've probably heard horror stories about bizarre questions college admission officers have asked during interviews. Most—but not all—are apocryphal. (Yes, a friend of ours who served brilliantly as a senior person in the admission office of two Ivy League colleges used to ask, "If you could be any vegetable, which would it be and why?" But those days—and those wonderfully quirky personalities—are generally long-gone.

It is very important that you plan your strategy for the interview (see pages 107–108) The interview can be an important element in your positioning, and it is an essential factor in your packaging and communication. So be prepared!

Common Questions

Here are some of the more commonly asked questions we've heard about. Obviously no list can include all the questions you should at least think about before going on an interview, but these are a pretty good start. Questions 5, 11, 12, and 13 have "right" answers; see page 106.

1. Why are you considering this college?

2. How did you come to include us among your choices?

3. What makes you think this college and you are right for each other?

4. Where else are you applying and why?

5. Which is your first choice?

6. What do you hope to major in? Why?

7. What are your plans for the future? What do you expect to be doing 10 years from now?

8. What have you liked or disliked about your high school?

9. If you were the principal of your school, what would you change?

10. What would you like to tell us about yourself?

11. What newspapers, magazines, and websites do you read? How often?

12. What books not required by your courses have you read recently?

13. What television shows do you watch?

14. Tell me about your family.

15. How do you spend a typical afternoon after school? Evening? Weekend?

16. What extracurricular activities have you found most satisfying?

17. What are your strengths? Weaknesses?

18. Do you have any heroes, contemporary or historical?

19. How would your best friend describe you?

20. If you could talk with any one living person, who would it be and why?

21. How do you feel about:
    - Nuclear power
    - The use of drugs and alcohol
    - Advertising
    - Gun control

22. What events have been crucial in your life?

23. What is the most significant contribution you've made to your school or community?

24. What is the most important thing you've learned in high school?

25. What historical event do you feel has had the most impact on the twentieth century?

26. Tell me about your innermost fears.

27. What do you want to get out of your college experience?

28. If you could sit down with any professor here, who would it be?

29. What would you like to share with us?

The "Right" Answers

Some interview questions have "right" answers.

If the interview is at Haverford and the admission officer notes you are applying to Amherst, Middlebury, Harvard, and Swarthmore, you've somehow got to convince the admission officer that Haverford really is your first choice. Or at least that you are really gung-ho about the place. You should be honest and candid but not too naive. Admission officers know that over 70% of those who get into Harvard go there.

Don't try to impress an interviewer by pretending you've read books still sitting untouched on your shelf because they may have read them and might ask you about them. Similarly, don't profess to be addicted to the *New York Times* Op-Ed page if you're not prepared to discuss the recurring themes in Tom Friedman's columns or the political differences between Maureen Dowd and David Brooks.

If science fiction is your favorite escape, admit it. If the last book you read was by Dan Brown or Lee Child, that is OK. But don't pretend that they are serious history or serious literature. Reading is imperative to success in college, and you should get used to it in high school despite all your coursework, test-prep, and extracurricular activities. And under no circumstances should you ever say that you don't like to read!

If you are asked to discuss your favorite films or television shows, don't fake it. If only half the people who claim to watch *The NewsHour* with Jim Lehrer actually even turned it on, its Nielsen audience ratings would match those of *Lost*. Admission officers don't award extra points to students who say they love the films of Ingmar Bergman. Nor do they subtract points for those who admit to crying during *E.T.* or laughing hysterically during *Zohan*. Be yourself!

Interview Do's and Don'ts

1. **Arrive on time.** Sound obvious? You'd be shocked to know how many people don't! Actually, you should show up early.

2. **Dress conservatively and comfortably.** No tank tops, no bare midriffs, no cut-off jeans. But suits aren't necessary either.

3. **Listen.** You shouldn't do all the talking. If you ask the interviewer a question, listen to the answer. And, if possible, ask a follow-up question to show that you were listening and know how to probe deeper. And make good eye contact with the interviewer.

4. **Be positive.** Stress your strengths and explain your weaknesses, but don't dwell on the negative. And don't complain.

5. **Don't fight with the interviewer.** It is one thing to be feisty, and another to be acrimonious. If you are discussing something about which you feel strongly and the interviewer disagrees with you, stick to your position but don't berate or condemn his. You might humorously suggest a future conversation in which you can try to convert the interviewer to your position. Remember, the interviewer may be seeking to determine your flexibility and ability to think on your feet.

6. **Answer all questions.** Try to respond to all the interviewer's concerns. If you are confused, ask for clarification.

7. **Keep the conversation going.** Don't be afraid of a few pauses, but be sure you're not taxing the admission officer by making him ask all the questions.

8. **Be prepared to ask questions.** The interview is a two-way process; take advantage of it. You are there—in part—to figure out if this college is the right place for you. Don't be afraid of appearing stupid! Admission officers are pretty tolerant. But do prepare some thoughtful questions before you set foot into that interview room. You can be essentially guaranteed that the admission officer is going to

ask you, "So what would like to ask me?"

9. **Try not to lead the conversation into a "trouble" area.** If you know little about current events, don't direct the talk to that area.

10. **Be honest.** Always. And don't try to kid anyone. You can't win. If you don't know the answer to a question, say so.

11. **Enjoy yourself.** You'll survive the interview and many more. Turn the session to your advantage. Don't get psyched out and don't worry too much. If you try to do your best, you probably will be successful.

12. **Send a thank-you note.** A personalized thank-you note to your interviewer never hurts. Just make sure you spell the admission officer's name correctly.

Ranking the Colleges—Your Way

You've put together a master list of colleges. You've done some real research. You've talked to people. Now you have to do two more things:

- Evaluate the colleges and rank them based on your research.

- Make a rough assessment of your own desirability to colleges. (This means juxtaposing your self-assessment with a college's median SAT/ACT scores. This, admittedly, is a blunt instrument, but it is a realistic place to start.)

Worksheet 4-4 on pages 110–115 pulls together many of the questions you've asked about the colleges on your master list and provides spaces to note the results of your research about each school. As we said earlier, we suggest you use this worksheet as a dashboard, not as a scorecard. That's because the scoring system we propose works for us—but it may not work for you! Take what we have provided and customize it so that it works for you. As you'll see, we include room for only six colleges on this book version of the worksheet. You probably have investigated and are still considering far more than six schools, so just make as many copies of the worksheet as you need.

For those of you who prefer a more powerful (and flexible) tool, we have posted an interactive version of this on Zinch at www.Zinch.com/gettingin-worksheet.

Use whichever format—or tool—you prefer, but use something to help you sort through your choices and preferences.

The Scoring System for Ranking Colleges

Here's the scoring system you should use to rank the colleges your way. It's the one provided on Zinch for the interactive tool and works for Worksheet 4-4 as well.

Scoring: Please score each question on a 1 to 5 scale. (Yes, a 2.5 or other fraction is OK.) Examples of what the extremes mean are included with each question.

Scoring Criteria: The scoring system we include in this tool reflects our judgment. The criteria and their relative importance are subjective. They may or may not be what is important to you, so feel free to change criteria or the weighting (importance) we give them. We strongly encourage you to be rigorous and consistent in your thinking and assessment. That is, don't "stack the deck" because someone (a parent, teacher, counselor, or friend) likes a particular college or because you want to attend a place with a boyfriend or girlfriend. Choosing the right college is about what you want, not what someone else thinks might be right for you.

Worksheet 4-4 College Evaluation Worksheet

Your Initial College List

In the boxes to the right, list the colleges you're interested in; and colleges that your parents, counselor, teachers, or friends think you should look at.

Source of College Recommendation

Who recommended it?

How much do you trust or value this person's recommendation?
Score 1 = Not at all; Score 5 = Complete trust

Did anyone else suggest you attend or at least look at this college?
Score 1 = no one else; Score 5 = everyone you know

Gut Reaction

What was your immediate gut reaction to this place?
Score 1 = Hate it! Score 5 = Love it!

Research

FISKE GUIDE
Check out the *Fiske Guide* for each of the colleges on your list. What was your reaction? Were you more or less interested?
Score 1 = Totally turned off; Score = 5 Completely turned on

COLLEGE WEBSITE
Visit the college's website. Spend some time exploring it.
Score 1 = Totally turned off; Score = 5 Completely turned on

OTHER WEBSITES OR SOURCES
Did you get information from any other source which you trust?

THE COLLEGE NEWSPAPER
Go online and check out a few issues of the college newspaper. Did what you read interest you or bore you? Score 1 = Boring!; Score 5 = Very cool!

MAJOR OR COURSE OF STUDY
Let's assume you have some idea of what you want to major in or study.
From your research, how well is your initial academic interest satisfied?
Score 1 = Couldn't find my desired major or initial course of study;
Score 5 = Perfect fit

College 1	College 2	College 3	College 4	College 5	College 6

continued

Colleges

Research *(continued)*

DISTRIBUTION REQUIREMENTS

Some colleges have a core curriculum all students have to take. Others have a range of distribution requirements that can often be filled from a broad array of courses. And a few have no distribution requirements at all. For each college on your list, check carefully to see what the distribution requirements are for graduation. And then compare those requirements to your own interests.

Score 1 = Hate them; for example, you'll have to take something—math, a language, a science course—you can't stand; Score 5 = Way cool; no problem!

COLLEGE SIZE FLEXIBILITY

Many students are advised — or decide on their own — to look (principally) at particular size schools. For example, some students look only at smaller colleges while others consider only larger universities. How comfortable do you personally feel about the size of a college, and is that comfort level based on any personal experience?

Score 1 = You're absolutely certain about the size of school you want—whether it is large or small; Score 5 = Absolutely flexible about size

ACTUAL COLLEGE SIZE

For each college you've listed, how does that school's size correlate to your initial preference about college size?

Score 1 = No correlation to the size you're interested in; Score 5 = Absolute fit

LOCATION & SETTING

Schools— like homes — exist in an environmental context. Generally, they are either in an urban setting; a suburban setting; or a rural setting. (Some colleges which are "in" a particular city, are really in a suburb anywhere from 10 to 30 minutes from that city.) How attractive do you find the location of each college?

Score 1 = UGH! Score 5 = Really attractive to you

College Visit

Have you visited the college? We strongly, strongly urge you to visit as many colleges as possible — even if you have no interest in applying to a particular place. The more colleges you visit, the better your frame of reference will be. Just remember to keep notes about each visit. After the first few, visits will start to meld together in your mind.

Score 1 = No; Score 5 = Yes

College 1	College 2	College 3	College 4	College 5	College 6

continued

Colleges

College Visit

Have you visited the college? We strongly, strongly urge you to visit as many colleges as possible — even if you have no interest in applying to a particular place. The more colleges you visit, the better your frame of reference will be. Just remember to keep notes about each visit. After the first few, visits will start to meld together in your mind.
Score 1 = No; Score 5 = Yes

FIRST IMPRESSION
Many students have an immediate reaction to a school. What was your immediate overall reaction to each place?
Score 1 = Hated it; Score 5 = Loved it

THE STUDENTS
Score 1 = Hated them;couldn't see yourself among them for 10 minutes much less 4 years; Score 5 = Loved them

TOUR GUIDE
Some tour guides are great and others can turn you off—unfairly but completely—to a particular school. While it is important—and easy to say—"look beyond" the particular tour guide, it is useful to be candid and explicit about how much that person influenced your impression of the school.
Score 1 = Hated him or her; Score 5 = Your newest best friend

ADMISSIONS STAFF
The admissions staff represent but one tiny piece of a campus' "culture." But they can have a significant impact on how you initially view a school. Again, look beyond them, but record your impression, and decide later how much they influenced your perception of a place.
Score 1 = UGH!; Score 5 = Great people

THE PHYSICAL CAMPUS
How did you react to the campus itself?
Score 1 = Awful; Score 5 = Great!

THE "VIBE"
Just walking around on a campus you can sometimes get a feel for what the place or the kids are like. After spending time on campus, what was your reaction? (This is different from your initial gut reaction.)
Score 1 = Awful; Score 5 = Great!

College 1	College 2	College 3	College 4	College 5	College 6

Ranking Yourself the College's Way

Of course you are more than a test score, but your grades and SATs/ACTs will be a significant factor in where you should consider applying. In particular, your grades will be a very important factor.

Our friends at Zinch have pioneered a college-matching service based on an important belief: everyone really is more than their test score. Sure, SAT and ACT scores count (although they are less and less important at more and more colleges). But one of the factors you should consider. That's because most colleges typically refer to your SAT/ACT score as your "numerical shorthand."

What are your grades and SAT/ACT scores? If you haven't taken the SAT/ACT yet, what were your PSAT scores? And what is your grade-point average? Don't worry about the details yet; but quick: are you an "A" student? A "B+" student? What type of student are you?

Colleges publish their average SAT/ACT scores. They usually do this as a range of scores, reflecting the 25th and 75th percentiles—in other words, the scores largely in the middle. Thus it excludes the super-high scorers as well as the lowest.

Take your own scores— whether SAT, ACT, or PSAT— and see how they compare to the college's 50th percentile—the average of their 25th and 75th percentile.. If you are above their 50th percentile score, you're probably in the ballpark for admission (assuming your grades are commensurate with your SAT/ACT scores). Of course, that doesn't mean you're getting in; it means you've got a shot.

Reaches, Cores, and Safeties

We discuss reaches, core schools (possibles), and safeties in great depth in Chapter 5. But as you start to categorize the places you may consider applying to, it is useful to start grouping colleges according to their historic selectivity and your relative academic strengths.

We use an absolutely unfair shorthand when "categorizing" colleges and one's chances of admission. We base this solely on your SAT/ACT scores. (We know you're more than a test score; and we thank our smart friends at Zinch for helping the colleges de-emphasize their reliance on SAT/ACT scores. There are far more meaningful factors.) But our shorthand categorizes schools as reaches, cores, and safeties. Remember, we do this absent of any student attributes other than SAT/ACT scores. We're ignoring grades, athletics, extracurricular activities, legacy status, and everything else. But this is a useful starting point!

Now is when your college evaluation worksheet (Worksheet 4-4) comes into play. Look at Worksheet 4-5 below. It is a very coarse, rough-cut tool to help you assess three things:

- Your interest in a school
- The college's selectivity
- Your grades/SATs/ACTs

Fill in the worksheet for however many colleges you like and consider it your semifinal list. After you do, you'll have a simplified dashboard that compares your interest in a school with its selectivity and your rough competitive standing. This dashboard should not be treated as a hard-and-fast cut-off device. Instead, it should help you determine whether your colleges fall into the reach, core, or safety category.

Worksheet 4-5 Semifinal List of Colleges

Name of the College	College's Total Score from Worksheet 4-3	College's Median SAT/ACT Score	Your SAT/ACT Score	Gut Guess: Is This a Reach, Core, or Safety?
College 1				
College 2				
College . . .				

Deciding Where to Apply—Your Final List

How do you go from the semifinal list of colleges you created in Worksheet 4-5 to a final list of colleges to which you'll actually apply? Through a dynamic process of conversations with your parents and guidance counselor. Believe it or not, just getting this far was the hard part. Getting to a semifinal list means you've done your homework. The final step may seem monumental, but it's not. Where you finally apply is, of course, important. But if you've done smart research—and you have—you really can't go too wrong. You might get rejected at a place or two—in fact you should if you've included real reaches on your list—but you'll be fine.

Take the semifinal list and sit down with your guidance counselor. Be prepared to discuss why certain places are on the list and other schools didn't make the cut. And now talk strategy.

In Chapter 5 we discuss crafting your strategy. And in Chapter 6 we discuss tactics and the hook. Once you've read through those two chapters—and really thought about a positioning, a hook, and packaging—you, your parents, and your guidance counselor will be more easily able to settle on that final list.

5

CHAPTER 5
Your Application Strategy

You think you may know where you want to go to college. Now, how do you get in?

What is past is past; and yet all that is past is prelude. Yes, your high school course selection is pretty much set. Most of your grades that will be going to the admission committee are engraved on your transcript. You've taken some standardized tests and probably have a plan whether to take them again. The extracurricular activities that you've pursued have added to your overall high school experience and helped "define" or "position" you as a candidate for admission. And you understand, generally, what colleges are looking for and how they make decisions. So what do you do now?

Let's first define what "now" is. If you—or your parents—are reading this now, it is a pretty safe bet that it is the middle (or end) of your junior year, the summer before senior year, or the beginning of senior year. Whenever it is, don't worry. You have time to plan and implement a smart application strategy.

Improving Your Odds

We recommend an eight-step approach that comprises an effective application strategy. We go into more detail in this and the next chapter, but try to keep this big picture in mind as you assemble the various components and tactically execute the plan.

Step 1: Put together a realistic self-assessment.

Step 2: From the college research you've done, put together a starter list of reaches, core schools, and safeties.

Step 3: Evaluate your "early" options.

Step 4: Meet with your guidance counselor or college advisor for a reality check.

Step 5: Refine and settle on a list of schools to apply to.

Step 6: Create your application schedule.

Step 7: Figure out your positioning and packaging, and what we call the "hook," which is discussed in Chapter 7.

Step 8: Execute, execute, execute! Be thorough, accurate, and, of course, on time.

Step 1: Do a Self-Assessment

We tell all kids to take a step back and fill out what we like to call a "brag sheet." What have you done with your high school experience? What courses did you take and what grades did you achieve? What subjects did you really enjoy, and which ones did you just manage to get through? What were your SAT/ACT test scores?

What extracurricular activities have you participated in and which ones did you love? Have you won any awards? Were you elected to leadership positions? Did you have after-school or summer jobs? Did you volunteer? Travel?

List everything on a single sheet of paper. Then rank your activities, experiences, and awards from most to least important. (The Common App and most colleges will ask you to do the same on your application.)

Now take a step back. At first glance, how strong a candidate are you going to be? Yes, that answer will depend on which colleges you're considering applying to. But one key question is where do you rank in your class—are you a top-10% candidate or a top-25% or top-50%? There may be lots of factors that will affect your chances of admission, but it is important to make a candid self-assessment right up front.

Step 2: Create Your Starter List

Your master list of colleges should be complete now and all your basic research done. Now's the time for you to organize that list to better enable you to decide which schools—and how many—to apply to.

For the purposes of this starter list, we group colleges into three categories: reaches, core schools, and safeties. These categories are a function of the college's traditional selectivity—the average SAT or ACT scores and grades of their entering class—and your relative strength as a candidate based on your grades and SAT scores.

Reaches

Reaches are those places you dream about attending—and which are usually super-competitive in their admission practices. And your grades/scores may be just below what they typically accept. Even so, you still want to take a shot at these places and hope they find a reason to admit you.

Perhaps it is the school your mom and dad have talked about for years. Maybe it is a place where one of them attended, or where they met. Perhaps you've heard about it from friends since you started high school. Or it is that name school whose banner has been up on your wall—perhaps as an inspiration—since ... forever. However a place winds up on your dream list, be realistic about the odds, especially if it is a reach. You will definitely need a good "hook," that piece of the application puzzle that might make a reach school more realistic. (We cover hooks in detail in Chapter 7.) But you absolutely shouldn't focus all of your effort on reaches. Reaches should comprise about a quarter of your application list.

Core Schools

Core schools (or possibles) are those where you are certainly competitive, but there is a lower chance of admission. Your qualifications may fall squarely in their admission standards, but this school may have a more competitive applicant pool, with many applicants with credentials similar to yours.

You should have a pretty good shot at admission (let's say 50-50), as compared to the virtual guarantee of your "safe" schools.

Core schools should comprise about half of your application list. You have a very solid chance of gaining admission to these schools. And you should really love these places. Whether it is the curriculum, the feel, or even the prestige associated with these schools that excite you, they should be the focus of your effort. So make sure you research them thoroughly

Safeties

Safeties are your "best bets" for admission; those that are most likely to admit you. Again, based solely on your grades and SAT/ACT scores—and the college's historical admission data—you have an excellent shot at admission.

Safeties should not overload your application list. Find two or three you truly like—about 25% of the total number of schools you apply to. There should be fewer schools in the safety category than in your core or reach categories. A safety should be a place where you can see yourself fitting in

and getting a solid education. The most important thing is that you honestly believe you can be happy there.

A safety might be a smaller version of either a core or reach school. It could be located in a particular city or geographic area that is really important to you. Or it might be defined by a special approach to a curriculum— St. John's "Great books" curriculum, for example— or a specific academic major offering. One of the very real upsides of safety schools is that you might be very pleasantly surprised to see how interested they are in you. These schools genuinely appreciate your interest.

Remember this cardinal principle: treat your safety schools just as you do your core and reach schools. From initial contact through your application, and in all subsequent contact with the school, treat them respectfully, thoughtfully, and with attention to detail. There is no easier way to turn a safety school into a reach than by submitting a poorly written application or by ignoring their communications with you. And who knows, you might even receive a merit aid award from one of these safety schools. Remember, these "lower ranked" schools are often trying to raise their position—by attracting more attractive, better qualified students. So they may try to convince you to matriculate there instead of a "higher ranked" or more expensive competitor—a college that may be on your core or reach lists.

Rating Schools as Reaches, Cores, and Safeties

As we said, you're way more than a test score, but scores are a great way to rate the schools on your master list to come up with your application shortlist. By comparing the college's published mean SAT/ACT scores to your own (see Table 5-1), you'll get a rough idea whether the college is a reach, a core school, or a safety.

For example, based on SAT scores alone (on a combined 2400 point scale), here's how the colleges would stack up:

- More than 100 points lower, that college is a reach.
- From 50 points lower to 200 points higher, that school should be a core school or possible.
- 300 points or more higher than the college's mean scores, that school should be a safety.

Factoring in your grades may change things a bit. For example, having an A or A– average will allow you to have slightly weaker SATs. Conversely, if your grades are a B or B+, you'll have little leeway with respect to deviation from average SAT scores.

For example, Table 5-1 shows how your grades and SAT scores combine to determine the school's rating for you. We refer to SAT scores to make this exercise a little easier. If you have taken the ACT rather than the SAT or the college publishes statistics for only one of the standardized tests, use Table 2-1 on page 26 to convert your score first.

Table 5-1 Your "Numbers" Trigger the Basic Categories of Reaches, Cores, and Safeties

Your SAT Scores Compared to College Mean Scores (Combined 2400-Point Scale)

Your Grades	200 Points or More LOWER	100–200 Points LOWER	50 Points LOWER	Same as College Mean Score	100 Points HIGHER	200 Points HIGHER
A or A– average	Reach	Reach	Core	Core	Safety	Safety
B or B+ average	Long Shot	Long Shot	Possible	Possible	Core	Safety
B– or C+ average	Fughetaboutit	Real Long Shot	Reach	Still a Reach	Possible	Almost a Safety

Source: Princeton Review

How Many Colleges Should You Apply To?

We recommend applying to three safeties, six cores, and three reaches. That is a pretty good target. There is obviously no magic or ideal number of schools to which you should apply. Every student is different, but 12 schools is a reasonable place to start. Remember, you're balancing cost and effort—yours and the work that people who you'll be asking to write recommendations have to do—against the "odds" of admission.

A word on mathematical odds: increasing the number of reach schools you apply to does *not* improve your odds. It's like buying one more "lottery" ticket—you are competing against thousands more students in that school's application pool. We discourage kids from overloading the number of reach schools for one more reason: you don't want to set yourself up for too much disappointment in the spring when acceptance and rejection letters are sent out. (Or posted on the school's website.) You may think you can handle rejection well, but it is a different story if it really happens.

It is also important to check your high school's application policies. Some high schools limit how many applications you can file. In this techno-logical age where a push of a button can mean applying to another school, we urge you to resist the temptation. Only apply to those schools you could honestly see yourself attending.

Remember that your goal is to get a hearing at all the schools you apply to. Getting that full (even enthusiastic) hearing should be relatively easy at your safety schools. But you must take the time and put in the effort to prepare their applications well. You need to show genuine interest and enthusiasm as well! This may be a bit harder for you than for your core or reach schools. But if you apply to a college—any college, but especially safeties—you had better really want to go there. Which means you have to be willing to do what it takes to show that school why you're an attractive candidate. You want to make it easy for the college to put you into the applicant pool that commands real attention and discussion for admission consideration.

Step 3: Evaluate "Early" Options

One of the most important strategic decisions for many of you will be whether to apply "early" to a particular school and to know how that decision might impact your application strategy. First we're going to clarify what these early options are, and then we discuss how they might refine your personal admission strategy. There are three major variations on the early theme and a few less-common ones, which we address below. But the basic idea is that you apply earlier in your senior year, and you hear decisions from those colleges early on as well—usually by December 15. Here are the big three:

- **Early decision:** You make a commitment to a particular school and sign a contract. This agreement is signed by you, your parents, and your school counselor, and it legally binds you to that school if you are accepted. You're allowed to apply to just one of these schools.

- **Early action:** You apply to a school and receive a decision early in the process, but you are not legally bound to attend that institution. You may apply to more than one of these schools.

- **Rolling admission:** You apply to a school as part of the regular application process. The college evaluates applications as they are received—or roll in—and notify you within weeks of receiving the application. The earlier you apply, the earlier you hear back, and you are not legally bound to attend. You may apply to more than one school.

The "early" scene changes from year to year, as colleges change their policies. It is essential that you check a college's website to determine what their policy is that particular year. Several years ago when Harvard, Princeton, and Virginia all did away with their early programs, it was expected that many other schools might follow their example. Surprisingly, few did. And if anything, the early fervor—among both colleges and kids—has increased. (Note: Harvard, Princeton, and Virginia reinstated their early action programs for Fall 2011.)

Early Decision (ED)

Early decision is a process that favors kids who "know" where they want to go. (We put "know" in quotes because, as we've said, most kids change their minds—about lots of things—as they proceed through college. Maturity and experience has a habit of causing that.) But early decision is also a proven method of improving one's chances of getting into a particular college—assuming you have a reasonable chance of admission at that school in the first place. Remember, you can apply to only one school as ED.

We want to address (and dispel) the philosophical criticism of early decision right up front. (Our objective with this book is not to debate philosophical or political issues surrounding education. It is to help you get into the right college for you.) One of the major arguments against early decision programs is that they discriminate against poorer families. The argument is that kids in poorer school districts don't have adequate college counseling to know about early decision programs. And to compound the problem, these families can't or don't visit colleges early enough to make informed decisions—and thus are not prepared to make an early commitment.

In response to this criticism, many colleges try to provide that access earlier in the process. In addition, we have launched a nonprofit initiative called iCollegeBound.org which provides no-cost access to essential information and resources on the Internet. We believe in a level playing field. But it is up to high school guidance counselors and principals to make sure their families know about these resources and these options.

That said, both universities and students/families find the ED option useful. Let's look at it first from the college's perspective. The reality of early decision is that kids who apply ED are a self-selected group. These students see themselves as viable candidates for admission based on their own credentials and the college's historical standards. These kids—and their guidance counselors—believe they have a pretty reasonable chance at acceptance. The flip side of the equation is that kids who apply ED are still in a *very* competitive pool.

The competitive advantage to the student applying ED is that you are committing to that school. Any smart Dean of Admission or Vice President for Enrollment Management loves that commitment. They know that it positively affects their yield number—which affects their position in some of the magazine rankings. It also reduces their marketing costs. Because once acceptance letters go out to high school seniors, the power shifts from the college to the family. Colleges know they are competing with other colleges that have accepted you—all trying to get you to show up on their campus in the fall. Having that 100% guarantee you are coming makes their lives easier. So from their perspective, they would prefer to "front load" admissions through ED as much as possible—even if that means there will be fewer spaces available for an even larger group of applicants in the regular decision pool.

There is one group that is often well represented in the ED process, and it benefits both the college and the students. Those folks are student athletes. Here is the bottom line as it relates to ED. Division III colleges—and these are schools that range from Amherst to Williams in the northeast, to Colorado College and Pomona out west, plus hundred of other great, smaller colleges in between—have no athletic scholarships. So the only way in which a coach can get a binding commitment from an athlete that he or she wants is through ED. Early decision is the major athletic recruiting tool at smaller colleges. Whether or not financial aid is also available to that prospect is a separate matter. But in terms of getting in, ED and athletics are joined at the hip.

Does ED make sense for you? If you have started the college search process in your junior year, had the opportunity to visit a selection of colleges, and done real research into a variety of schools, then the ED option may make sense.

The statistics speak for themselves. Most colleges using ED have a somewhat higher admit rate, often combined with slightly lower academic standards for those admitted through ED. Take a look at Table 5-2 on pages 130–131. It compares the admit rates—under early versus regular admission programs—for the Ivy League and five other highly competitive schools.

Table 5–2. Early Decision Statistics for Top Colleges

| College | Year | Acceptance Rate | | Regular Decision Volume | |
		Regular Decision	Early Decision	Applications	Acceptances
Brown	2014	8.2%	19.9%	27,300	2,237
Columbia	2014	7.6%	21.0%	23,200	1,765
Cornell	2014	15.1%	32.7%	36,350	5,502
Dartmouth	2014	9.9%	28.8%	17,200	1,704
Harvard	2014	6.9%	N/A	30,500	2,110
Penn	2014	11.4%	31.2%	23,100	2,630
Princeton	2014	8.2%	N/A	26,250	2,148
Yale*	2014	5.9%	13.9%	20,600	1,210
Williams	2013	20.4%	36.5%	6,017	1,229
Colgate	2014	33.0%	57.8%	7,871	2,596
Kenyon	2014	38.1%	53.2%	3,723	1,417
Lafayette	2013	44.5%	61.9%	5,189	2,307
Rice	2013	21.5%	34.0%	10,463	2,254

* Yale uses single choice, not early action.

Early Decision Volume		Class Statistics	
Applications	Acceptances	Percentage Filled by ED Acceptances	Expected Size of Freshman Class
2,850	567	38%	1,485
3,000	631	59%	1,070
3,600	1,176	37%	3,150
1,600	461	42%	1,090
N/A	N/A	N/A	1,655
3,850	1,200	50%	2,420
N/A	N/A	N/A	1,300
5,260	730	56%	1,310
614	224	41%	549
651	376	43%	875
340	181	38%	473
446	276	43%	616
709	241	27%	894

ED Rounds 1 and 2

A few schools offer two rounds of early decision: a first round with a November deadline and second round with a December deadline. The idea is to give (often disadvantaged) students who did not have great college access a bit more time and to give kids sitting on the fence a bit more time before committing to the ED's legally binding process. Some of the colleges that offer this option are Connecticut College, Franklin & Marshall, Oberlin, Rollins, and Wesleyan, among many others.

With most ED round 2 programs, you are allowed to apply to other colleges in the regular application process. You commit to the ED2 school in January and hear from them in February. If you're successful, you will be required to withdraw your other applications.

Some college counselors have figured out how to "game" the system just a bit. They have kids apply ED round 1—with the earlier deadline—to a reach school. If the student gets in, great. If not, then he or she has time to apply to a core school ED in round 2. You still have better odds in the ED2 pool than in the general applicant pool, but you have to be really organized to take advantage of this tactic.

A few words of advice. Use early decision wisely. Just because a college may take a large percentage of its class early doesn't mean you'll get in—if your credentials are marginal. ED can improve your odds, but make sure you really want to go there. Remember, you sign a legally binding contract when you apply!

Visit the campus one more time if at all possible. Stay overnight, sit in on classes, talk to students before making that commitment. And be realistic about your early chances.

Remember too that a significant percentage of ED applicants are deferred to the regular pool. Do not take that as a rejection; it is a deferment and means you still have a shot! Most ED schools will outright reject you in the early round if they think you have little chance of being admitted in the regular pool. (They don't want to review an application a second time if they think the student doesn't have a real shot; that is additional work they'd rather not do.)

If you're deferred in the ED round, there are things you can do to enhance your prospects in the regular round. Think strategically what you might do to enhance your application. It could start with a strong letter of interest and intent from you that updates the college on any significant changes since filing your ED application. It might mean a letter from your favorite senior-year teacher or an updated addendum from your counselor about your first-semester work. Remember that senior midyear grades were not part of your application package or the college's ED review. So getting a few As in those courses can make a world of difference. (Just one more reason why you should take your senior-year courses seriously and avoid senior slump!)

Early Action (EA)

Many colleges prefer to offer an early action option, rather than early decision. Boston College, Chicago, Georgetown, MIT, Notre Dame, and Villanova are just a handful of top schools that only use EA. Under the EA option, you typically apply by November 1 and hear by December 15. Most importantly, you don't have a legally binding commitment to attend that school. Under most EA programs, you are usually allowed to apply to other EA (and regular decision) schools. You are not, however, allowed to apply to an ED school. (We think you can see the logic in that: you're asking the EA school to take the time to evaluate and tell you early; but if you were allowed to apply to an ED school, you'd secretly be saying to that college that you love them more. No one likes to be two-timed and jilted.)

Some schools, like Yale and Stanford, have their own, somewhat modified, and very particular approaches to EA. They use a hybrid version called **single-choice early action.** This program restricts the applicant from applying EA to any other school. It does, however, allow them to pursue other schools in the regular decision process. So your application to either of these colleges sends a message that you love them most—or pretty close to most—and they, in turn, have a pretty good sense that you will matriculate on their campus.

What complicates the EA picture is that Harvard and Princeton are now joining Yale and Stanford in single-choice early action. And in the rarefied air of Harvard-Yale-Princeton-Stanford, there is, believe it or not, competition among those schools to attract the very best students. So showing early love to one of the big four can lead to earlier bonding, if not outright commitment.

Check with each school you are interested in to see what they allow. There are real differences among colleges with respect to application deadlines and notification dates.

EA is much more popular with students who aren't ready to make that binding ED commitment. But your application sends the school a clear message that they are most likely your top choice. The philosophy behind EA is pretty clear. It allows a college to tell you that you will have a place in the class at that school, but take your time to think about it and explore other options if you like, and let us know your decision by May 1. It makes you feel good and makes you feel good about that school.

Strategically, it also allows you to revisit and reshape your master list. Very often a student who wants to attend an Ivy League school might get an EA acceptance at Boston College, Chicago, or Georgetown. Having an EA acceptance at a top school will often allow a student to adjust the regular decision application process, particularly for safeties.

On the flip side of the equation, unlike some ED schools, most EA schools cut little slack in their standards for their EA applicants. They often accept only the top of their applicant pool, and in most cases they defer a significant proportion of EA applicants. EA schools rarely deny in big numbers—they want a large pool to revisit during the regular decision process. They also know that a significant number of applicants may be using them as a safety or core school in that student's application strategy. Also unlike ED, EA can be an enrollment manager's nightmare because there are no guarantees of who will attend from the admitted group.

If you are accepted EA, you can be can be sure the college will direct some heavy-duty (though subtle) marketing in your direction—all designed to convince you to matriculate on their campus.

Rolling Admission (RA)

Rolling admission is a process popular with many public institutions and is growing in popularity with private schools as well. Very simply, RA means that the earlier you apply, the earlier you hear the school's decision. Sometimes that decision can come just weeks after your application is submitted. To this day, Steve can remember getting that fat envelope from the University of Michigan on October 17. And a generation later, his son Jacob heard from Arizona State the second day of his senior year! There is nothing better to relieve the stress of the admissions process than a very early acceptance from a college you really want to attend.

Some kids use RA schools as safeties. Others use a school as a top choice, and they know their odds of admission are better the earlier they apply.

From the admission officer's perspective, RA is a terrific tool to manage large numbers of applications. Rather than waiting until the application deadline to evaluate a whole cohort of applicants, RA allows a school to admit qualified kids as their applications come in. Selective schools like Michigan and Wisconsin are known for "rolling early." That means they will look at significant numbers of applicants, especially those of out-of-staters, in the late fall and make decisions on those applicants.

The downside for students who procrastinate is that openings sometimes close out early as qualified kids are accepted. We've seen several popular SUNY New York campuses, such as Binghamton and Geneseo, close off applications ahead of their posted deadlines. That's because they know they are close to capacity or may even be overenrolled. So remember this important rule about schools with rolling applications: apply early! The more selective the school, the earlier you should apply. Waiting too long to send in your application is a stupid way to turn a safety or core school into a reach, so don't delay! If there is no room left, it won't matter how qualified you are.

Step 4: Meet with Your College Advisor

This might seem like a no-brainer—of course you're going to meet with your college counselor, you say. The question is when? And how prepared will you be in order to make that session productive?

Most high schools which are on top of the college process try to meet with juniors in order to educate them about the process. Unfortunately, many school districts have seen their counseling budgets slashed. Consequently, it is not uncommon for a single college counselor to have a student load of 300 to 400 students, or even more. With that sort of caseload, it is not unusual for students not to get to see their college counselor until senior year. And it is not unusual for those sessions to be brief. So what should you do?

1. Be pushy but polite. Squeaky wheels do get more attention. But broken wheels tend to get sent off to the junkyard. Recognize that your counselor probably has a substantial workload. Be respectful of that burden. But make sure that you—and the counseling office—don't miss any deadlines.

2. Determine what sort of help you really need. You want your counselor's attention where it counts. At the very least, you will want a great school recommendation—which often comes from your college counselor. Do you really need your counselor to explain the admission process to you? Not if you've read this book you don't! You do want to know if there are colleges which look favorably at kids from your high school. And you want to know about your attractiveness as a candidate relative to others from your high school class. In short, you don't want to "waste" time on basics. Instead you want insights and customized recommendations.

3. Be prepared. When you get your appointment with your college counselor, make sure you arrive prepared. That means if your counselor asked you to complete or submit any forms in advance—such as a brag sheet—make sure you've done so. Then, go in with a printed list of the schools that comprise your reaches, core schools, and safeties. (It doesn't hurt to have a list of other schools you looked at and have rejected.) If you've used our evaluation tool, it would probably help to share that with your counselor as well. Let her see what criteria you used and how you assessed each prospective school. If she thinks you've misjudged a place or should add another school to your starter list, listen to her. This discussion will prepare you for Step 5 of your strategy, when you refine and settle on the final list of schools to apply to. Finalizing the list shouldn't take place during this first substantive conversation with your counselor, but the process of refining that list should now get underway.

4. **Be ready to discuss the early options with respect to your list.** Just make sure you've read and digested the pros and cons of each option.

5. **Be prepared to discuss your positioning, your packaging, and your hook.** (Positioning and packaging are addressed later in this chapter, and Chapter 7 is dedicated to the hook.) So when you meet with your guidance counselor, make sure you've thought about possible positionings and hooks.

6. **Leave the meeting with a list of concrete next steps.** What do you have to do next; and what does the counselor have to do? You should have a specific "to do " list.

Step 5: Make Your Final Where-to-Apply List

At some point, you have to make some hard decisions. And the toughest is where to apply. You (or your parents) may think this is a do-or-die, life-altering decision. It really isn't; but we're not going to be able to convince of that, so we won't try. Instead, we'll encourage you to make some decisions—and move on!

Here is a simple checklist. But remember, these are recommended numbers. You might, for example, choose to add an extra core or remove a safety. The final choice is yours.

✔ Have you identified 3 or 4 reaches?

✔ Have you settled on 5 or 6 core schools?

✔ Have you figured out 3 safeties where you could really be happy?

✔ Have you fully evaluated an early-option strategy?

If you've done your research and (relatively) objectively assessed your options, it shouldn't be too painful to make that final list. (Even if you've decided to apply ED, you still need to have a full list. There are no truly "guaranteed" admissions. Because if you do apply early—and then don't get in—you need to move pretty quickly to get those applications off to regular-admission schools.)

Step 6: Create Your Application Schedule

Don't miss deadlines! There is no dumber way to miss out on a possible acceptance than to miss a deadline. Schools are not flexible about this. Remember, colleges look for reasons to reject kids, and the easiest reason is a student's inability to make a deadline.

If you, your parents, and your counselor think that an early option makes sense for you, don't procrastinate. The odds of admission under early programs are somewhat better at most schools. But many kids

forego this opportunity because they don't think they're really "sure" about a particular school. Big question to ask yourself: How much more sure do you think you'll be in two months when all applications are due? Or will you have one more credential— great first-semester grades or an athletic award, for example—in January/ February that you won't have in December?

Once you've made that early-option decision, make

a realistic schedule. And remember: everything takes longer than expected. Leave time for editing and rewriting your essays, for "nudging" teachers to write those recommendations, and for presenting supplemental materials. Write out a realistic schedule and stick by it. It will reduce the stress.

Step 7: Determine Your Positioning and Packaging

Positioning and packaging are very important—and often misunderstood—concepts. We didn't invent them. But we did introduce them to the admissions lexicon more than 25 years ago. And since then they have been used and abused by a generation of kids, parents, and counselors. We want to make sure you understand what they really mean and how to use them intelligently and to your advantage.

Remember the first myth we presented way back in Chapter 2—that colleges are looking for the well-rounded individual? As you've now heard way too many times, colleges are looking for a well-rounded class. Every school needs to fill out academic departments, music and arts programs, and athletic teams. Admission offices are sensitive to development and legacy concerns, diversity and financial constraints. Consequently, the class they admit reflects these competing institutional needs and constituent pressures.

The admission directors at all of the top schools report that they could easily fill their entering class with only valedictorians or only kids with straight 800 SAT scores or 4.0 averages. And indeed the admissions job would be a lot easier. Instead, they look for individuals with talent and passion. The goal of the well-rounded class is the true challenge for that admission office.

And your goal is to present the admission office with a clearly defined position in an attention-getting application package. Some aspects of your positioning and packaging are beyond your control, like your socioeconomic status and your SAT/ACT scores. Other elements, like your essay and your extracurricular activities, are under your control. We focus here on the ones you have control over so you can use them all to your best advantage.

Positioning

Positioning refers to how the admission committee "sees" you in their collective mind. What position they slot you into. What niche you fill. Or, to be even blunter, what need you satisfy.

Are you a super-science student? Or a talented quarterback? Are you a first-generation kid whose parents don't speak English at home? Or a development prospect whose family can and will help build a new language lab? Are you going to thrill the professor who teaches James Joyce? Or the kid who will organize students to clean up the next oil spill in the Gulf?

Your positioning affects how they see you as an individual and how they see you in comparison to other kids applying to that school. Positioning is not a concept or effort in isolation. It is a reflection of what you say, what others say about you, and what other applicants say about themselves. It is a competitive effort to secure a preferred place in the prospect's—the admission officer's—mind. Positioning is a function of what the committee takes away from your application. And that, in turn, is a function of how you "package" the information in your folder.

Got all that? Don't worry, it's not easy. But neither is it that complicated.

Think about it this way: the admission committee sits down to discuss applications from George Washington High School in Anytown, USA. The admission officer responsible for Anytown presents the candidates from Anytown. Her presentation may go something like this:

> "Mary Jones is the kid from George Washington who . . . "

How you help the admission officer fill in that sentence is your positioning.

If the admission officer completes the sentence with "is the 3.8 student who's taken three science APs getting fives on each," you know Mary's positioning. She's the female science whiz.

How about if the admission officer presents Mary this way? "Mary Jones is the kid from George Washington who's got a 3.3 but went to the state music competition as a clarinetist. She didn't win, but her teachers love her and say she's in the stands for every football, basketball, and baseball game cheering on her friends with her clarinet." Musical positioning? Probably not. Pep squad? You bet!

Few colleges get excited today about the three-sport athlete who also writes for the school paper and belongs to five clubs at school. That might be a great kid, but it isn't easy for the admission officer to slot this kid. There is no clear positioning that helps the admission officer put together the well-rounded class mosaic.

To position yourself, the college needs to see your passion, to see how you tick and where you lead. In which of those three sports are you a star? And will you serve the coach's needs? Which of your organizations made a real impact in your high school community? And were you responsible for that impact?

Packaging

Packaging is the tactical companion to the strategic positioning. Packaging focuses on how you influence that desired positioning. It includes what you say about yourself and what others say about you in your recommendations. Packaging involves two elements: the substance and the presentation. What you say in your essay and what you list as your most important activities can make a critical difference in the admission committee's perception of you and in their decision. Consequently you want to make sure your presentation is clear and concise. You want it to be well organized and well written and to get your major points across easily. Don't take two pages to say what you can say in a paragraph.

To position yourself, you might consider what a college is looking for. Does a kid from New York have more geographical appeal in Ohio than to a college on the East Coast? It does, and you shouldn't be afraid to say you want to study in a different part of the country from where you grew up. If a school historically looks for a certain type of applicant, don't be afraid to say you are that type of candidate. (For example, if it is a religious college.) Colleges want to see and hear the right things from you, but it is what they remember about you that really counts.

If packaging is done right, it should feel natural to both you and the admission committee. Packaging is not about a fancy wrapping around a disappointing gift inside. Rather, it is about ensuring that the box is easy to open in order to appreciate the contents. Think about how Apple packages all of its products. Simple, elegant, functional. Now compare that to some of the items you've purchased that require scissors, knives, or a veritable chain-saw to open their small clear-plastic packages. By the time you get the packaging open, the quality of the product inside is almost forgotten. Similarly, think about the large cardboard boxes with tons of Styrofoam cushioning. How often have you said to yourself, "I know they have to protect the product during shipping, but really, there's got to be a better way."

That's what packaging—even in the college admission context—is all about. In an ideal application, you shouldn't even have to think about packaging—it should all be sincere and real. Your extracurricular and summer activities would complement your academic profile and say something memorable about you. Your volunteer work might have given you valuable experience in the field you wish to study. But how do you get that information across clearly and convincingly?

You don't want to be like a holiday gift—where the beautiful wrappings intrigue and entice you to open it first—but then it disappoints when you finally get it open. It is what is inside that really matters. You want it to be attractive and intriguing at first glance, with content that lives up to the created expectations—and more. Better still, you want it to generate the right response: "This student is exactly what we're looking for."

The Essay

The essay is the most important piece of your positioning and packaging. It is the one piece of the application where you are fully in control. (Yes, you get to choose who writes your recommendations, and you can subtly influence what your teachers say. But they are in control, not you.)

A well-written essay—versus a poorly written essay—can make or break an application. Many an admission officer who has been impressed by your transcript can be equally disappointed by your essay. Though a well-written essay may not overcome a weak transcript, it might make the difference on an application where the admission committee is torn which way to go.

The essay is the single most important element of the application that you can use to directly influence the committee's perception of you. If you position yourself as an aspiring journalist, that essay better

read like a well-tuned Pulitzer prize contender. It better be clear, and structured like a fine piece of journalism. If you are an aspiring playwright, your essay should probably be dramatic or comedic. If your positioning involves being perceived as a sensitive, reflective type, your essay's topic should echo that sentiment. And if your desired positioning is as a math whiz, you should take great pains to communicate the basis of that passion—in terms that non-math folks can appreciate. (The perfect math-whiz essay would also connect with the math major on the admission committee who would see your brilliance and communicate it to her admission colleagues—and perhaps to the math department itself.)

Many applicants misuse the essay. Not only are their topics boring, but they usually don't tell the committee anything of value to help their cause. Too many students try to appear intellectual and wind up sounding like shallow pseudo intellectuals. Or they write about an extracurricular activity or summer job and what they learned from it. This is tame, forgettable stuff. You want the admission reader to remember you.

Again, put yourself in the position of the admission officer. She may have 50 folders to read every night! (Is it better to be the first or the 50th essay she reads? Neither if it is boring, and it doesn't matter if it is great.) If your essay is boring or pretentious, eyes will glaze over and you've lost an important opportunity to make an ally. And believe us, way too many are boring or pretentious! We cannot overemphasize how many essays we've read where the student thinks he is being funny or at least witty. In

Your Essay Speaks Volumes

Unlike many college admission officers who look at the transcript first, I always read the essay. When I was doing a first read on a file and would bring 30–40 files home a night to read, I'd stack them on my bed and start reading essays. To me, the essay gave me that first glimpse into who the candidate was—what was their passion, what motivated them, and how they spoke from the heart and soul. It was their chance to tell their story. As I read them, I separated them into three piles—the great essay, the OK essay, and the poorly written essay. And I did this only on what the applicant had written—no judgment for spelling, punctuation, or writing (remember, Brown used to require a handwritten essay).

After I made those piles, I made my second pass through them. I reopened the files of the essays I loved to the transcript page, hoping it might mirror the quality of the essay. If it did, they moved into a new first file and got my highest ratings. The rest went into new piles two and three—two meant still in good shape and three meant less likely because of a transcript that would not stand out in the Brown pool. I'd go next to the OK essays, and it would take a spectacular transcript to vault into pile one, while the others would fall into their respective places in piles two and three. Finally, I'd turn to the poorer essays, and rarely, if ever, would they climb into my pile one.

I would then complete the read of the rest of each file, slightly tweaking where a file might fall if recommendations or other reasons might warrant that change. But for me, the essay set the tone and told the story and often the fate of that applicant.

—MM

fact, he is being neither; it is a lame, sophomoric attempt. Just because your mother or best friend thinks you're funny doesn't mean you are. Humor is a great tool in an essay—if it's really funny.

Find a tough critic to read your essay and give you honest feedback. Ask that person to tell you the first thing that comes to his mind about you after reading it. Is that your intended positioning? Try the same exercise on a second person. And stress to each of these readers that you're not looking for sugar-coated niceties. You want candor. And, unlike Jack Nicholson's admonition, "You *can* handle the truth!"

If you need inspiration for an essay topic, check out the Common App online. It includes a variety of essay questions that the colleges use. Last year's questions offered a range of options:

1. Evaluate a significant experience, achievement, risk you have taken, or ethical dilemma you have faced and its impact on you.

2. Discuss some issue of personal, local, national, or international concern and its importance to you.

College Essay Organizer

Several of our friends have created a very useful web service called the College Essay Organizer. It includes some very cool tools that help you organize the various essays required by different colleges. It is worth checking out: www.collegeessayorganizer.com.

3. Indicate a person who has had a significant influence on you and describe that influence.

4. Describe a character in fiction, a historical figure, or a creative work of art (as in art, music, science, etc.) that has had an influence on you and explain that influence.

5. A range of academic interests, personal perspectives, and life experiences adds much to the educational mix. Given your personal background, describe either an experience that illustrates what you would bring to the diversity in a college community or an encounter that demonstrated the importance of diversity to you.

6. Topic of your choice.

Question 6 will rescue many of you, even though it's hard to believe you couldn't find a response for one of the other questions. The questions on the Common App rarely change, so you have plenty of time to think about what you might write. And though a well-written essay can cover almost any topic well, many admission officers advise against writing about the three Ds—death, disease, and divorce.

Your goal in your essay should be to share something that the admission committee cannot find out about you elsewhere in the application. Alternatively, you can use the essay to provide greater insight into some aspect of the application that reinforces your positioning. Let your essay show your passion and who you are, giving them a window into your heart and soul.

We cannot emphasize enough how much brevity is appreciated by harried admission officers. Write short! There is a brilliant quote often misattributed to Mark Twain: "If I had more time I would have written you a shorter letter." (Voltaire, Pascale, and Cicero are all credited with the original quote.) The more you can say in fewer words is a true talent the admission officer will appreciate.

Take the time to investigate each college, and write an essay that is specific to that school's educational philosophy, curriculum, and approach. That research can only help you—even to help you eliminate certain "name" colleges. The University of Pennsylvania, for example, has asked applicants to discuss a professor the applicant might enjoy studying with. That requires a little bit of research. The University of Chicago has been renowned for its essay questions—different and unique each year. You can rest assured you won't be using a generic essay to respond to their question. And heaven help the student who tells Columbia they love the freedom of their freshman curriculum—an answer that might work well at Brown—but doesn't jibe with Columbia's highly structured core course requirement philosophy.

Make sure, too, that the essay is in your own words and your own voice. In your angst about writing the perfect essay, you'll ask peers, family members, teachers, tutors, and perhaps independent counselors to read it. Most will have different ideas about what to change. Listen to their criticism, but also listen to yourself. If your final draft is so different from your first draft—where you truly said what you wanted to say—go back to that first draft and simply clean it up. Only an essay that is truly from you—and in your personal voice—will say what you want to say. And that will impress a committee.

Admission officers—even brand-new ones—have read a gazillion essays. They've seen it all. Most of them have a pretty good antenna that tells them when an essay isn't in a kid's own voice, or when it has received a little too much "proofing" by a parent or advisor. And heaven forbid if you are tempted to use a "successful" essay written by someone else and used at a different college—forget it! If it is even suspected, it will hurt your chances of admission. And if it proven, you're

Video Essays

In some cases, colleges have allowed students to submit video essays versus written essays. The fact that many video applications are made public has raised questions about whether video essays can result in an "American Idol" popularity contest.

There's also a debate about whether video essays favor students with the financial means to have equipment or obtain professional editing (or even to employ professional helpers), but the trend toward allowing optional video will likely continue.

The Common Application has supplements for arts and athletic videos. The Common App suggests you use privacy settings for videos you post online. (And we agree!) If you search YouTube or Vimeo for "common application arts supplements," you can find sample videos that were made public.

Importantly, many arts and athletic programs have separate instructions for prescreening or supplements as part of their application processes. It's best to confirm the school's policies on their website or, if necessary, by phone or e-mail.

There are many YouTube celebrities with lots of YouTube subscribers. If this is your passion and a dimension where you stand out, include a link in your application!

finished—no matter how impressive the rest of your application is.

Martha Allman, Director of Admission at Wake Forest, sums up the goal of the essay quite nicely. She writes on Wake Forest's website, "I look for beautiful, clear writing that comes to life on the page and offers insight into the character and personality of the student." She goes on to say that she hopes the student voice is not lost in the process of review by others. If you believe your essay is indeed what she describes—and is in your own voice—it's ready to send.

Supplemental Materials and Additional Essays

Don't forget that the Common App also provides you a place to "share anything else you might like the committee to know about you." Use that opportunity wisely.

In the discussion of the Common App (pages 158–159), we mentioned that many schools request a supplemental essay. It is common for a school to ask you to write about why you want to attend that particular college. They want to gauge your interest in

Plagiarism and Academic Integrity in the Digital Age

For years, colleges and universities have been using the TurnItIn for Admissions website to screen papers completed by their undergrad and graduate student body (TurnItInAdmissions.com). Last year, TurnItIn launched a new service for admission offices to use in screening admissions essays, personal statements, and application questions as well.

Sixty-seven percent of admissions offices surveyed by Kaplan indicated that they have discovered claims on an application to be exaggerated or untrue.

TurnItIn tested 450,000 admissions essays and found that 36% had "significant matching text," leading them to suspect that the essays were plagiarized.

Now students can check their own work using TurnItIn's new service called-WriteCheck, which enables students to check their writing for improperly used content, inadvertent plagiarism, or quotation errors. Check it out at writeCheck.com. Other free services exist, such as Viper, which is available at www.scanmyessay.com.

their school and see if you've adequately researched their program. This can be a trap that many applicants fall into. They hurt themselves by writing a generic response to the question that they think can be used at multiple colleges. It can't be. And if you fall into that trap, it can destroy your chances of getting into a particular school.

Recommendations

Recommendations are read—carefully! But remember the adage: the thicker the folder, the thicker the kid. Many colleges are making it very clear what they want in terms of recommendations. And it is not in your best interest to exceed those instructions. Check each school's policy. The more explicit they are, the more important it is for you to heed their advice closely.

Most colleges expect a counselor or school letter of recommendation, plus one or two letters from your teachers. The purpose of the school/counselor letter is to paint the broader picture of your time at your high school. It might be written by a senior school administrator or student's advisor. Each high school typically has its own

process, and it often depends upon the student-counselor ratio and who best knows the individual student.

The letter will often include quotes from your teachers, insight into your extracurricular activities, and your role as a member of your high school community. The counselors at Phillips Andover used to call them their "stories." Each one was unique to that particular student, and it was the tale of their journey and transformation through their years at the school.

For any counselors reading this, a wise old Dean of Admission at Trinity, Larry Dow, reminds you to be concise, just as we ask the students to be. He jokes that the letters of former college admission people who have gone into college counseling get longer each year that they are away from their old profession. It can all be said in a page.

The teacher letters, on the other hand, should be more classroom specific. They should not be a repeat of what the school letter contains. Selecting who writes your letter(s) of recommendation is normally up to you. We encourage you to put careful thought into whom you select. Normally it will be a teacher who taught you during junior year. They had the opportunity to work with you for a full year, and they usually have a pretty good perspective of you as a student. Teachers you had during sophomore year are OK too, but the rigor of 10th-grade work is usually a bit less strenuous than 11th-grade courses. Don't use 9th-grade teachers for your recommendations.

It is important that the teachers who write your recommendations know how you think, participate, and get excited about your studies. If you are reading this at the end of your junior year or at the beginning of your senior year, it is too late to start or influence that (intellectual) relationship with a teacher. But what you want your recommenders to do is help an admission committee see how you will succeed in a demanding college seminar or get the most out of a larger, lecture setting.

Think about how your recommendations fit into your packaging. If you intend to be a classics major, there better be a letter from your Latin teacher. A potential engineer might select advanced math and science teachers. Remember, too, that a teacher can say no or be reluctant to write your letter. If a teacher expresses hesitation, or suggests she might be too busy, look elsewhere!

If you are not applying early or if you are in a bind, you can certainly ask a senior-year teacher—late in the first semester. It is particularly useful to ask a teacher who taught you in freshman or sophomore year and again in your senior year. They often can provide real insight into your maturity and growth as a student.

Another issue applicants often wrestle with is whether to submit additional letters to the college. The most common rule-of-thumb is that it is OK to submit one more recommendation than the school requests. This letter should be an opportunity for someone—usually from outside the school—to share information about you that school authorities might not know about or provide. A work or internship supervisor, a church or community service coordinator, or someone who taught you in an area outside the school (art, music, language) might provide the admission committee with valuable information.

Conversely, a letter from someone "important" who knows your parents but doesn't know you is a definite no-no. ("If Steve is anything like his father, he'll be a great addition to your class, blah, blah, blah.") Don't do it!

Your parents may be justifiably proud of all the awards you've won. Don't send them to the admission committee. Well-crafted school recommendations, along with the section of the application that asks about awards, will suffice.

Extracurricular Activities

Extracurricular activities are important—to your development as an individual and for what they say about you—i.e., your positioning. But you don't want to send a college a laundry list of activities!

Go for quality rather than quantity. Find your passion and make sure the college knows what it is. This is an essential part of your positioning and packaging. Applications—including the Common App—typically ask you to list your extracurricular activities "in their order of importance to you."

What and how you list these activities says a great deal about you. Think how you want the admission committee to see you and remember you. Is the activity you wrote about in the Common App as your most rewarding near the top of your list? It should be.

If you devote an incredible amount of time to one activity, make sure there is a way you are communicating that. Student-athletes who participate in a sport year-round may often appear "lighter" in the extracurricular realm. Colleges want to see focus and dedication, but they also don't particularly like one-dimensional candidates. If you've worked at a summer sports camp—even if you spent 80% of the time lifting weights—make sure that additional dimension makes it onto your activity list.

We can't stress too much how colleges like leadership and initiative. Make sure you list your leadership roles in your extracurricular activity list. If you work in student government, tell them what you do and what programs you have developed. If you lead a club or organization, make sure the committee knows what the club does and how you influence their work. If you're a team captain, say it. And if you are an editor of a school publication, you should probably send the committee a great editorial or short piece. Be sure to note it in the activity list too. The Common App allows you to attach a resume to more fully explain your extracurricular activities. Take advantage of that opportunity!

Remember to put proof of talent and passion in your file. You need to make sure this is included in your extracurricular list so that an admission officer or committee knows to look for these supplements in your folder.

Job, Volunteer Work, and Summer Activities

What you do in the summer and outside of school can often complement your application and complete the package. Though these summer activities are not as important as your transcript or essay, they can say a lot about who you are and how you use your free time. Admission committees appreciate the value of hard work, and not just in the classroom or your extracurricular activities. There are students who take jobs for experience. These often include volunteer jobs at hospitals as a way to see if medicine is truly a field they wish to pursue. It would be rare for the Cornell Hotel School to accept someone who hasn't had some kind of experience in the hospitality industry.

An important note: there are lots of students who work at McDonald's after school and on the weekends to help pay for their own expenses—or even to help pay the family bills. Don't think an admission committee won't think that is important. It is; tell them about it. They will appreciate knowing it.

Summer academic experiences—often at colleges—can accomplish much the same thing. There are great summer programs across the country that help students figure out what they might want to study in college. Summer study in engineering or architecture may indeed help you decide whether you wish to pursue careers in these fields. They may also help convince

How Your Application File Is Reviewed

In the "old" days of college admission—when the first edition of this book was published—your file was a manila folder that contained a sheaf of paper documents. They were very similar to the digital components of the Common App. Papers were filed in a set order: usually the transcript came first, followed by test scores, essays, recommendations, an interview report, and supplementary materials. If papers were out of order, they were put back in the correct sequence by the committee chair, reflecting the priority put on each element. On the outside of the folder were notations indicating who had read your folder, the scores they had assigned to your academic and personal qualities, and any special designations, such as whether you were a minority candidate or of interest to the athletic department and whether your family was likely to endow a new building on campus.

When the Columbia (or Brown or Northwestern or Pomona) admissions committee used to sit down, your file was physically in the hands of your area representative. The area rep. was the admission officer who knew your file best and who presented the reasons for the committee to consider your application. In fact, that area rep. typically presented all the kids from your high school along with the applicants from kids in all the surrounding towns. Their job was—and still is—to know the high schools in their region: which ones inflated grades, which had really tough graders, which turned out grinds, and which produced nice kids. Your area rep would have made notes in the file, perhaps a quote from a teacher recommendation or a line or two from your essay. Someone else in the room might ask to see the file, and the presenter would pass it to them. That might be followed by another request from across the table, and your folder would be passed to another admission officer for a quick read. In the meantime, the conversation about you would continue, and a decision made in a matter of minutes.

Wow, how some things have changed! In our introduction to this book, we discussed many things that haven't changed in the admission process: the role of constituencies, how admission officers want the well-rounded class rather than the well-rounded kid, the value of your presenting a hook. Well, your file still has that transcript, your essay, some recommendations, and supporting materials. But walk into that Columbia committee room today, and your file is on everyone's computer screen. Any paper documents you've submitted have been scanned, and there might even be a link to your YouTube video or the website you asked an admission officer to look at. Papers in the file rarely get misplaced, and there are few secrets that a reader may miss. In fact, in this technological age, very little is truly private, and there is a fair chance the embarrassing Facebook photo you thought was private is now part of your application folder. (Beware what you post!) That folder should also include the supplementary material that demonstrates your true passion or talent. Students no longer submit slides of their artwork—they submit links to their websites. Though many music programs still require live auditions, you might submit a link to your performance piece. Student-athletes typically submit DVD highlight reels to coaches with proof of their talents. But a link for the admissions team that demonstrates your leadership on the field can never hurt. One warning: many an admission officer has collected the worst videos and links to share with colleagues. Make sure what you submit really does—objectively and in context—show you in a positive light!

Let's take that a step further. It is very important to put yourself in the role of the admission officer. (We devote a whole chapter—Chapter 6—to that critical role-playing.) But as you think about putting together your application strategy and its components, you have to remember that you can never really be sure who is reading your folder, who your audience is. The person assigned to be your area rep.

might be a veteran admissions person or might be a recent graduate of the college. That person might be black or white, gay or straight, male or female, a liberal arts major or a science whiz. Although the admissions dean has articulated the school's admission goals for the current year and specific criteria they're trying to achieve in the next year, every reader will have a personal and different way of looking at your file. You certainly don't want to be so bland as to blend into the carpet. But you also don't want to stand out for the wrong reasons—or worse yet, stupid reasons.

Your e-mails and correspondence with the school will become part of your file. So if your e-mail address is HotStuff69, you probably should change it—now! There is no reason to be paranoid or reticent about sending an e-mail asking a question or alerting the committee to an accomplishment. But think first and reread it before you send something. If your YouTube link or Facebook page is publicly accessible with things you wouldn't want your parents to see, you might not want an admission officer to see them either.

Many colleges create Facebook pages and friend prospective applicants. They often like to connect prospective students with current students or have you communicate with young admission officers. Exercise some discretion about what you post! Your application file is not limited to that simple manila folder any more.

the admission committee of your genuine interest in a field as well as convey that you have some sense of reality about what you are getting yourself into. Summer academic programs are also opportunities to study things your school might not offer or to build upon what you have already studied. The budding author who takes an enriching summer writing program at Kenyon or the University of the South might spark your interest in those schools. And they might also enable you to produce a piece you could publish and make part of your admission file.

Privilege is a wonderful thing. But it's what you do with it that matters in the eyes of an admissions committee. If you're fortunate to come from a family that has the resources to allow you to travel or attend a summer session at a college, you are lucky and should appreciate your good fortune. These are terrific opportunities that you should not squander, but they won't make a bit of difference to the admission committee unless you convert that privilege to something truly positive. Recognizing that you are privileged is a start.

Your Experience Matters

Years ago, I remember an applicant to Brown from New Bedford High School in Massachusetts. He was a first-generation, hard-working student of Portuguese descent who stood second in a class of 700 students. Test scores were not at our norms, but everyone raved about this student's work ethic. No one explained, however, why he had no extracurricular activities or anything about his family situation. I remember calling the counselor at the school who reluctantly told me that the applicant didn't really want his story known—that his father was a disabled fisherman and that the young man worked every day after school and on the weekends to support his family, while still achieving his impressive academic record. In his case, work, to us, was the sacred thing he did. I can guess you know what our decision was and the kind of aid we gave him to make his dreams come true.

—MM

Admission officers often joke about the number of kids who spend a summer in an impoverished Central American country digging latrines or building . . . something. So many kids brag about digging those latrines that there really should be a giant latrine stretching from the Atlantic to the Pacific. (One of our kids spent a summer in the Virgin Islands helping a local Rastafarian farmer cultivate his marijuana crop.) Simply writing about this summer-of privilege is not a great topic for the all-important essay!

There are, however, students who have come back from these trips and held fundraisers to build a school or dig a well in an impoverished place they visited. If the summer trip to the eco-forest stimulated you to get a recycling program going at your school or put solar panels on the school's roof, say so. There will be admission officers at many schools who came from limited means who will want to see how you made a difference. That quote, "From those to whom much is given, much is expected," rings true in many an admission committee room.

Scrub your Face(book)!

It's a good idea to view your Facebook profile, or other online accounts, as the public see them to ensure you're putting your best foot forward. Here's how:

1. Go to http://zesty.ca/facebook/.

2. Enter your Facebook username. (Your username is the text that appears after www.Facebook.com/ in the web address for your Facebook profile.

If there's anything you need to remove from public view, change your privacy settings by going to www.facebook.com/help/?page=419.

Many schools require students to do a certain amount of community service. Other high schools do not. What is important in the college process is what you do, why you do it, and how you communicate it. The passion a student can show when they write or talk about their community service work can sway many an admission committee.

Think about these two scenarios. Student A goes to a private school in Boston and does his required hours of community service. He mentions it in a college interview, but with little enthusiasm. And then he places it on his activities list below JV tennis. Student B goes to the same school but continues his volunteer work into the summer. He is proud about it in his interview and writes about it in the Common App as his most important activity. His supervisor even offers to write a letter of recommendation to the admission office on his behalf. Putting yourself in the role of the admission officer, evaluate these two candidates. If all else is fairly equal between these two candidates, which one would you prefer?

Whatever you choose to do as an extracurricular or summer activity should be because it is important to you, not to help get you into college. Honesty and sincerity throughout your application isn't false or misleading packaging. Communicating who you are, what's important to you, and what you care about is important to the admission committee. Packaging is only about communicating it clearly. And the admission committee will appreciate it.

Step 8: Execute, Execute, Execute

Smart, organized planning is essential. Getting all the pieces together, making decisions, writing the essays, rewriting them, proofing them, and getting them out the door— or more accurately, off the computer desktop—is more important. If you don't actually get all the work done and submit every required piece of the application, you simply won't be considered. It sounds ridiculously simple but it isn't. Too many kids make really dumb mistakes, like forgetting to submit a required document or not correcting a misspelling. So the bottom line is: just do it! With real attention to detail. And, of course, on time!

The Common Application

The one thing that has really changed since your parents applied to college using a typewriter to fill in their applications, is the use of technology in the application process. Most colleges now prefer submission of materials electronically by both you and your high school. The most common (no pun intended) application used is "The Common Application," also known as the Common App, (www.commonapp.org). Over 400 colleges in 42 states used in the Fall of 2010, including all eight Ivy League schools. In fact, a large number of colleges, including many selective private and public institutions, have stopped printing their own application materials. They now rely on the Common App as their sole means of accepting applications.

Take a moment to review The Common Application at their website. It will help give you a sense of how the college application works and how your file is created. You can download all the Common App's forms and see what is required without having to register. You'll see that the first section requires your basic information, future plans, demographics, family history, academics, and testing history. Next, you're prompted to discuss honors won and extracurricular activities and to highlight your favorite activity or work experience. Then you're asked

to write an essay. When it is time to submit the Common App, you're asked to register.

You are required to report any disciplinary action taken against you. If you answer in the affirmative—meaning yes you were in trouble—you will be asked to attach an explanation. And lastly, you'll be invited to provide any additional information you'd like to share that might assist the admission committee with their decision.

Finally, don't forget to pay the required fee or to submit a fee-waiver form. (Check with your counselor to see if you might be eligible for the fee waiver.) You will get a "you need to pay" prompt from the program.

Subsequent sections of the Common App include teacher recommendations and school forms for your counselor. (There are sections for initial, midyear, and final reports from your school.)

The Common App also includes application deadlines for specific schools using the Common App. It indicates other criteria too: whether the college uses Early Decision, Early Action, or Rolling Admission, and whether it requires an application fee, an SAT/ACT test, or supplemental materials—such as, in many cases, an additional essay. If a school has a test-optional policy, the Common App will typically refer you to that school's website.

The beauty *and* the danger of the Common App is how easy it has become to apply to more schools with just the push of a button. The beauty is that it is now much easier to complete the college application process. The danger is that you will be tempted to apply to more schools than you would have in the past—when packets of preprinted forms had to be completed by hand or typewritten. The danger is also that you're more likely to submit an application to schools you have little interest in attending. (After all, it is "only" money—typically your parents'. But those application fees—often $75 per school—add up.) Remember our rule about treating each school like it is your top choice. Before you hit that "add school" and "submit" button, make sure you can honestly say you want to attend!

One note of caution about the Common App test section. If you intend to submit applications both to schools that require SAT/ACT testing and to those that are test-optional, you may have to create two separate versions of the Common App. As of Summer 2010, the Common App software does not allow you to mix and match. We assume they will correct this. But at the moment there is a glitch. And remember too that even though the Common App requires you to list your SAT/ACT scores, you will have to get the College Board and ACT folks to send official scores to each college.

The Special Division/School Strategy

One myth that needs to be dispelled is that there are "special"—easier—ways to get into selective schools. In the old days—probably when your parents were applying —it was often called "getting in the back door." Sorry folks, those days are gone. For example, at Cornell, years ago, it might have been the Agriculture School (now called Agriculture and Life Sciences School) or Industrial Labor Relations (ILR). Both were branches of the New York State system and seen as less competitive than Arts and Science or Engineering.

This is definitely no longer the case! The biology program in the AG school and business program in ILR are as competitive as any program to get into at Cornell. And the fact that these programs have slightly lower tuition makes them even more popular and thus competitive.

You'll find that programs like Columbia's School of General Education (often also called Continuing Studies) or Harvard's School of General Studies are indeed easier to get into. But they are not intended for recent high school graduates. Rather, they are for somewhat older students—often mid-career professionals who never received a college degree. NYU does have a Liberal Studies Program that it refers some students to who are not quite ready for regular admission. (Boston University has one as well.) But you will be limited in course choice for your first two years. And you'll be required to complete core work for your final two years in a major.

Not surprisingly, it is easier to get into Johns Hopkins in a major other than biology or pre-med or into Carnegie Mellon in Arts and Science. But there are no guarantees you'll ever switch over to their more selective programs. So if you decide to apply to the nursing school at Boston College or Georgetown thinking those specialized programs are your ticket into those name colleges—don't. Unless you really want to be a nurse.

6

CHAPTER 6

The Hook:
Putting It All Together

The key to a better of more effective application is a **hook.** And that's why we devote nearly a whole chapter to it. So what's a hook? It is something about you that is positive and memorable. It enables the admission committee to "hang their hat" on you—the shorthand reason to admit you.

The hook grows out of a bigger (marketing) concept known as positioning. It may sound crass, but the application process is really all about marketing yourself to the admission committee. (If you feel compelled to yell—as Patrick McGoohan did at the beginning of every episode of *The Prisoner*—"I am not a number; I am a free man!" go ahead. Now get over it and recognize the competitive environment you are playing in and man-up or woman-up. If you want to compete in this ballpark, you need to play by the rules.)

OK, so back to the bigger concept: positioning. Positioning is the place you achieve in the mind of your target audience: the individual admission officers reading your file. It is your niche, and it is derived from your strengths and weaknesses, how you influence that perception of you, and the competitive landscape— the other kids who are also applying.

The last piece of this marketing triumvirate is known as packaging. That is how you communicate your positioning and hook. Sometimes your optimal positioning will emerge from a hook—a favorite activity, an award, a unique experience. Packaging is about ensuring that your entire application supports that positioning and effectively communicates the hook.

In an advertising campaign, the hook is the iconic image and/or slogan that's immediately recognizable and stays in people's minds. In college admissions, it's the experience, activity, or accomplishment that makes you memorable. Its purpose is to both garner attention and convince the college to choose you because you meet their specific needs. This chapter is all about the specifics of positioning, the hook, and packaging in order to create the most successful application you possibly can— so that the admission committee looks at your candidacy and says, "Yes we want this kid."

Positioning

Imagine that it is 1960 and you work for a small foreign-car manufacturer that is trying to sell its automobiles in the United States. American carmakers are producing large, fast models with cool designs and giant engines. More importantly, Americans like the models coming out of Detroit, and the autos are selling well.

Unfortunately, your model is, to put it gently, ugly! It's small, unusually shaped, and underpowered. How are you going to convince the American car buyer to even consider your automobile, much less buy it?

Well, if you're Volkswagen, you establish a positioning for yourself in the marketplace, and then package your communications—principally through your advertising—to reinforce that positioning niche. Positioning requires you to take into consideration not only your own assets and weaknesses, but the competitions' as well. If you're Volkswagen, you realize that your design might be out of vogue, but you do have positive attributes. In fact, your strengths are directly related to your size and shape. Very simply, your cars are much more *economical* than Detroit's gas-guzzlers.

How do you convince the public of this? By packaging your communications believably and memorably. You run ads with unusual, surprising headlines, like "Think small," as shown in Figure 6-1.

Figure 6-1. Set a clear and memorable hook.
© Volkswagen of America.

When we say "Think small," for example, we are suddenly making a credible argument for economy. Wouldn't it be nice to get 30 miles to the gallon instead of eight? We've positioned ourselves as *the* economical automobile.

That's what you're going to do with "your brand"—you—as well.

But first, a couple more points about VW. A few years after VW entered the American market, the Japanese auto companies Toyota and Honda decided to crack the U.S. market as well. Their positioning, however, was different from VW's. They didn't "own" the "economy" positioning but had a pretty good head start. So the positioning that Honda and Toyota tried to secure for themselves was "reliability."

In fact, it worked so well—particularly compared to VW's less reliable quirkiness—that VW decided to address its own weakness head-on. It ran one of the most memorable ads of the 20th century: "Lemon," as shown in Figure 6-2. It admitted that it occasionally had a car that came off the assembly line that wasn't perfect. By acknowledging a "small" problem, however, it was able to reestablish its credibility

Lemon.

Figure 6-2. Embrace your weakness.
© Volkswagen of America.

with American consumers. You've seen similar moves more recently by Toyota after its series of recalls.

In fact, the success of the Lemon ad allowed VW to focus on—and counter—its other weakness: the car was bizarre looking, at least compared to the new Japanese models. They addressed their body design head-on with the two ads shown in Figures 6-3 and 6-4. (American car companies were completely asleep at the wheel, not believing that macho Americans would give up chrome and horsepower for economy and reliability.)

Figure 6-3. Celebrate your style.
© Volkswagen of America.

Figure 6-4. Convince them to "just say yes."
© Volkswagen of America.

Figure 6-5. Focus on your core strengths.
© Apple Inc.

Why are we focusing on old ad campaigns? Because as you think about your own strengths and weaknesses, you could do a lot worse than to learn a lesson from some master marketers. Let's take a look at one more example—one you are probably more familiar with: Apple Macintosh computers.

One of the most popular and successful ad campaigns of the last five years is the Apple Macintosh "I'm a Mac and I'm a PC" campaign, as shown in Figure 6-5.

Think about what Apple did with this campaign and why. Apple is much, much smaller than Microsoft and sells far fewer computers than most of the other PC computer manufacturers. But Apple focused on its core strengths: reliability and ease of use. In fact, if you go all the way back to 1984 when the first Mac computer was just being introduced, it was exactly the same positioning: the anti-PC. Its iconic image is shown in Figure 6-6. Check out the entire commercial at www.youtube.com/watch?v=OYecfV3ubP8.

So now that you've been subjected to a 10-minute history of the best positioning and ad campaigns of the last

Figure 6-6. Set yourself apart from the competition. © Apple Inc.

half-century, put them aside. And think about how you want to be seen and remembered by the admission committees of your favorite colleges. You're not a breakfast cereal to be sold; but you are your own brand. When people hear your name or think about you or read your application, they think of certain attributes. You hold a position in their mind. Your job is to help form that impression.

At first glance, positioning and hook may seem the same. They're not. But they are linked. Your positioning is the niche you occupy in someone's mind. The hook is the experience or activity or accomplishment that makes you memorable, that enables you to achieve that positioning.

Don't get hung up on them!

Positioning is a sophisticated concept that even most professional marketers and advertising executives misunderstand. You're not expected to master its intricacies at this stage of your life. But even a modest understanding of the concept can help you craft a more effective strategy. The hook is easier: what is that one thing that allows an admission officer to hang their hat on your candidacy, to say yes, we want this kid?

If you can identify a hook for yourself, that is great. If you can build that into a positioning, even better.

Hooks Thanks to Fate or Good Fortune

Some of you may have hooks by virtue of birth or good fortune. They fall into three basic areas:

- Diversity hook
- Legacy and extended legacy hook
- Development hook

There is really little positioning involved with these—they are what they are, and you benefit from them. But you do need to develop a strategy about how to use them best.

Diversity Hook

At first glance, the diversity hook might seem rather obvious: it would be based on race. But diversity is actually defined in different ways by various colleges. The most obvious may be race or ethnicity, but schools can also define diversity in terms of socio-economic status, geographic origin (or current address,) or cultural background.

Race and Ethnicity

There are many schools that want to create a campus microcosm of today's changing society, They want the college community to reflect the face and color of today's world—not as it once was, but as it will be. The days of the all-male, white, Ivy League campuses are long gone. American society is growing more diverse, and many colleges want to create a learning environment where students study and grow in this more diverse community.

That means being a student "of color"—through it's many shades—will most likely be a hook for some of you. Most state schools—and virtually all private colleges—ask about and use race/ethnicity as a factor in the admissions process. (California is one of the few states that excludes race as a "plus-factor.") So, if you are a "minority," make sure that you check that box on the Common Application and wherever else it is asked.

In your research of various schools, don't be afraid to ask how race is addressed and whether it may impact your application. Many admission offices have a full-time person dedicated to minority/diversity recruitment. And a fair number of colleges even have special programs that might bring you to campus for a visit—at no expense to you. Other schools run special "minority" days on campus—along with special orientation programs after you're admitted—so that students of color will have a better sense of what support and experiences they will have at that school.

Remember, however, that race will be viewed differently at different colleges. A Latino-from-Texas applicant to a school in Texas might be viewed more as a "majority" applicant. But that same applicant to a northeastern private school would gain an admission advantage. Because Asian-Americans make up a significant portion of the population that applies to highly selective schools, they are usually not given an "application-plus." At some liberal arts colleges in the north, however, there are far fewer Asian-American applicants, and that "scarcity" triggers a diversity consideration that translates into a plus-factor in committee.

Economic "Privilege"

More accurately, it is the *absence* of financial privilege that is also a factor, both in and outside the context of race. Although many schools seek the face of color in their population—regardless of socioeconomic background—the most selective colleges see economic diversity as a desirable category in its own right. The top schools prefer kids who have achieved—both in academics and in extracurricular activities—without having had the advantages of family wealth. And this is true both for kids who are minorities and those who are not.

Tom Parker, the veteran Dean of Admissions at Amherst College, calls "first-gen" kids—kids whose parents didn't go to college—the type of diversity he hopes to enroll at Amherst. And this could include the white coal-miner's daughter from West Virginia or the Bosnian refugee's child who arrived in the United States speaking no English.

Legacy Hook

Some of you have grown up, hearing—seemingly all your life—about the wonderful college experience that your parents had. You've gone to football games and tailgates and tagged along with them during their reunions. They might have expressed their desire to have you follow in their footsteps, or you might have just decided that on your own. (If you choose to apply to OldU, hopefully it is because you've actually done some good research and decided it is a good fit, instead of merely wanting to please your parents.)

But if you do decide to apply to OldU, the legacy hook is something that *may* be open to you. We say "may" because the legacy hook is most effective when your parents have remained involved with their alma mater. That involvement could be in campus and alumni activities as alumni admission interviewers, class agents, or reunion event planners. Other parents have donated financially—some more generously than others.

Both of these approaches to alumni involvement will be a plus for you. (And if your parents contributed both time and money, that is even better.) But being a legacy only works if your academic credentials are competitive with *today's* admission standards at that school. Too many parents look back upon their own academic credentials as the standard for admission. Don't do that! In many cases, the admissions standards were less competitive when your parents applied, Or, the school

was all male back in the "old days," and that means perhaps 50% or more of the places in today's class will now go to females.

Most schools do a good job explaining their legacy policies. At the University of Pennsylvania, for example, they are quite explicit in stating that legacy applicants who truly desire to attend there should apply early decision. Georgetown states that legacy status will not impact an early application, but it may be an advantage in the regular decision process. Remember too that colleges ask (on the Common App) where your parents went to college. That means that other schools will see where your legacy status is.

Schools try their best not to disappoint legacy families. Many schools—Brown among them—have a full-time person dedicated to working with alumni families. These alumni reps often run summer (and reunion weekend) workshops and give counseling advice to legacy families. But they also often cushion the blow if it looks like admission is not going to happen.

The most significant legacy impact is through parents, but attendance by siblings, grandparents, and extended family members will also be taken into account. In the case of siblings, many admission committees will actually have the high school transcript and record of the older sibling to see how they compare with the younger applicant.

We mention the term "extended legacy" because many families have relationships with employers, neighbors, or business colleagues who might encourage you to look at their alma mater. In some cases, they may well be a person of influence on that campus and offer to assist you with admission. (To have genuine impact, the person usually needs to be a trustee, board member, or significant donor.) Most well-meaning neighbors-friends-colleagues don't have any real impact. So, as delicately as possible, you should try to gauge the real level of impact they may have. But you must remember: you'll still need to be competitive in the applicant pool. And if you are competitive, their support will depend on your firm commitment to attend the college. So choose wisely.

Development Hook

If you are fortunate to come from a family of means—i.e., your folks are rich—this can also be a hook. The reality of our society is that money still talks, and in this tough financial climate, many colleges are not adverse to admitting a borderline applicant with donor potential. That financial donor potential is known as a being a "development" prospect. Colleges are not shy about identifying such families, and it is pretty easy for them do so since most charitable giving records are in the public record and easily accessible over the Internet.

Just having money is not as important as having a record of giving money—particularly to other educational institutions. Families who have supported other educational endeavors over the years are usually seen in the most positive light. Colleges know that this is a risky business: there is rarely an outright quid-pro-quo: we'll admit young Pat and you'll build a new library. And schools have often been "burned" by families that the admissions-development folks thought would make generous contributions to the school. (Even when stiffed by parents, colleges still have hope in the next generation—the kid who has actually been admitted.) The dance that takes place involving development prospects is a delicate one, and the use of extended legacies can come into play here. If your parents have the means and intention to contribute to NewU if you get admitted, it is very useful to communicate that commitment through someone the school knows and trusts—and who knows your parents.

Hooks That Work

This section is devoted to exploring how you can identify and package effective hooks—when you weren't born into wealth, legacy status, or a desired ethnic/racial/ geographic group.

Finding Your Hook

Ask yourself three questions:

1. What excites you?

2. What have you done that someone who doesn't know you would react to by saying, "That's interesting"?

3. What will excite a college admission officer given their need to satisfy key constituencies?

The last two questions seem pretty obvious. But why the first question? Because if you think about what you really care about, what excites you and motivates you, you will probably have more success in identifying both a hook and a positioning that is "organic." It should be one that really comes from within and that you can support throughout all the elements of the application process.

Academic Hook

You've worked hard in high school. You've taken the most demanding curriculum in a wide range of disciplines, gotten excellent grades, high scores on your AP exams, and

SAT subject tests that speak to your success in these courses. You're exactly the kind of student every college wants. That's an academic hook. Now think how to best use that success.

Some colleges ask you on the application what you wish to major in. Others require that you apply to a specific school or program. If you *think* you know what you want to major in, terrific. Most admissions people know that once you get to college there is a 50% chance you are going to change your mind—and that is perfectly OK. College is supposed to be about intellectual exploration.

But the designation of an intended field of study should be a guide for the committee about who you are. If, for example, you're trying to position yourself as a being passionate about history but check off "mathematics" as your intended major, that sends a confusing message to the committee.

Conversely, if you are trying to convince the committee that you are a biblical scholar-in-the-making and plan to major in Egyptology—yes, that is a real department

at Brown—but have never taken a language beyond basic Spanish or attended a religious school, you probably don't have a legitimate hook. Don't try to pull a fast one on the committee.

Activity/Special Interest Hooks

Hooks based on experience and interests rather than academics are also effective. Here are some real kids we've known over the years and the hooks/positionings they used to get into terrific—and well-suited—colleges.

- **The Linguist:** Alan took a dual language tract, Spanish and Latin, throughout high school. He took each through the final course offered by his high school and did well in both languages. Interestingly, he majored in music when he got to college.

- **The Classicist:** Kelly took Latin right up through her senior year and took a Greek course at the local college during the summer.

- **The Math Nerd:** Jennifer spent two summers going to a camp that offered intensive programs in math.

- **The Tutor:** Mark volunteered for three years tutoring middle school kids from a poor neighborhood.
- **The Coach:** John, a high school football player, volunteered at a local Pop Warner league as an assistant, helping younger kids learn the basics.
- **The Lab Rat:** Lizzie spent two summers volunteering in medical labs: first in a dentist's office learning how to sterilize surgical instruments, and later in a hospital assisting the technicians doing routine analysis.
- **The Writer:** Randy got two articles published in his local paper about a zoning fight pitting a building developer against local residents.
- **The Trombonist:** Oliver was the lead trombonist in his school orchestra. He applied to big state schools that were very proud of their marching bands and saw the potential in having a talented, dedicated trombonist to lead the parade.
- **The Ship Designer:** Sam loved ships and boats, and he not only entered every science fair that could showcase his design ideas, but also corresponded with leading naval architects around the country.
- **The Filmmaker:** Daniel created three funny films about school life that were shown during school assemblies.
- **The Fund-Raiser:** Martha, an upper-middle-class kid, went to Africa on a "service learning" trip: not that uncommon among wealthier families, and not very impressive to admission offices. But when she returned, she spent a year holding school events in order to fund the building of a school library in the town she had visited.

So, think about what distinguishes you from others. It may be something you have taken for granted but that demonstrates your real passion and interest. It just may separate you from the pack in the final review process.

A Case Study: The Extracurricular Hook

Both the Common App and most individual college applications ask for extracurricular activities to be listed "in order of their interest or importance to you." In fact, the Common App asks you to write a short essay about your favorite and why. The choices you make can create decidedly different pictures of who you are in the minds of the admission committee. For example, consider the case in Table 6-1. The same activities are listed in both columns, but in different order.

Jessie Hunter's lists present two very different portraits. Version A suggests that she may be a little preoccupied with what she thinks the admission committee will consider an impressive list of credentials. She ranks National Honor Society first—despite the fact that it is little more than an honorary organization, a recognition of good grades, and no felony convictions. Similarly, Jessie probably thinks Key Club will be viewed favorably because it is a service organization.

Lower down the list are activities that touch on the full range of her high school experience. The overall impression, however, may be one of "breadth without depth," or even of an individual who is a bit unfocused. Of course, this single piece of information will be fit into the rest of the puzzle to form the complete picture of

Jessie Hunter. But the initial reaction to this element may not trigger a notably positive or memorable impression. Remember that colleges are not seeking a well-rounded individual, but rather a well-rounded class.

Version B creates a rather different impression. Jessie is now someone who is very interested in writing. She may not be a star reporter or editor, but she shows perseverance and consistency. She downplays the National Honor Society and the Key Club, and may even add credibility to her application because of this.

Table 6-1 Jessie Hunter's Extracurricular Activities

Version A
National Honor Society 3, 4
Varsity Soccer 2, 3, 4
Student Council 3, 4
Key Club 3, 4
Literary Magazine 2, 3, 4
Associate Editor 4
Band 2, 3, 4
School Newspaper Staff Writer 2,3,4

Version B
Associate Editor, Literary Magazine 4
Literary Magazine 2, 3, 4
Staff Writer, School Newspaper 2, 3, 4
Varsity Soccer 2, 3, 4
Student Council 3, 4
Key Club 3, 4
Band 2, 3, 4
National Honor Society 3, 4

The 10 Essential Rules to a Better Application

1. Tell the truth, the whole truth, and nothing but the truth.

Sound like *Law & Order?* It should. Don't lie, exaggerate, or make things up! Not only is it wrong, but you will get caught!

Volkswagen recognized the most important rules of positioning and packaging. Don't pretend to be something or someone you are not. Not only is such deception wrong, but it is dangerous. For one thing, you almost certainly will be found out. We're not offering you a morality lesson, but we are offering some pretty sound advice to anyone who is even "thinking" about tinkering with their records, inflating their awards, or sweetening their extracurricular record. Don't! You will get caught.

Prepare your application yourself. Discuss it with your parents, counselor, anyone you want. Argue about it; ask for feedback. But do it yourself!

You may think that a slight exaggeration will improve your chances of admission at highly selective schools and that the risk is so minimal as to be worth it. Don't! You'll find yourself disqualified from applying at all. It happens all the time. There's nothing unethical about seeking advice from others—even asking them to read your essay and giving you detailed feedback. But, ultimately, you have to present yourself as you are, and only you can do that in the best and most authentic way.

Completing the Application

With all this discussion about positioning and hooks and packaging, it is important not to overlook the basics: the nuts and bolts of actually filling out the application. You need to assemble all the components into a cohesive package—and get those applications in before the deadline! This section provides you with pointers for creating that successful application package and managing the application process. And it includes a reminder about things you definitely want to avoid saying or doing.

Avis is only No.2 in rent a cars. So why go with us?

We try harder.
(When you're not the biggest, you have to.)
We just can't afford dirty ashtrays. Or half-empty gas tanks. Or worn wipers. Or unwashed cars. Or low tires. Or anything less than seat-adjusters that adjust. Heaters that heat. Defrosters that defrost.
Obviously, the thing we try hardest for is just to be nice. To start you out right with a new car, like a lively, super-torque Ford, and a pleasant smile. To know, say, where you get a good pastrami sandwich in Duluth. Why?
Because we can't afford to take you for granted.
Go with us next time.
The line at our counter is shorter.

Figure 6-7. Be realistic about the competitive arena. © Avis Rent A Car System, LLC

2. You DO want to be remembered— for something!

The more pieces of your application that reinforce this "something" about you, the better! Consider another example from the 1960s. (We love the 1960s, for lots of reasons, but most importantly, there was some really smart positioning and packaging taking place.)

Back then Avis Rent-a-Car was struggling. Hertz was the dominant company in the field, and Avis was a distant number two. In fact, it was neck-and-neck with National Car Rental for the number two slot. Suddenly Avis recognized that it could improve its competitive position by establishing a unique positioning. It would call itself "number two" to Hertz's number one, as shown in Figure 6-7. It would position itself as the company that "tries harder"—because it was determined to move from number two to number one.

Avis packaged its communication of this positioning by saying, "We have to try harder, we're number two." Suddenly it was perceived as being in competition with Hertz, whereas before it was really in competition with National for that number two slot. The result? Avis grew and prospered, not really at Hertz's expense but at National's.

What the Avis example shows us is that you can define the arena you want to compete in, at least to a certain extent. If you have some reasonable credentials, you can influence the way people perceive you.

3. Give the admission committee a reason to vote FOR you—A HOOK!

Remember that the vast majority of admission officers don't take any pleasure rejecting you. In fact, they know that most of their applicants are qualified and could succeed admirably on their campus, but they have way too many kids applying and far too few open slots. Which means you have to give the committee a hook upon which to hang their acceptance hat. Sound silly? It's not!

Most kids do nothing to help their own cause by failing to provide the committee with this hook. Help the admission officer presenting your folder to the committee by filling in the following sentence:

"This is Pat Smith, the kid who . . . "

That incomplete sentence is the key. What is it that you're going to help the admission officer say? This is the kid who:

- won the regional science fair with a project on ship design.
- got the school government to vote *for* a dress code.
- wants to major in archaeology and studied Greek on her own.
- emigrated from Kosovo and didn't speak a word of English till 9th grade but became deputy editor of the school newspaper.
- worked at McDonald's 30 hours a week since he was 14 to help support his single mom and younger siblings. Not only did he become the assistant manager when he was 17, but he still got straight Bs.

This is the essence of the hook. Something easily memorable, credible, and impressive—and most effectively communicated in the essay! And despite all the hype that has surrounded packaging and positioning for the last 25 years, most kids don't do it. So think about your assets and experiences, and look for that hook.

4. Test your positioning and hook.

Just because you think your positioning or hook is credible or memorable doesn't mean much. Test it out on your parents, friends, and counselor. Is it really unique? (Or will five other kids in your class say the same thing—possibly to the same college?) Is it credible? Do you have the academic record or extracurricular history to support the positioning? And which constituency at the college does it appeal to?

If your positioning or hook doesn't pass the "smell test," try another one.

5. Make it easy for the admission committee to REMEMBER you.

This is the packaging piece of the hook. Are you communicating that positioning and hook effectively? Most kids don't! Too often they forget that an admission officer will read 50 folders a night. (Which means that one applicant's record begins to look very much like another's.) So don't be boring or pretentious!

You shouldn't shout "Remember me!" But you can present your hook in a clear, compelling, memorable way.

6. Don't give them a reason to reject you!

Just as you want to give the committee a reason to remember you, you don't want to be remembered for the wrong things. You don't want anything in your application folder that suggests you are snide,

"You Can't Handle the Truth!"*

Recently, we read two essays written by a smart high school senior. He intended one essay to be funny, the other politically insightful. They were neither. The so-called funny essay was sarcastic, and the political essay sophomoric and pretentious. We told him so, specifying what didn't work for us. (His mother thought they were brilliant and witty. Then again, she might have been wearing rose-colored glasses and really hasn't read too many college essays.) Anyway, he didn't listen to our feedback and submitted the essays with a few minor tweaks. Needless to say, he was rejected—both early decision and in the regular pool—by his first-choice school.

Would he have been accepted if he had "heard" our feedback? No way to say. But we knew he was shooting himself in the foot with the essays he was submitting.

So what's the message here? Find people who will give you honest, candid, critical feedback. It might be painful and result in your having to do a lot more rewriting, but in the long run, having such a sounding board is an extraordinarily valuable asset. Search hard for one, and then listen!

*Apologies to Aaron Sorkin for appropriating his line, delivered brilliantly by Jack Nicholson, in *A Few Good Men*.

sarcastic, or arrogant. You don't want to be pegged as a not-very-nice person. Niceness counts.

So does accuracy, completeness, neatness, grammar, and spelling. Which means don't make any silly or careless mistakes!

7. It is not what you say, but what the committee "hears" that counts.

This is one of the most important rules you can learn about any form of communication. And it is one that most people never really master. It is what separates great speakers from the merely adequate and superb writers from the rest of us.

We've worn many hats: teachers, editors, writers, producers, entrepreneurs. Whatever the role, we see the same mistakes over and over again. People think they're saying (or writing) something clearly or persuasively. They're not! Just because it appears on the paper or the screen doesn't mean that it is coming off that page into the reader's mind.

Here's the hard part: most readers—teachers, parents, friends—are not sufficiently "honest" in their criticism. They look for "good" or "nice" things to say about what you've written. Have you ever heard the expression, "If you don't have something nice to say, don't say anything at all?" If feedback is vague or nonexistent, throw that essay out the window and start over. This is when you want absolute, unvarnished, candid criticism!

8. One size DOESN'T fit all.

You do not have to use one positioning for all of the colleges you apply to, but each alternative positioning must be fully supportable. There is nothing wrong with positioning yourself as a science whiz—with a hook that focuses on your winning the regional science fair—to a school seeking engineers; and as a "geo" to a different school outside your locale. Just make sure that your record bolsters your contention by tailoring your applications to reflect each positioning. You won't be telling a different story to every college, but rather highlighting alternative aspects of your record and personality. You are simply matching your assets with each college's needs.

9. Play offense, but never be offensive.

If you had a problem—for example, a suspension or a failing grade—find a place in the application to explain it (the Common App provides such a space). But don't sacrifice your essay as a defensive maneuver. The essay should be on the offensive—used to bring out what you want to emphasize and enhance your positioning. There are usually other places in every application—or via an attachment—to explain discipline issues or aberrations in your record.

10. Start early and stay organized!

Figuring out your positioning, testing your hook, and refining your packaging takes time. Each should probably involve a few dead-end efforts and require numerous drafts. Don't wait until the weekend before an application is due!

Several years ago, a young woman we know and her family had an experience that is not terribly uncommon. But it was terrible! The student was really well organized, with application materials laid out on the living room floor, couch, and table according to reach, core, and safety schools. She was all set to file everything electronically. These were just the back-up materials! The family went away for the Christmas holidays, with the daughter toting her computer and files. And then disaster struck—literally. There was a terrible storm where they were vacationing, and all Internet access from the region was knocked out—for days! Desperate, the family called us, told us where to find the hidden house key, how to disarm the alarm, and which supporting materials, checks, and essays were to go with each school's application. It took hours, and we barely got everything out on the last FedEx plane. The experience almost ruined the family vacation and the kid's college plans. (Yes, she got in and is attending her top choice.)

But the lesson is: don't procrastinate and do stay organized!

That also means giving your recommenders plenty of advance notice and the materials or tools they need—or ask for—to write your recommendations.

Your Positioning and Packaging Checklist

1. Have you identified your optimal positioning?

2. Is it credible and supported by the evidence?

3. Have you tested your positioning on an honest critic?

4. Do your essays contribute new information, or are they merely repetitious?

5. Have you gotten honest feedback on your essays? Did you objectively consider that feedback?

6. Did you double- and triple-check the essay for spelling and grammatical errors?

7. How many other applicants will write about the same subject?

8. Do you sound like you're whining or complaining?

9. Will an admission officer say to his colleague, "Hey Jane, you've got to read this one?" And will he be saying it admiringly or critically?

10. Have you addressed issues that the committee wants answered?

Application Do's and Don'ts

The Do's

1. Find out everything you can about a school. Make sure that the program or major you're applying for is actually offered. Identify courses and a professor who you might like to study with—that's a great plus in an interview and a question on the University of Pennsylvania application.

2. Find a positioning and a hook for yourself, something the admission committee can remember you by. Make sure it is consistent with and supported by your application.

3. Try to set yourself off from other students applying from your high school, and from the applicant pool in general.

4. Show interest in the school to which you're applying and emphasize the positive reasons for your application to that school.

5. Provide your guidance counselor and teachers with sufficient information about your reasons for applying to each school and your intended positioning. Do they know about all your awards, activities, and interests, especially outside of school? Have you chosen recommendation writers wisely?

6. Try to establish a personal relationship with an individual admission officer. That person can act as your advocate before the committee. At the very least, establish a relationship with an alumnus who can lobby on your behalf. And always send a thank-you note or e-mail after meeting with them!

7. Schedule your interviews so the least important come first. (Remember, you want to give yourself some practice and build your self-confidence for the schools that you most want to attend.)

8. Write your essays early to allow time to put them away for a week, then review them with fresh eyes and rewrite if necessary.

9. Show your essay to an amenable teacher or counselor who will give you critical, objective comments.

10. Ask admission people about specific programs and requirements—or even whether to include something in your folder.

11. Send supplementary application materials if they are relevant to your positioning and if they show genuine ability. Make sure you know what a school will accept or review. In fact, many are more happy today for a website link or a YouTube video than actual hard-copy materials.

12. Feel free to ask your admissions interviewer (politely) about the committee's composition. (Traditionally, the more faculty involvement, the greater the emphasis on scholarliness.)

13. Make a copy of everything you submit. There's always the possibility that a form will be lost via e-mail, in the mail, or in the admission office itself. Then if you need to resubmit a form, you can do so quickly and efficiently. This is especially crucial for your essays. Always save your online work in two places.

The Don'ts

1. Don't assume all colleges are alike in their approach and admission standards. They are different. Research them as best you can.

2. Don't ever be boring! Never repeat information already in your folder—in your essay, your list of activities, your recommendations. Use each opportunity to add something important. Entertain the committee. Make sure that your application is a pleasure to read.

3. Don't ever try to put one over on the admission committee. Don't exaggerate or take credit for things that are not yours.

4. Don't be arrogant or pushy or driven. Show grace and charm in your writing and personal dealings. Be assertive but not aggressive.

5. Don't overload your folder. Send only the best examples of your work if you're including supplementary materials. And ask for the best, most in-depth recommendations. What counts is quality, not quantity. Remember that to many admission folks, "The thicker the file, the thicker the kid." Send your best article, not a collection of them.

6. Don't ask to have access to your recommendations. (You have this right under the Buckley Amendment, but we suggest you waive it.) Admission officers will take your teachers' comments more seriously—and your teachers will write more candidly—if the recommendations remain confidential. Comments that stress both your strengths and weaknesses work more for you than colorless, guarded references. And even with the Buckley Amendment, you'd probably never see them because most schools destroy admission materials after committee review.

7. Don't read from a list of questions during your interview. And don't come out with a memorized speech. Spontaneity is important But bringing along a resume to share with the interviewer is fine.

8. Don't telephone the admission office between January and April unless you have an urgent problem or something crucial to determine (e.g., has a missing form arrived?). Admission officers are very busy during this period and resent unnecessary intrusions.

9. Don't telephone the admission office with new information. If you want to ensure that something about your latest achievement makes it into your folder, send an e-mail or write a letter. In this way, the update will go right into your folder—which is essentially "you" to the admission committee. Or, ask your counselor to send a note to reinforce the significance of any new information.

10. Don't pretend you're super-human. You're an individual with feelings, fears, and subtleties of character. But don't dwell on your problems—either in your essay or during an interview. Be positive!

11. Don't write superficially. Whether in your essays or when answering an application's short questions, explain in detail what various experiences meant to you.

10 Tips for College Applicants in Social Media Age

1 Don't worry. Social media is evolutionary, not revolutionary.

Social media simply makes it easier to get different perspectives on colleges, and to reach experts, admissions' decision-makers and insiders (such as students currently attending a college). While word-of-mouth is limited to your circle of friends and family, social media is "word-of-mouse" that lets you view or connect with a network of people.

2 Use social media to research colleges.

The "official" channels of the college: website, blogs, YouTube Channel, Facebook page can help you understand what life's really like on campus and whether a particular college might be a good fit for you. Unofficial sources can be interesting, too, provided you follow #3 (below).

3 Be a savvy consumer of social media.

Don't believe everything you read. Consider the source. Verify information (especially deadlines and requirements) with the admissions office or official admissions website. Real, raw perspectives on a college can shed light, but they might not be true or representative.

4 Use social media to get on the radar of schools you're considering.

"Liking" or "following" a college on social media sites can get you noticed. Depending on the college, you may be able to engage directly with admissions staff at a college by posting questions. Creating a Zinch profile can help because it's a network designed expressly to let you showcase yourself to admission officers. They use it; so should you.

5 Use social media to stay updated on colleges you're considering.

Subscribing to RSS feeds, "liking" or following a college, can make it easy to stay informed on events, deadlines, or even changes in admissions policies. At Zinch, you have a stream that lets you see updates from all the colleges you've "liked."

6   Be a smart producer of online content.

Privacy is decreasing. Assume that what you post on a social media site could become public. Ask yourself, "Would I want this information to appear on a poster in a school hallway?" If that's concerning, think twice. Also, Google yourself and, as shown in this chapter, check your privacy settings on sites like Facebook.

7   Know your interviewer or others you meet in the admissions process.

Google the people you meet in the admissions process. Got an interview with an alumni interviewer? Be prepared by understanding their background.

8   Know that constant change is here to stay. Embrace it!

If this book was written five years ago, we'd talk about MySpace. Now, we (and colleges) focus much more time on Facebook. New technologies to stay informed and connected will certainly arise. Instead of resisting, use them to your advantage!

9   Manage your online identity.

Your online identity consists of what you post about yourself and what others post about you. Yes, colleges do (occasionally) check out your profile. They're not doing it because they think you're cool or cute. They're doing it to resolve inconsistencies and to make sure they're not embarrassed if they admit you or award you a scholarship.

You can track what others are posting about you through services such as Google Grader from Brand-Yourself, Google Alerts (plugging in your own name), and SocialMention.com.

There is an old adage that is still very good advice: you don't want to say or write anything that you wouldn't want to appear on the front page of the newspaper. And since your sensibilities are probably a little more casual than admission officers, assume that newspaper headline will be read by your parents or grandparents.

10 Don't be fooled.

Online entrepreneurs—and scammers—are always coming up with new ways to try to get your attention, your time, and sometimes your personal information. (Take a look at the discussion of the "college" Facebook scam on page 91 for a good example.) So, use social media, but use it intelligently!

7

CHAPTER 7

Athletic Recruiting and College Admission

The College Athlete

We write this chapter with a somewhat different style from the others. That's because unlike other "hooks," there are indeed a set of rules and structures that exist within the college athlete's world. This chapter will apply to a smaller—but not small—audience. It is first for kids who want to play intercollegiate sports—and who have the talent to be recruited. Second, it is for kids for whom high school athletics have been an important part of their lives and are wondering about two things. First, can they play on the college level? And second, can that dedication to a sport help them in their college application? This chapter is also very important for parents who have often invested thousands of hours supporting and shlepping their kids to practices and events. Our hope is that we'll clearly dispel myths about college recruiting, scholarships, and admission policies—on both the Division I and Division III levels. If our tone sounds more factual and less folksy than some of what we've written elsewhere, we apologize. But much of this world—and thus this material—is rule-based.

More than 100,000 college freshmen will play on NCAA teams next year, and about 30% of those kids will receive athletic scholarships. Do you hope to be among them? And do your parents hope to see an athletic scholarship? Or are you just hoping that your athletic prowess will make a difference in the admissions process? Rumors abound. Half-truths take on the power of gospel. And dreams of glory are as often made real as they are shattered. Although the process differs a bit from college to college, and division to division, there are some "truths" that are important to understand.

The Lay of the Land

The NCAA (the National Collegiate Athletic Association) is the major governing body of intercollegiate athletics. It divides schools into three divisions. Division I includes all those big-time athletic programs you hear about: the schools in the conferences you see playing football on television every Saturday, the colleges in the bowl games, and those pounding the floorboards during the NCAA March Madness basketball tournament. Division I schools range from the Ivy League to the Big Ten to the Pac 10 to the Southeast Conference, and so on. There are about 350 schools classified as Division I. Division I used to be known as the University Division, while smaller schools were in the College Division, or Division II.

Division II schools are normally somewhat smaller universities and are not willing or able to make that financial commitment to "Big Time" intercollegiate sports. But they still offer athletic scholarships. The distinction is really a matter of scale. A Division II school might give up to 36 football scholarships per year, while a Division I university would typically have about 85. There are several hundred schools classified as Division II, ranging from perennial lacrosse champions like Lemoyne and C.W. Post in the East to the perennial multisport powerhouses of the California state college system. Division II schools often play Division I colleges in basketball, typically early in the season. Although they rarely win these match-ups, they are essentially warm-up games for the Division I schools and "money games" for the Division II colleges.

There are more than 500 Division III schools, and they range from smaller universities to some of the most selective private colleges in the country. Here's the key take-away: there are no Division III athletic scholarships! Forget what you heard—your neighbor's kid did not receive an athletic scholarship to Amherst, Williams, Bates, Carleton, Pomona, or any other Division III school. In fact, the NCAA has cracked down on schools which use buzz words like "leadership" awards—or other merit scholarships—which are really athletic scholarships in disguise. Simply put, athletics has no bearing on the financial award that a Division III athlete may receive, and any merit award must be consistent with all other students awarded those grants. A few Division III schools do have one or two particular sports that compete at the Division I level and award scholarships in that sport. Hockey is a good example (Clarkson, Colorado College, RPI, St. Lawrence, and Union are a few examples). But those are the exception rather than the rule.

There are also 287 smaller colleges that belong to a group called the NAIA (National Association of Intercollegiate Athletics)—rather than the NCAA—and 90% of these schools do offer athletic scholarships. Similarly, junior colleges have their own governing body and set of rules.

We focus our remarks on Division I and III schools for a simple reason: the rules of the game for Division II schools are pretty much the same as for Division I.

Basic Eligibility

The NCAA serves as a clearing house for athletic eligibility for Divisions I and II. A student-athlete who hopes to be recruited or to compete on these levels should register at www.ncaa.org by the completion of their junior year in high school. You will not be allowed to take an official visit to any school if you are not registered. The NCAA sets a sliding scale of GPA versus standardized testing (SAT or ACT) that establishes eligibility. For example, a student with a high school grade point average of 3.0 needs a combined SAT score of 620 (on a 1600-point scale [verbal and math only—the writing section is not currently utilized!]) A student with a 2.5 GPA, needs a combined 820 SAT score. Division II schools don't use a sliding scale. Students simply have to have a minimum GPA of 2.0 and an SAT combined score of 820.

(For more information, and to see whether the NCAA has changed its standards, go to www.ncaa.org. We also post up-to-date information at www.zinch.com/athletes.)

The easiest way to make sense of the formula is to remember that for Division I schools, the higher a student's GPA, the lower their standardized testing can be, and vice versa. The NCAA also sets up a series of 16 core courses (increased from 14 in 2008) that a student must also pass in order to qualify for athletic eligibility. This includes four full years of English; three years of math, two each in science and one social science; and six additional courses. Since most college coaches begin looking at prospective recruits well before the student's senior year in high school, they are very concerned about a prospect's ability to successfully pass their core courses and achieve the minimum testing scores. Many schools will not recruit a prospective student-athlete who they fear won't be eligible to play because of their high school grades or SAT/ACT scores.

Student-athletes who intend to apply only to Division III schools do not need to register with the NCAA Clearinghouse. Division III schools utilize their own individual standards for admission and eligibility, which most coaches will share with you. In most cases, if you have the grades and SAT/ACT scores to be admitted to a Division III school—without the athletic hook—you've met the sports-eligibility standards for that college. You might wonder how far below typical admission standards a Division III school might go to admit an athlete—that varies from school to school. But you must continue to make satisfactory progress at the college in order to continue to compete, and it would be a disservice for that school to accept a student, especially without an athletic scholarship (remember Division III schools cannot give athletic scholarships), who could not do the work there. Unfortunately some schools do.

Getting Started with the Recruiting Process

You've received that first letter from a college coach—what does it all mean? The reality is that you are one of many receiving that initial letter. The test is to see how that interest continues to develop. Unfortunately, many coaches lie. We say that not out of disrespect, but because the system pretty much forces them to. If you are a national-class, blue-chip athletic prospect, you probably won't be lied to. Every coach would love to have you, and they'll try to offer you the world. That world, however, is only an athletic scholarship, and anything more would be an NCAA violation. (And if you don't think colleges are sticking way closer to the NCAA rules, just take a look at the turmoil surrounding USC. Forcing USC to return Reggie Bush's Heisman Trophy shows just how serious the NCAA is.)

Most high school athletes, however, are not blue-chip prospects. Rather, they are student-athletes with the ability to play at the college level. And that prospect may—or may not—be worthy of an athletic scholarship at that particular school in that particular year! In short, individual kids are part of the food chain of college sports, and the coaches are trying to figure out whether and where that prospect might best fit in. And for that reason, coaches must lie.

Let's explain. Division I coaches have a certain number of scholarships they can award in a given year. Many Division III coaches have "admission slots." (Yes, they negotiate with the admission office over how many places in the next freshman class they'll be allowed to fill.) And most coaches will be "pretty honest" about how many slots they have and where a prospect stands on the list.

They might need a pitcher more than a catcher or an outfielder. But they need to keep all three prospective recruits interested because the pitcher (or one of the others) is being recruited by multiple schools. The coach is also recruiting a backup for each of those three positions. In fact, the coach probably has a list of five prospects for each position, even though the pitcher is the priority. And the coach has to convince each of the 15 that he wants that particular kid. Or more accurately, the coach has to do that early in the process. As the recruiting/admissions process grinds on, the funnel—and the prospect pool—gets smaller. Some students commit to other schools, and others fail to meet admission standards. The list gets smaller—and you may still be on it—but you still may not be the prospect of choice.

Think of it in terms of casting a wide net. An Ivy League track coach (with no athletic scholarships) will write to many student-athletes. They would be identified by their athletic performances—state meet or league results,

performance lists, etc. From those who replied, the coach would then narrow down the group for academic reasons and then prioritize them based on what events the program needed most.

Each year the coach would start with a list of the track team's needs. Did he need distance runners more than sprinters? Sprinters more than field event people? Then he'd establish a priority list of the prospects he'd been talking to and turn it over to the admission office. In most cases, the admission office would respect the coach's wishes. Sometimes the admission committee would balk over a particular kid, fearing that a student wouldn't be able to survive

Coaches May Lose Even When They Win

I suspect it's a bit easier for schools with scholarships to recruit than those without. I remember a year at Auburn when, as track coach, I looked at the national rankings for high school mile times. I went after three of the best, offering each a scholarship. I also encouraged each of them to get in touch with each other, hoping that might encourage them to come together. (As a group, they would have been the dominant mile team in the conference.) The strategy worked, and they all committed to Auburn. But I had no money left for the other students I had kept on hold, since I hadn't expected to land all three. My next group prospects were cut loose, and then picked up by other schools.

—MM

the academic rigor of an Ivy League institution. Occasionally the coach would be given the chance to make the case on behalf of the kid. But the ultimate up-down decision remained with the admission office.

Now, let's look at that process in terms of numbers. That initial prospect group of 500 good high school athletes might drop to 100 who had the grades and SAT scores for a realistic hope of admission. From there, the coaches would narrow it further to a group of 40 who they'd submit on a priority list to the admissions office. And from that priority list, maybe 20 might be admitted. But the coaches would still have to keep those 100 interested until they narrowed the list to the 40. And they'd have to keep those 40 interested until they learned which of the 20 might make it through the admission process. And even then, they'd have to see how many of the 20 chose to commit. Often,

at the last minute, a coach might hear that a prospect was going elsewhere. The coach would then inform the admission office and have a decision changed. A kid who was about to receive an acceptance letter would now get a rejection. That's because the admission office cares a great deal about yield—remember that the magazine rankings of "best" colleges are typically heavily influenced by yield. So the admission offices rely on the coaches to keep them informed. No one wants to waste an admission slot on a kid who will go elsewhere and negatively impact yield.

Also, be aware that at many schools, the Director of Admission and the Director of Athletics may discuss the needs, success, and priority of each team each year and decide whether to award a particular sport more or fewer admission spaces. This can also affect recruiting late in the process and is out of your control.

Ivy League Colleges Are Different!

One important note about the Ivy League: the Ivies have a formula called the academic index (AI), which throws another set of rules into the process. It combines your GPA with standardized test scores. Not surprisingly, the AI standards are much tougher than the NCAA eligibility requirements. If you are being recruited by an Ivy League school, the coach will explain it to you. The highest possible individual AI score is a 240 total. That would reflect an A+ student/valedictorian with straight 800 scores on both the SAT1 and the two required subject tests. Typically a student with high 600s in all tests and a solid A–/B+ average falls in the median range for most Ivy League school athletic recruits. That might be an AI in the range of 200 to 210. If you are far below that, it is highly unlikely you will be recruited. But like the NCAA sliding formula, higher SATs might allow for a slightly lower GPA.

The Ivy League rules require that a school's average AI team scores be within one standard deviation of that school's overall entering class score. That means if the entering class overall has a median SAT score of 2200, the athletes on most teams other than football, basketball, and hockey might need to still average in the 2000 range. What it actually means is that the Ivy League really is looking for smart student-athletes. Consequently, an Ivy League coach might balance a great athletic prospect who has a slightly lower AI with a lesser prospect who has a higher score. Each school has the flexibility to approach this mix differently. So, for example, an athletic director might require the track team to have a higher team index than a wrestling team.

The coach may also suggest that you take the SAT again, not only to raise your AI score—and improve your chance of admission—but to help the "team score" as well. To further complicate matters, football, basketball, and hockey are limited in other ways too. They have restrictions on the number of weaker students they can recruit over a four-year period. And to manage this, they use **bands**—essentially categories—that group the number of athletes into a band based on the student's academic strength. So if a coach "suggests" that you take the SAT one more time, take the hint—even if you'd prefer not to.

Several books and articles over the last few years have drawn attention to the admission practices for student-athletes in Division III schools. In response, college presidents have reacted to those criticisms by reducing the number of admitted student-athletes and raising academic standards for those who are admitted. Division III schools typically use a process pretty similar to the one described above for the Ivies. There is no defined AI, but a banding process is used, limiting the number of weaker students a school might admit for primarily athletic reasons. The process is often further complicated by coaches having to wait to see who commits to a school after financial aid packages go out to admitted students.

Remember, at Division III schools there are no athletic scholarships, so the financial aid offers are truly a function of a family's need.

If a coach at a Division III school encourages you to apply early decision, you should consider that advice very seriously. Early decision is the Division III coach's equivalent of the Division I scholarship letter of intent. (Remember that you can apply to only one school ED; and if you're admitted, you are legally bound to attend that school.)

A coach's support of an ED applicant significantly improves the student-athlete's chance of admission. The NESCAC (New England Small College Athletic Conference) schools are best known for this practice, and it is little surprise that great academic schools like Amherst, Williams, and Middlebury contend for national athletic titles through the use of this process.

Trade-Offs

Why does banding and academic index (AI) matter to an Ivy League coach? In many sports, there are team averages as well as individual AI scores that must be achieved. For example, an Ivy recruit in wrestling might need to be part of a team average of 200. If his score is 180, there better be another recruit at 220 to get that team average. Unfortunately, there are very few genuine superstar athletes—with very high academic index numbers—who can help a program achieve that team average. A 220 index requires roughly a 730 on all SAT tests and an A– average in high school. So, for years, Ivy League colleges accepted many more just-okay athletes in their most visible sports—but who had super-high indexes. These kids counter-balanced the exceptionally talented athletes (who had lower indexes).

These less-talented athletes used up valuable spaces in the admission class to achieve a team average. I remember a hockey player from Lake Placid who had a 235 AI. (He was actually the hockey team manager and rarely played.) But with such a high AI, he appeared on the lists of five Ivy League coaches and admission offices as a hot prospect that year. Did he deserve admission? Probably. But as a student, and not as a heavily recruited —"listed"—athlete, whose presence on the list was solely to help the team's overall academic index.

To fix this "average score" system—and reduce the number of athletic admits in football, basketball, and ice hockey—the Ivy schools went to a banding concept. This allowed schools to accept a certain number of athletes in a specific academic range, called *bands*. The lower the credentials, the fewer allowed; the higher the credentials, the more allowed. Limits were also set on how many could be admitted over a range of years. Since banding was implemented, no spaces in the class are used to balance off a lower AI. That means more spaces in the class for nonathletes. The NESCAC also uses a similar banding concept to limit the number of athletic admits. So don't be surprised if a coach asks you to take the SAT/ACT again to raise your score to get into that higher band.

—MM

The Student's "Play"

As a savvy student-athlete prospect, you should not be afraid of letting a college know you are interested in that school. A short letter to the coach along with a resume can be an effective first step. (Yes, e-mail is OK.) Just make sure you convey why you're interested in that school's program. So make sure that you don't get sloppy with mass mailings or e-mails!

The resume should include:

- Personal information: name, address, phone, e-mail address, high school

- Basic academic info: GPA, SAT/ACT, or PSAT if you haven't taken SATs yet

- Athletic information: sport, position, top stats, high school/club coach/team

If you hear back from the coach, immediately fill out the questionnaire the coach is likely to send to you. And don't be afraid to stay in contact; you want to stay on the coach's radar screen. If it is a school you really like and you don't hear back from the coach, it's fine to try again. Or have your high school coach follow up.

NCAA rules mandate that until July 1 after your junior year, the majority of any contact with a college coach must be initiated by you. After July 1, you hopefully will be hearing from them.

You—probably along with a parent's help—should plan on producing a CD/DVD highlight reel. (A YouTube link or website with highlights is helpful as well, because it allows the admission officers to see you in action too.) Many college coaches are also very interested in seeing an entire game, not just your highlight reel. They want to see what and how you do when not being the star. Typically your high school or club coach should have a game tape. If not, ask a friend to video an entire game; it doesn't have to be Academy Award quality. Finally, you should also have your high school or club coach get in touch with the college coach to discuss your talent level and potential.

It is important that you do some real research about a program. Assess the level of play of that program. Times and distances don't lie. Do you need to be a nationally ranked tennis player to really have a chance at consideration? And if so, how high? If you are a swimmer or track athlete, see how your times compare with athletes already in the program. You can often learn that you might be more competitive in a weaker Division I program than a strong Division III program. Get a sense of squad size, year in school of current team members, and what positions they play. If both catchers will be seniors, you can rest assured the coach will be looking to replace that position. As for squad size, a golf or tennis coach might only add one or two players each year. But a football or lacrosse coach has much greater needs, meaning more spaces in admission too.

In addition to conveying your interest in a particular school, it is also very useful to alert a college coach that you are participating in a summer showcase or holiday tournament. Showcases come in all varieties and locations in many sports. They are often set up for student-athletes with higher academic credentials. Coaches from institutions who recruit from that pool—the Ivies and NESCAC, for example—are often inclined to come and observe the student-athletes in action. Going to a showcase outside your region could open up a new set of schools that might be interested in you. Finally, it can be useful to find out which summer camps, tournaments, or showcases the college coach of your top choice college plans to attend. Then you should try to participate in those events. Remember that few college coaches have the time to come and see a high school contest—unless you are the absolute blue-chip top prospect. And in those cases, they already know how good you are. They're visiting in order to get you to think more highly of them and their program; they're trying to enhance their chances of enrolling you.

The level of the coach's response might also help you realize what level of interest there may be in you. Or in some cases, the high school coach can find out what skills you may need to work on. Remember, NCAA rules prevent direct contact between a college coach and most prospects until July 1 prior to senior year. (There some exceptions to this rule that apply to football, basketball, and ice hockey.) If the phone doesn't start ringing by July 2, it may be time to reassess whether athletics will play a significant role in your admission process, regardless of level.

One more thought—be able to look yourself in the mirror and make an honest assessment of where you really belong. Too often, a true Division III prospect chases the Division I dream and realizes too late that the Division III coaches have moved on to other prospects. Perhaps the most difficult thing to accept is that even though you enjoyed playing in high school—and were pretty good there—there may not be college interest in you. If that's the case, move on. There are plenty of schools that will love to have you become a star in their intramural leagues. And you'll probably enjoy it enormously.

Should Students "Lie" Too?

One of the most significant dilemmas of this process is whether students should "lie" just as coaches do. Should students "inflate" their level of interest in a particular school until they can determine the coach's real level of interest in them? And, although there are both ethical and practical problems here, the answer is yes. The student-athlete is well advised to play it "close to the vest," telling several schools they are really interested in that school—until he or she gets the green light from the college. One word of caution, however. In many sports, coaches talk among themselves, and a student-athlete would be wise not to cast the net in too many places. The word often gets out in certain circles (squash is a great example) where you need to be very careful what you say in the recruiting process.

Both Ivy League and Division III schools utilize the school's regular financial aid process to assist families with the cost of attending their schools. These financial aid packages really are based on the financial need of the family—not how badly the school "needs" that athlete. In the old days, the Ivy League actually compared aid packages to make sure they were consistent from school to school. While that process is now forbidden by federal rules, few schools will risk the wrath of their fellow members—or Justice Department or NCAA probes—by offering a financial aid package way out of line with the family's "demonstrated need."

A family's demonstrated need is the flip side of the family's "expected family contribution." (See Chapter 8 for a full explanation.) The federal government calculates these numbers based on financial information provided by the family when they file the FAFSA or Profile forms. (FAFSA is the government's Free Application for Federal Student Aid. The Profile refers to the College Board's financial aid form. Both are typically required for families seeking aid, and both are discussed in detail in Chapter 8.) The formula is at once arcane, predictable, and unrealistic about actual cost-of-living expenses. For example, a family with a $100,000 income and $20,000 in assets would be expected to contribute about $9,000 a year to a child's college costs.

It is very important to understand that virtually all families can receive some form of financial aid—but it might be in the form of student loans rather than grants. (A grant is the official financial aid buzzword for a scholarship.) Colleges have some discretion in the mix of grants and loans that comprise a student's financial aid package. So, a prospect can certainly share the details of a financial aid award with another school to see whether the second school might match or improve upon it. But colleges are very unlikely to go way outside the aid package prescribed by the FAFSA and expected family contribution.

Division III schools are highly unlikely to award any additional financial aid if it would appear that athletic ability might have been a factor. Division I schools obviously have more flexibility in their aid awards—because they do award athletic scholarships. Thus, they can decide how to spend their dollars. In many sports, colleges can divide scholarships between kids in order to stretch their dollars further and fill out a team. That means you shouldn't necessarily expect a full scholarship. Rather, your award may be balanced by a low-interest loan.

At some schools, a small scholarship award may be used to get a good-but-not-great athlete. The coach may want this kid, but not enough to use up a larger chunk of his available scholarship dollars. Larger scholarships will go toward more promising athletes. The coach's strategy may also be sending a message to the admission office itself. By allocating a small piece of the scholarship pot to a specific kid, the coach is saying to the admission office: take this kid. I'm allocating some of my scholarship money on him; you need to make sure he is admitted.

And then there are the non-scholarship athletes. These are kids whom a coach likes—but doesn't *love.* The coach won't attach an athletic scholarship to this prospect. But the kid may receive a financial aid award based on need. And that financial aid package will be similar to those given to non-athletes with similar FAFSA profiles. Or, if the student is eligible for a merit (academic) scholarship, this "second-tier" athlete will get an award similar to those given to non-athletes with similar academic credentials.

The recruiting process is nuanced. Never be afraid to involve your high school coach or college counselor in the process. College coaches are much more likely to be truthful with high school coaches and counselors—because they'll probably want to "do business" with that high school again in the future. But realize too, that your high school coach or counselor—while your advocate—needs to be "pretty" honest with the college as well. They don't want to lose credibility with that college coach that might affect future recruits. So be sure to keep the high school coach and counselor in the loop as your priorities and interests change.

Title IX—Women Athletes

The world of college athletics changed forever in 1972. That was the year Congress passed a series of Education Amendments designed to reduce discrimination against women in hiring and employment. There was almost no discussion of athletics in the hearings and Congressional Committee reports. But in the intervening years, as a result of both Department of Education rulings and lawsuits, the impact of what has become known as Title IX (nine for you rusty on your Roman numerals) on college athletics has been monumental. This section is not written as a criticism of Title IX. When instituted appropriately by a college, it creates opportunities for female athletes that were denied for years. We write this simply to make you aware that different schools have approached Title IX in different ways.

Title IX has been both a blessing and a curse for many athletic programs. The basic intent of Title IX was to increase opportunities for female student-athletes. When it was enacted, many colleges were spending disproportionate amounts of money on men's football and basketball programs—when compared to "non-revenue" sports. (Sports like track or squash.) And the disparity was even greater when compared to the tiny sums being spent by colleges on women's athletics.

Back in 1972 when Title IX came into effect, women's athletic programs existed under a different organization, called the AIAW—the Association for Intercollegiate Athletics for Women. Today, the AIAW is gone, having been absorbed into the NCAA, and women's sports are regulated by the NCAA.

Title IX requires colleges to offer their female student-athletes similar opportunities to those given to the men. The law's implementation takes into account the percentage of the campus population that is female, the number of men's sports compared to the number of women's sports offered, the budgets for men's and women's sports, and the school's history of growth in creating more opportunities for women. That could mean adding more sports, improving facilities, and increasing budgets. It has been a boon for woman's programs, as many schools have added sports, increased roster size, and boosted athletic scholarships. We mention this in detail because there are opportunities for female athletes that never existed before. In fact, when considering your hook, there may be even more opportunities for women than men in today's college athletic arena.

Here's a good example. The University of Virginia is recognized as one of the finest academic institutions in the country. They also have an outstanding athletic program. The men's lacrosse team is always a national championship contender, and the football team competes against some of the top football schools in the country, including USC, Georgia Tech, Miami, and Florida State. To compete in those top-tier leagues, the university spends scholarship dollars on 85 football players and more than 20 lacrosse players.

To be in compliance under Title IX, the university needed to fund a similar number of female athletes. As a result, Virginia added and has funded a varsity crew program for women that now ranks annually among the best in the country. It also gave more scholarship aid to other women's teams. In fact there are now more varsity women's teams at Virginia than men's. Without Title IX, this never would have happened. (The men have a nonvarsity club crew team, but they must fund it themselves. This is a fairly common occurrence at colleges that added varsity crew for women.) Not surprisingly, compliance with Title IX is not as difficult or costly for those schools without Division I football.

There is a downside of Title IX for male athletes. Instead of spending more money to support women's growth, many schools have sacrificed men's nonrevenue programs. They've simply chosen to limit opportunities for male athletes. You'll find a number of schools that sponsor women's swimming, track and field, or gymnastics that do not sponsor similar men's programs. Another consequence of Title IX is that many schools limit the squad size of the men's team but not the women's team. Particular sports without a female equivalency, like wrestling, are often the first to be eliminated in order to achieve Title IX balance.

Many schools put more scholarship dollars into non-revenue women's teams than into the men's team. This is done to offset the scholarship dollars spent on football. The NCAA itself even recognizes and supports the inequity. It allows 20 scholarships for women in crew compared to none for men. You'll see that the NCAA allows more scholarships for women than men in sports like track and swimming to achieve Title IX compliance and gender equity.

We call attention to this for what must now be pretty obvious reasons. There are more opportunities available to female student-athletes—particularly in "more obscure" sports. (So get rowing!) It also means there may be fewer roster spots for men. And that is true even at non-scholarship schools like the Ivies. It also means there are fewer scholarships available in non-revenue sports.

It is in your best interest to inquire how Title IX has been implemented at the school you're interested in, and how it might affect your opportunities to compete at that school. Don't be afraid to ask the college coach!

The College Walk-On

The movie *Rudy* is probably the best-known flick ever about a college walk-on. And in that spirit, we're happy to tell you that there is hope for you as a walk-on. You can make it onto some pretty good Division I and Division III teams simply by walking on. There are basically two types of walk-ons: invited walk-ons and self-initiated walk-ons. Neither approach will have any impact in your college admission. But it may impact your decision about where you might attend.

Here's the good news: many Division I programs have limited scholarships. That means the teams often need bodies to fill out their rosters. This is more likely in sports that require greater numbers of players like football, lacrosse, or rugby. There are also sports like crew where a novice might even take up the sport as a walk-on. Many a tall lanky male or female has been recruited on campus by a savvy crew coach during freshman orientation.

An invited walk-on is someone who is encouraged to come out for the team by the coach and is given a very good chance of remaining on the team. There may be contact during the admission process. And although the coach was unable to support or assist you in getting in, they encouraged you to try out for the team if you're admitted. These are serious invitations, and if you want to play at the college level, follow up with the coach even before you arrive on campus.

When you walk on—on your own—your odds of making the team are tougher. But if you've continued to hone your skills and maintain your conditioning, the coach will be more open-minded about a true walk-on. Most coaches have their team from last year, know their recruits, and may have encouraged a few others to try out. Not being in that group may put you at a serious disadvantage. So don't be afraid to ask the coach for an honest evaluation of your skills; and what you might need to do to make the team. Many a walk-on has heeded a coach's comments, worked hard in the off season, and come back to make the team the following year.

One last point about walk-ons and Title IX: At some schools, the coach might not even be allowed to keep a male walk-on in an effort to reduce the number of male athletes in that program. Conversely, in order to be in compliance with Title IX, the coach might be encouraged to try to add as many females as their team can accommodate.

Big Fish in a Little Pond, or Little Fish in a Big One?

If you're the true blue-chip recruit, this is not an issue—you'll most likely be the big fish in the big pond. For most other athletes, however, this is something you'll need to wrestle with. If you've been honest with yourself through the process—and coaches have been candid with you too—you should pretty much know where you'll stand in a program. Is there a realistic chance you'll start? As a freshman? Get playing time? Or is it a program where you are expected to pay your dues, and the coach plays upperclassmen who have been loyal to the program over the years? As long as you know the rules and what you are getting yourself into, then you should feel comfortable with the possibility of being that small fish in a big pond for a few years.

For many of you, however, that might not be good enough. You may really want to play, not just be on the team. If so, you need to step back and factor that into your decision.

Should you accept the smaller scholarship in the bigger program, or a richer scholarship in a less successful program? And where will you get more playing time and have a greater impact? Would you be better off playing at a Division III school where you might be an All-American? And would you even have such an opportunity on the Division I level? There are very real differences: an NCAA Division III champion's mark in many track events would not even qualify you for the Division I meet.

It is important to listen to a college coach's candid assessment and advice. Too often we've heard stories about high school athletes not "hearing" a coach's advice and becoming obsessed about proving the coach wrong. Determination is a great thing. But so is realistic self-assessment and keeping an open mind. Sometimes being the big fish in that little pond isn't so bad.

8

CHAPTER 8
Paying for College

First the good news: you can almost always "find" money to pay for college. And now the bad news: you will almost always have to pay some of it back over time. Every family is different in its comfort level about whether to take on student loan debt. We are not about to suggest how much debt you should incur to go to college—or even whether you should take on any debt at all. But you almost never have to say that you don't have access to funds to pay for college.

Think of paying for college like paying for an airplane ticket. Some of you can pay full price and do. Others buy far in advance or use a discount company like Expedia or Priceline to get a better rate. You never really know what the person next to you might have paid for their ticket. Financial aid (and merit awards) work the same way. No two people pay exactly the same amount or even use precisely the same financial instruments. Many of you will even pay different amounts each year.

And just as with the airplane ticket, some of you will pay with a credit card, spreading the payment out over time. Others will use a debit card

Big Warning

As of this writing—Winter 2011—much of the college financial aid world is in flux. That's because the federal government has made major changes in the way financial aid gets administered and distributed. So while this chapter is quite up-to-date, you should check our website for the latest developments: www.zinch.com/financialaid.

and pay for the flight all at once. Financial aid packages are similar. The goal and destination remain the same— you want to attend CollegeU. There are just different rates and ways of paying for it.

There are, not surprisingly, smarter ways—as opposed to less productive ways—to go about securing money for college. Let's start with a basic assumption: your family, like most families, probably has not saved enough to pay for four years of college. Something has probably been put aside. But most families find it beyond their means to write a check for $30,000 or $50,000 every year for four years—for each child.

The first question families typically ask is: Is that how much college really costs? ($30,000 is the typical cost at a state university; $50,000 the cost of tuition and room and board at many private colleges.) The answer is no; and we discuss what that cost really is in the next section called, appropriately enough, "The *Real* Cost of College."

From there we'll take you on the emotional roller coaster that begins with the gentle climb of in-state versus out-of-state tuition. The real fun begins when you have to face reality with what the government calls the Expected Family Contribution. That calculation is often like the steepest, scariest part of the roller-coaster ride. But it soon gets a little better—if not more fun—when you consider different types of funding available to you. And then there is that stomach-turning final swoop as your family has to complete the myriad financial aid forms. You'll all survive the ride. And when it's over, you may actually say, "That wasn't so bad." But don't worry: you'll have to do it all again next year when it is time to reapply for financial aid.

So let's get started, but hang on: it's going to be a bumpy ride. (Yes, we borrowed that from *All About Eve*.)

The REAL Cost of College

You've probably heard the expression "sticker price" in the context of buying a new car. (For those of you who haven't actually experienced the process of purchasing a new car, the autos in a show room have a giant paper sticker—usually two feet square—affixed to the driver's side rear window. It details the base price of the car along with the price of every option included in that particular auto, from upgraded sound system to delivery fees. The total is the sticker price; from which you start haggling with the dealer to arrive at the final price.)

Colleges have a sticker price too. Just go to any college's website and you'll find the annual tuition charge, along with required fees (student organization fees, health fees, perhaps recreation fees). Plus there are living and eating costs—whether you live in a dorm, in off-campus housing, or at home—plus the cost of books. That's the college's sticker price.

Most colleges are completely transparent about the cost of attending, and many include online calculators that help you really understand how much that school is going to cost. These online tools ask simple questions about your intended program of study, expected living arrangements, distance your home is from campus, etc. It then provides you with a pretty good estimate of the final cost.

Important reminder: Make sure you calculate the cost of a full year at the college, not just a single semester! Some colleges list semester costs, not annual costs.

You may be asking yourself shouldn't I be calculating the cost of four full years of college and not just one year? The answer is that you should. But in terms of the financial aid process itself, it is really only an annual process. In fact, because it is an annual process, you—and especially your parents—will have to go through it every year. It is a

major pain in the butt! But it is important to remember that family circumstances can change each year—for the better or for the worse. And colleges will take that into consideration as they evaluate you yearly for financial aid.

It is important that you calculate the total estimated cost of attending a particular college for a pretty obvious reason: Does your family have the savings to send you to four years of that college? What if you take an extra year to get through school? Or choose to study abroad? Do you have siblings already in college or coming up behind you in high school?

These are all reasonable questions that you and your family will have to address. And as we said earlier, if your family doesn't have a savings account (or investments) set aside for college, then you'll have to come up with alternative ways to pay that college bill. And that typically involves loans. So you'll all have to have some candid conversations about your comfort level with debt. That's because some college loan options place the responsibility for repayment on the children's shoulders while others saddle the parent with the debt.

But let's return to the single-year tuition, room-and-board, and expenses calculation. Is that the *real* cost of attending the college? It is and it isn't. That's what the sticker price is. But it may not be the real cost to you. And that's because colleges use different types of scholarship or merit aid to entice certain students to attend their institution. (We discuss different types of financial aid later in the chapter.) Your real cost, however, will be the sticker price minus any outright grants or scholarships the college gives you.

Starting in October 2011, colleges will be required by federal law to post "net-price calculators" on their websites. These tools, which are supposed to be interactive, will show the actual cost of attendance. And importantly, they are supposed to include an estimate of what a family would actually pay after all grants. It's difficult to find anyone who dislikes the basic intent of the rule. But the jury is still out on how effectively—or compliant—all schools will be in implementing the program.

As defined by the government, net price is a straightforward concept. You add up the published price of tuition, room and board, and fees. Then you toss in the estimated cost of indirect expenses like books, travel, and miscellaneous living expenses to arrive at a figure for cost of attendance. Then you subtract the median amount of grant aid given to a group of similar students, and there it is: your estimated net price. Sounds easy, but it won't be. The good news, however, is that it will create an opportunity for colleges to communicate and work with families as they implement the rule.

In-State vs. Out-of-State Residence

Another very common question is whether a student who gets accepted at a state university can change his residence to in-state status after the freshman year.

Tuition at fine state universities for out-of-state residents is often two to three times what in-state kids pay. Not surprisingly, parents wonder if they can change their kid's legal residence and save a bundle. After all, the student actually does live there, may have changed his driver's license and registered to vote in the university town, and may even plan to remain there after graduation.

Unfortunately, it is *very* difficult in most states to change residency sufficient to trigger the lower in-state tuition. State legislators and school administrators are well aware of parents' desire to do it and consequently have either passed stringent regulations or tightened up loopholes.

And both the legislators and the college love the higher tuitions that out-of-staters pay. We remember taking the college tour at the University of Colorado, Boulder, when one of the touring parents asked about establishing in-state residence after the freshman year. "Absolutely impossible," said the tour guide. Most university websites will delineate what is required to establish legal residence—for tuition purposes. It may be possible, but be prepared for it to be very difficult at the very least.

The "Big Picture" Process

Colleges usually don't just throw money at you; you have to apply for it. We say usually because there are two major exceptions: athletic scholarships and merit (academic) scholarships. If you're a super-athlete, you've probably already read Chapter 7. If you're an academic superstar, you should pay attention here.

Colleges do award merit scholarships to kids they really want to attend their school. This is different from being awarded a grant

or scholarship based on academic merit *after* you've applied for financial aid. Merit awards can be used by the college to attract kids who have no "demonstrated financial need." It is simply a way for colleges to attract top scholars and encourage them to attend OldU rather than CompetitiveU.

Think of the colleges like a food chain. The most competitive colleges—like the Ivies and other extremely selective schools—simply don't give any merit awards. Pretty much every student they admit would be deserving of a merit award for one reason or another. As you move down the college "prestige food chain," however, the next-lower level of schools might become more aggressive with merit aid. They are hoping to entice you away from attending that more prestigious school where you'd have to pay the full tuition. And the further down you go in the food chain, the more aggressive a school with resources may be in their attempt to attract you.

At this stage of the discussion about paying for college, we will ignore non-need-based merit scholarships. If a college comes after you with a merit award, super! We'll discuss what to do with those offers later in this chapter. In the meantime, we want to focus on the process of looking for money.

In short, if you want help paying for college—other than from your parents' piggy bank—you have to ask for it. This whole world is known as the financial aid process. And it is a real pain in the butt.

To get financial aid—money from just about any type of scholarship, loan, or work-study program—you will have to complete and file several horrendous forms.

The FAFSA

The FAFSA is a government form. It looks like and feels like a federal income tax form, except it is even more confusing. Hard to believe? Trust us. FAFSA stands for Free Application for Federal Student Aid. While it doesn't cost money to file this form, it costs plenty in terms of the hours it takes to complete. There is no way around it: if you want any sort of loan or scholarship, you and your parents have to fill out this thing.

You can find it here: www. fafsa.ed.gov/, and you must complete it online. Welcome to the modern age.

Be forewarned: Both parents and students need to apply for PIN numbers as well. And before you sit down to tackle the FAFSA, gather all your tax information—your parents' completed tax forms and yours. You need them in order to answer the FAFSA questions.

You can't submit a FAFSA until after January 1 of your

senior year. But you should do so as soon after January 1 as possible.

FAFSA and Early Decision— Yep, there's a timing conflict. Early decision deadlines are typically November 1 and November 15 for many smaller liberal arts colleges. And you hear the college's decision—which is binding—in early December. But what if the college's financial aid package doesn't meet your perceived need? Happily, most colleges offering early decision options also are committed to meeting a student's financial need. If they admit you, the school will work with you to find the money to attend. But you still have to submit the bloody FAFSA forms.

"Release" from an Early Decision Commitment—It is important to know that most colleges will release you from your early decision commitment if you honestly believe you can't afford to pay for that college with the financial aid package they've given you. You must realize, however, that you give up your spot there, and your financial aid awards may not end up being any better elsewhere.

The CSS/Profile

The CSS/Profile is a second financial aid form required by about 600 colleges. Most selective colleges use the CSS/Profile. CSS stands for College Scholarship Service, and it is part of the College Board. Yes, the CSS/Profile has to be completed and submitted *in addition* to the FAFSA. But if a particular college requires the CSS/Profile, they typically don't require a school-specific financial aid form. While the FAFSA is free, the CSS/Profile is not. It costs $24 to file the form and have it sent to one college. It costs $18 for each additional college you want the report sent to. You can, and should, submit the CSS/Profile early in the fall of your senior year. Preliminary financial aid offers—particularly for those applying early decision or early action—will be based on the CSS/Profile. Unlike the FAFSA, which focuses more on annual income, the CSS/Profile looks more closely at family assets.

The CSS Profile also does a better job than the FAFSA in alerting colleges about other education expenses your family might have. In addition to listing a sibling in college, it also allows you to list a parent who may have returned to school; graduate, medical, or law school expenses for an older sibling; or costs of private education for younger siblings. Although the colleges are not required to factor this information into your award package (though most will for a sibling in college), it can certainly be of benefit to a college to be aware of these expenses if you later appeal your award.

Tax Forms

Most colleges require you to submit copies of your parents' (and probably your) federal income tax forms. Just get 'em ready. Sometimes they just ask for the Form 1040. And other times they require information from other supporting forms or the forms themselves. So have an extra copy of them all handy. If your parents are separated or divorced, make sure your noncustodial parent has their taxes done early too—most colleges will request this information from them.

Special Circumstances Documentation

Most colleges—along with the CSS/Profile folks—allow you to submit explanations and documentation in support of special financial circumstances and requests. We strongly urge you to try to develop a relationship with someone in financial aid at

More Competition vs. Attack on Common Sense

Up until the early 1990s, the eight Ivy League schools and MIT met each year to compare the financial aid awards being given to kids who had applied to more than one college among that group of nine. The financial aid awards were then adjusted for the kid so that the family contribution was held constant. The philosophy was to take money out of the equation and enable students to select their school of choice based on the merits of the school and not what it cost. Makes sense right? Well, a federal antitrust suit was filed against the group for—are you ready—price fixing. And the schools were no longer allowed to meet. This explains why you now often get different packages from each of these nine schools.

your top-choice schools. Having a real, live contact person can be invaluable for both an appeal or review of your award each year. This may be especially important in documenting that one parent has failed to consistently meet their financial obligations in a divorced family. Schools may ask for proof—a statement from a lawyer or minister, for example—and will then use their professional judgment. That judgment call sometimes results in the college making an award that reduces, or even eliminates, a contribution from a noncustodial parent.

The Expected Family Contribution

The expected family contribution (EFC) is a calculation made by the government of how much your family is expected to provide—to contribute—to your college costs annually. You will hear, universally, that this is the most unrealistic calculation any government agency will ever make at any time. It is always being criticized as absolutely unrealistic. One of the biggest criticisms is that it typically fails to accurately take into account the *real* cost of living—no matter where you live. (The EFC sees no difference between living on the same $100,000 per year in New York City versus Fargo, North Dakota). It is also completely unrealistic about the amount of *disposable* income that families actually have.

And yet we all have to live with the EFC calculation if we want to apply for any sort of financial aid.

Independent vs. Dependent Students

The vast, vast majority of kids applying to college directly from high school will be classified as dependent children. It is even difficult for people in their early 20s to qualify as independent. We mention this right up front because lots of families think their child will qualify for more financial aid if the parents don't declare their child as a dependent on the federal tax form. And since most kids right out of high school have little in savings and few liquid financial assets, the financially savvy family often considers setting junior "adrift" financially—with perhaps some under-the-table, off-the-record assistance.

FUHGETABOUTIT!

Don't even think about it. Not only is it illegal and unethical, it doesn't work! (Nothing like adding the practical to the higher-road dimension.) For example, the University of Southern California is pretty typical in the criteria it uses to establish independence:

- An individual who is at least 24 years old by December 31 of the award year
- An orphan or ward of the court
- A veteran of the U.S. Armed Forces
- A graduate or professional student
- An individual with legal dependents other than a spouse
- A student for whom the school's Financial Aid Administrator determines and documents an independent status, based on the administrator's professional judgment of the student's unusual circumstances

So, it is not impossible, but it is not easy to establish financial independence.

Most Families Will Have an EFC

We debated how to phrase this headline. Should we have asked, "Will *all* families be expected to kick in an EFC to pay for college?" If we had, the answer would have been "no"—but it would also have been misleading. If your family earns over $30,000 annually, you can basically assume your family will have to contribute something.

Unfortunately, there is no simple way to estimate the EFC without answering a whole bunch of questions. That's because the formula is really quite convoluted. Parents' income, assets, expenses, and age all go into it. So does family composition: the number of kids in college; what state you live in; and what sort of savings, investments, and business your parents have. And finally, what you earn during your summer or part-time jobs comes into play as well.

There are two different sets of calculations that take place with the EFC: the federal methodology (FM) and the institutional methodology (IM). The FM is used to calculate your eligibility for federal aid and most types of state aid. For example, it's used by most public universities. Many private colleges and scholarship programs use the IM to determine your eligibility for their own grant funds. You'll also hear the expression "professional judgment (PJ)" used by many financial aid counselors. It simply means they used their PJ in determining your package. This often explains why awards may vary from school to school even though the schools are working from the same set of financial information from the family.

Here are some basic guidelines about how the EFC is calculated to help clarify matters. The formula used to calculate an EFC is primarily an income-based formula. Assets do affect the calculation but do not have the same impact as income. So if your family's income changes from one year to the next, that could have a significant impact on your annual EFC.

Your family's investments and assets also have an impact on the EFC, but to a lesser degree. Some examples of assets that must be reported are savings, checking, CDs,

stocks, bonds, mutual funds, college savings plans, real estate, business equity, and home equity. Other assets that are not included in determining the EFC are: the value of retirement plans (pension funds, annuities, non-education IRAs, Keogh plans) or the value of life insurance plans.

Student and parent investments are treated very differently in determining the EFC. A contribution of 20% of a student's assets is expected each year. So, for example, if you reported $10,000 in assets, you might be expected to contribute $2,000 of your savings. In fact, many selective schools may ask for up to 35% of your assets toward the first year. In comparison, your parents' expected contribution from assets typically does not exceed 6% of their assets.

So rather than try to explain a complex and convoluted formula "in print," we recommend you—or actually your parents—try one of the better online estimators. The College Board has a relatively easy one (www.collegeboard.com/ student/pay/add-it-up/ 401.html) as does Monster's FinAid site (www.finaid.org/). We link to these and other resources on our site as well: www.zinch.com/financialaid.

Can't we even give you a ballpark? Sure. Table 8-1 presents EFC scenarios you can use to gauge your own circumstances—roughly. It reflects a family of four living in New York. The college-bound child is 19, earns $1,500 from a summer job, and has no assets.

The family's assets, in all cases, reflect $50,000 in savings with the balance in real estate equity. Like hot sauce, use this table sparingly and with caution!

So are those expected family contributions realistic? We don't think so. But we warned you: this is how the formula plays out.

Table 8-1. Ballpark Estimator of Expected Family Contribution

Federal Methodology				
	FAMILY INCOME			
FAMILY ASSETS	$60,000	$100,000	$150,000	$250,000
$50,000	$3,089	$10,548	$25,436	$53,978
$150,000	$3,089	$10,548	$25,436	$53,978
$500,000	$3,089	$10,548	$25,436	$53,978
Institutional Methodology				
	FAMILY INCOME			
FAMILY ASSETS	$60,000	$100,000	$150,000	$250,000
$50,000	$1,689	$7,077	$17,225	$42,827
$150,000	$6,773	$10,212	$19,445	$44,552
$500,000	$24,273	$27,712	$36,900	$61,883

Types of Funding

There are three basic types of financial aid funding:

- Work-study money
- Scholarships and grants
- Loans

Everything else you are going to hear or read about are just variations on these.

We'll address where to find and apply for these monies later—as well as where these funds actually come from. But for now, let's just address the types of funding. Remember, however, that most colleges want to use money they receive from the federal government before they dip into their own financial resources. As a result, colleges utilize—and award—loans and work-study monies first.

Work-Study

Work-study money is the smallest pot of financial aid, and we want to address this one first, simply to get it out of the way. Many colleges include a small work-study component in the financial aid package they award students. Typically, work-study doesn't account for more than 10% of the aid package. Colleges include

it because a portion of the money comes from the federal government, not from the college's coffers. But on the flip side, most colleges don't want students to spend too many hours working (pretty menial) jobs on campus. The typical work-study pay is usually not much more than minimum wage and often no more than 10 hours per week. And colleges, while liking kids to have some work responsibility—and enjoying the productivity of college kids doing the college's basic labor at minimum wage—would prefer to have students actually studying or participating in campus activities.

"Special" Work-Study Programs

Perhaps the best-known "special" work-study programs are the military's ROTC programs. Each branch of the military has its own variations on the theme, but the basic approach is pretty consistent. If you are accepted—and both academic and physical standards are quite stringent—you receive a certain, usually significant, percentage of your college tuition and living expenses from the military. And in exchange, you agree to serve in the military (as an officer) for a set number of years. ROTC programs also require academic-year classes and drills in addition to summer "in-service" training. The Marine Corps has its own approach to officer training, which involves summer training. None of these programs are administered through the traditional financial aid process. So if this is something that interests you, be sure to investigate the branch of the service that appeals to you and find out whether that program exists on your (hoped for) college campus.

Scholarships and Grants

These are the "best" types of financial aid—right, you don't have to pay them back! Scholarships and grants come in all sizes for many reasons. Most, but not all, scholarships are awarded and administered by the colleges themselves. Colleges have access to many different pots of money that comprise the scholarship pool. Some are general and can be awarded to almost any student for almost any reason.

Others are restricted—by the recipient's background, academic major, high school or college accomplishments, interests, or almost anything. Sometimes—in fact often— there is no real exchange of cash. The college doesn't actually cut you a check, which you in turn deposit into your checking account and then write a check to the college to pay for tuition. Rather, your tuition bill is simply reduced by the amount of the scholarship award.

When many colleges put together your financial aid package, they typically include

Pell Grants

Many parents ask about the availability of Pell Grants— scholarship aid awarded by the federal government. Pell Grants are well known because they are often the subject of political speeches. Politicians love to tout how they are pushing for larger Pell Grants for their constituents. In fact, they are available only to the poorest Americans—families who earn less than $20,000 annually. The grants can be up to $5,550 annually.

some amount of scholarship aid. That's just smart marketing on their part. It says to you—and your parents—isn't junior smart; see how much we love him? They may designate the type of scholarship you are receiving—both for accounting and prestige reasons—or it may be a general "university" scholarship. (Names differ by college.) If you qualify for a very small package, however, they may use their federal funds to award you only a loan and/or work study.

Generally, there are no strings attached to scholarship aid other than acceptable academic performance once you are on campus. But if you fail to achieve a certain GPA after you've matriculated, you should expect your scholarship to be withdrawn!

Loans

Loans are the largest and most confusing category of financial aid monies. There are subsidized loans—with lower interest rates—and unsubsidized loans. There are need-based loans (which require your family income to be below a certain level) and open-to-all loans. There are loans that go directly to students and loans that go to your parents. Table 8.2 summarizes the types of loans available.

When you apply for financial aid—and the college's financial aid office sorts through all the applications and paperwork that you and your parents have submitted—they will determine which loans you qualify for and which you don't. They will then offer you loans, based on your eligibility, in order of the loans' "attractiveness." (Lower interest, "subsidized" loans are more attractive, and higher interest, unsubsidized loans are less attractive.)

Student Loans

A student's financial aid award will likely include one or more student loans. Both the Perkins and Stafford Loan programs are federal financial aid programs. These loans are taken in the student's name. You will need to complete a promissory note in order to have these loans processed. The actual interest rates can vary from year to year.

- **Perkins Loan**—Federal Perkins Loans are awarded by colleges to students with the highest need. Interest does not accrue while you

Table 8-2. Types of Education Loans

Loan Type	Need-Based & Subsidized?	Sponsor	Borrower	Interest Rate
Perkins	Yes	Federal government	Student	5% (fixed)
Subsidized Stafford	Yes	Federal government	Student	4.5% (fixed), effective July 1, 2010
Unsubsidized Stafford	No	Federal government	Student	6.8% (fixed)
Parent PLUS	No	Federal government	Parent	7.9% (fixed)
Private (Alternative) and State	No	Banks, colleges, foundations, state agencies	Usually student with creditworthy parental cosigner	Usually higher than federal rates (variable)

are enrolled at least half-time. The interest rate is fairly low—5%—and you don't make any loan payments while in school. Undergraduates can borrow up to $5,500 a year, totaling not more than $27,500 overall. Repayment begins nine months after you graduate or cease attending school at least half-time.

- **Subsidized Stafford Loan**—Federal subsidized Stafford Loans are also need-based loans. Interest does not accrue while

you are enrolled at least half-time. Currently, the fixed interest rate is 4.5%. The government pays the yearly interest while you're in school. Undergraduates with the greatest need can borrow up to $3,500 for their freshman year. This limit rises as you progress through school. Repayment begins six months after you graduate or cease attending school at least half-time.

- **Unsubsidized Stafford Loan**—Federal unsubsidized Stafford Loans are sponsored by the government but are not based on financial need. The interest rate is fixed at 6.8%. As a dependent undergraduate, you can borrow up to $5,500 minus the amount of your subsidized Stafford Loan, if you have one. That's for your freshman year; the limit rises as you progress through school. Interest does accrue while you are enrolled in school. Repayment begins six months after you graduate or cease attending school at least half-time.

Parent PLUS Loans

Many parents simply can't come up with their Expected Family Contribution. (We warned you earlier that the formula generates EFCs that have little relationship to reality.) Federal parent PLUS Loans are sponsored by the government but are not based on need. Generally, parents can borrow up to the total cost of education, minus any aid received. PLUS Loans are the largest source of parent loans. The interest rate is fixed at 7.9%. There is a credit check associated with the parent PLUS Loan.

Private (Alternative) and State Education Loans

Private (alternative) and state education loans are generally not subsidized or based on need. Although some colleges lend money to parents, private loans are most often intended for students. Still, a parent is usually a cosigner, since good credit tends to be a requirement. If you default on the loan, your parent is responsible for repaying it. Many—but not all—states offer special student loan programs. Typically you must either be a resident of the state or attending college in that state. Every program is different, so the best way to find out if there is a program and if you're eligible is to type in "state education loans"—and your state—into your favorite search engine.

Other Sources of Financial Aid

You've probably seen more than a few ads—on the Internet, in magazines, and in assorted brochures and guides—announcing the availability of millions of dollars in scholarships. You may have heard about scholarships that go "unawarded" and others that are, well, "weird" (scholarships, for example, for left-handed oboe players or students named Murphy who major in engineering.) Some of our good friends who run high school and college-oriented businesses are responsible for running these ads. And they are legit—but still somewhat misleading.

The vast majority of scholarships are, as we noted above, campus based. That means the school searches out who among their students (or prospective students) are eligible for these scholarships—and then makes those awards as part of the student's financial aid package. If you're eligible, you'll at least be in the running for the award.

The real question is: are these "matching services" worth using? Our answer is yes—if they are free! If a company asks you to pay for these matching services, move on. If it is free, it might be worth it. There are "special" scholarships that are not campus based, and you might be eligible for them. But there is an ulterior business motive behind the altruism of these free matching services. There is nothing wrong or sleazy about them, but you should know about the underlying business.

The business strategy behind these matching services is pretty simple: if you register with a company or even a nonprofit service saying that you are looking for scholarships, your name and contact information is pretty valuable to the company you've registered with. The information they collect about you is valuable to companies that have products and services which are pretty appropriate to college-bound families. The company you've registered with will "sell" or "rent" your name to these other companies, and you'll receive either direct mail brochures or e-mails with these offerings. You'll probably have no interest in many of these offers. But others will appeal to you, and they can range from computers to textbook rentals to parent loans.

For access to a terrific, free database of non-campus-based scholarships, go to www.zinch.com/scholarshipsearch.

The Link Between Admissions and Financial Aid

Does applying for financial aid affect your chances of admission? The answer is sometimes, and at some places. We're not being wishy-washy. That's really the answer—but we'll provide further explanation that should give you some clear black-and-white guidance.

Schools typically say somewhere on the admissions page of their website whether their admissions policy is **need-blind.** If it is indeed need-blind, that means that the yes/no decision on your application will be made irrespective of whether you apply for financial aid.

There are many nuances of this, however, in the award you might receive. A need-blind school that is flush in resources will meet 100% of your calculated need. But many need-blind schools do not have these resources and utilize something called **gapping.** What this means is that they want you to know you were qualified for admission, but they unfortunately don't have the resources to

fully fund all the students they have admitted. This often happens at schools with separate admission and financial aid offices. The admissions office makes its decisions, and then the financial aid office distributes what monies the school might have. The gapping terminology means simply there is a gap between your award and what you are expected to pay. Many colleges believe that if you really want to come, you'll find a way to make it work, through loans or an extra contribution from family. They are not being insensitive—they just don't have the resources to fund everyone.

Remember—always ask a need-blind school if they meet 100% of a calculated need. They are required to give you an honest answer.

If the admission office doesn't say it follows a need-blind policy, then it is pretty safe to assume that they do not. These schools are called **need-aware** and are sensitive to a family's ability to pay, and they factor that ability into the admission process. Which means you need to decide—strategically—whether you are going to check off the "Yes I plan to apply for financial aid" box on your admissions application. Because if you say "yes" you need financial aid and someone with very similar credentials is applying but says she doesn't need financial aid, then she is probably going to be admitted ahead of you. Many need-aware schools will share their policies with you. Often they have sufficient funds for most of their class and use need-aware policies for only the last 10% of those admitted. A school with lesser resources might need to do that with a much higher percentage of their class.

It may sound unfair, but it is a fact of life: colleges—especially those with smaller endowments—need a certain number of full-paying students. So if your family can afford to be one of those full-paying families—and you are applying to a need-aware college—it is going to work to your advantage.

The same logic holds true for out-of-staters applying to state universities. The standards for out-of-state applicants are normally more stringent than for in-state applicants at many selective state universities like Michigan, North Carolina, or Virginia. If you're an applicant who will be paying the full-freight, out-of-state tuition, some schools *might* cut you a little slack in these tight financial times—but not much. Check out the admissions requirements for most large state schools, and you'll readily see what we're talking about.

The question you have to ask your parents, of course, is how much of a burden it will be if you don't get financial aid for freshman year. Can they afford to pay? Note, however, that they will still be able to apply for a Parent PLUS loan, which can cover the full cost of freshman year. You should also know that even if you didn't apply for financial aid for freshman year—and you get admitted—you can *usually* still apply for aid in subsequent years. But some schools do require that you apply for aid for the freshman year to assure financial aid eligibility. So be sure to check out the school's rules! And if family circumstances change—like a younger sibling entering college—that can have a substantial impact on how much financial aid you're likely to receive. College financial aid offices are not heartless! They truly do understand the realities of middle-class finances—despite the government's Expected Family Contribution—and will do their best to help whenever possible.

Financial Aid Counselors

Among the various businesses that have cropped up around the college admission world are financial aid counselors. Many of these folks are accountants and CPAs who recognized that filling out the FAFSA and CSS/Profile was akin to root canal surgery without anesthesia. Or at least pretty similar to filling out tax forms.

Most of these consultants charge several hundred dollars for their service. And quite candidly, we've used them and been satisfied with their work. Could we have secured the same amount of financial aid without their help? Maybe. But at the time we were busy, stressed, and more than willing to pay a few hundred dollars to save ourselves the time and effort.

And now that we've written this chapter of the book—and really dug into the forms and methodologies—will we use their services again? It depends on how flush we feel—or how masochistic.

Making Sense of Aid Awards

Believe it or not, April will finally arrive, and notification of your acceptances will make you a very happy camper. Along with those letters, you will receive notification of your financial aid award. And every college will craft that financial aid package differently. Some will include large scholarships, while others may focus exclusively on loans. You typically will have about a month to decide where you want to attend. May 1 is the common agreed-upon date for most colleges to ask for your decision and deposit.

When you receive the various financial aid offers, there are several questions you should ask yourself about each one:

1. How much is the expected family contribution?

2. Can we handle that?

3. How will we handle it? From savings? From parent PLUS Loans?

4. How much has the school offered in grants/scholarships as opposed to loans?

5. Are the loans subsidized/lower interest or unsubsidized?

6. Based on this financial aid package, how much debt will I graduate with?

7. Do I feel comfortable with that amount of debt? And given what I think I may do after graduation, will I be able to make the payments?

You'll be surprised to know that the power has shifted from the college to you. If a college accepts you, they really do want you to attend. They know a certain percentage won't—that's the yield, remember? But they do want you. And they are willing to haggle—at least a little—on your financial aid package.

Remember that contact person we suggested you find in the financial aid office? Here is when they come in handy. You can tell the contact in the higher-choice school about the award you received from a lesser-choice college and ask them to review your award. Remember, however, that a need-based-only school will never match a merit award. There is nothing wrong with appealing an award. But when they say they're done, they're done. And the decision about where to attend is back to you.

9

CHAPTER 9

Getting In: The Final Chapter

Thriving (Not Just Surviving) During the Long Wait

This chapter is all about life after the application, starting with the long wait to find out whether you were accepted or not. Then we help you sort out what to do with the decisions when they arrive, including making a commitment, dealing with a waitlist, and appealing a decision. Should the worst happen and you're not admitted anywhere—or you're just not ready to start college yet—we give you useful pointers on making the most of your "gap year" to better position you for applying next year. And if you didn't get into your first-choice school or aren't happy after your first year if you did, we give you the scoop on making an effective college transfer.

Your App Is Submitted—Now What?

Let's assume it's February 1. So unless you've received good news from an early decision, early action, or rolling admission application, you're probably exhausted, relieved, or on pins and needles. And even if you got into a non-binding early-action school early, you're still anxious to hear from that dream school.

Prayer, meditation, or yoga can help. (We're not kidding.) But what if they really don't do the trick?

The reality is: you've done your work, and it is now time for the professionals to do theirs. You can, of course, reread our sections on how schools make their decisions. Or you can redo the case studies. Either can help pass the time while you wait.

Now here's the surprise: the months from late January until late March comprise a dynamic, ongoing process. And you can still do things to help your cause. *But*—and this is a *really big* but—do not try to pad or over-stuff your file. And don't over-bug the admission office. Here's how to use your time wisely and effectively.

Staying in Touch

With modern technology it is easy to stay in touch with admission offices. Your goal should be to do so in a helpful, unobtrusive way. If you developed a relationship with the admission officer responsible for your school (your area admission representative)—or someone else in the office—an occasional e-mail is totally appropriate. Be direct and to the point about why you are contacting them. (Some legitimate reasons are discussed below.) And remember that in this digital age it is easy to lose track of how often you are in contact with someone. You don't want to be perceived as pushy or a pain in the butt. So keep track of whom you're contacting, about what, and how often. And don't always expect an answer or reply. Remember that admissions folks are reading and reviewing hundreds of files. They may not be able to respond immediately or at all.

Here are a few things you might discuss with them.

Midyear School Reports

Every college's application—along with the Common App—requires you to submit midyear grades. For most of you, midyear grades aren't assembled until January—after you've submitted your applications. If your midyear report is full of As, this can be a real plus—particularly if you're applying to a highly competitive college. Telling the admission office about this first-semester accomplishment gives your admission representative more ammunition to argue on your behalf with the admission committee. So tell them: don't brag, but be sure to send an e-mail to your area representative pointing out your continuing hard work and interest in that college.

Unfortunately, the flip side is also true. A weaker set of senior grades—particularly after a strong junior

---

Finish Your Taxes

Make sure your family taxes are completed early. Many families wait until April 15 each year to file their taxes and consequently delay starting the financial aid process. No college will finalize their financial aid award until all your and your parents' current tax forms are filed. So the earlier you get them done, the better.

year—can really hurt. In this situation, you might want to point out a *legitimate* reason for your unexpectedly weaker performance. Perhaps it was illness or unusual family circumstances. You should also encourage your guidance counselor to communicate with the admission representative in order to reinforce your case.

Additional Recommendations

We're going to contradict ourselves a bit about our "stuffing the file" principle now. Most likely, you used a junior-year teacher to write the teacher recommendation that you sent in with your original application. Let's suppose you've really hit it off with a senior-year teacher, and you are now the star of her class. By January, you'll have been together for a full semester, and a letter from her might really add something to your file. So go for it. Importantly, if you were deferred at a college during an early-decision or early-action round, an additional teacher recommendation is a must. But it should shed new light on why the college should accept you in the regular decision round.

Special Achievement Updates

Many schools induct members into their honor societies in January. Again, this is typically after you've submitted your application. Similarly, many teams elect captains for their winter sports after you've applied. Or you may have just gotten the lead in the school play or received an art award. Let the admission officer know! An e-mail or letter should suffice; but don't be afraid to ask your counselor to send one too. It only makes that honor and award more important. Remember that new information will be added to your file to support your cause. If you don't notify them, it won't be in your file.

Disaster or Negative Updates

In your Common App, you signed a statement promising to report any disciplinary actions. Your school did the same. It is your obligation and your school's to report any such actions that occur after you apply. And it is much better for the college to hear it from you first! You will be much better served by addressing the issue than by pretending it doesn't exist or that it will magically go away.

If you are faced with this kind of unfortunate situation, it is imperative that you convince the admission committee that it was an isolated event and totally out of character. Tell them nothing like that will ever happen again. You'll need to reassure them that you've learned from your mistake—thereby making you a better person and perhaps even a better applicant after this real-life experience. It's a challenge to do that, but here are a few suggestions for handling the situation.

1. Be honest. Explain as best you can what happened and why. If there is no good reason for it and you were just being juvenile, say so. Admit your mistake, then go on to show how it won't happen again. Avoid sounding too defensive, and don't put the blame on others. Colleges will respect you more for taking responsibility.

2. Be forthcoming. Offer to provide further information or cooperate with the admission office in any way you can. If you are truly embarrassed or ashamed, provide the whole story. Your explanation will be kept confidential. Importantly, make clear how much you want to move past

this incident. You can offer to come to campus to meet with someone or to speak on the telephone at greater length if they want you to.

3. Find an advocate at school. If this was an incident totally out of character for you, the school may have felt obligated to take appropriate disciplinary action and report it to colleges but still believe you are a valued member of the community. A letter to that effect can go miles to repair the damage done by your action. It reassures a college that, despite your mistake, your present school can move past it, and they should be able to too.

Waiting Gracefully

Eventually, the only thing left for you to do is wait. Wait for the admission process to be over and not drive yourself crazy in the meantime. Waiting affects some kids—and parents—more than others. Some of you will rush home every day to check the mailbox. Or you'll call a parent at home asking if the mail carrier has shown up yet. You'll look at your e-mail incessantly, especially if you've been in contact with an admission officer. Maybe you'll check your electronic account on the college website, trying to make sure nothing is missing from your folder or to catch a subtle sign that your application has been processed or a decision made.

During this nerve-wracking period, try to concentrate on your other activities and your schoolwork. You'll never get your high school days back, so enjoy all those memories and moments. You'll soon be leaving it all—the victories, friends, teachers, and, in most cases, your parents and family. Since there is usually little more you can do about your applications, you might as well sit back, relax, and enjoy your last few months as a high school senior.

Don't Ask for an Early Notification

It is easy for us to say, "Don't let your anxiety get the best of you." We're not waiting. But we can say, with certainty: "Don't ask the college for an admission decision before their planned notification date." You may be tempted to try. Perhaps a classmate has received an early notification for a particular reason: they may have applied to a special program, may be a student of color and actively sought

Warning—Senioritis Is Bad for Your Academic Health!

Whatever you do, don't get an acute case of senioritis. Despite our recommendation to enjoy yourself, you'd be surprised how often senioritis can come back to haunt you. If you end up on a waitlist, a college may want to see your final-semester grades. If you ever consider transferring colleges in a year, every college will request your final high school transcript. Even if you got in early-decision, many schools will want to see your final grades. And they will ask for an explanation about why your grades dropped from what they saw in the fall. If they don't like your answer, they may rescind your acceptance and you may be scrambling for other options.

under an affirmative-action program, or may be a recruited athlete. And so you think you should hear too. If you think you fall into the same category, ask your counselor to make an inquiry call. Have her say that several students have heard and she is curious when the remaining students might hear. The worst call you could make is the one where you contact the college and say, "So and so heard from you, why haven't I?" This sort of call will give the admission office an impression of you as nervous and pushy—two qualities they typically frown upon. So don't do it! Just remember how busy these people are in the spring.

One of the dumbest tactics we've ever seen came from a family going away on vacation over spring break. Because they were going to be away from their mail, they wanted the college to give them a decision before they left. Put yourself in the place of that admission officer: they're working night and day to get their decisions done, and you're taking off on vacation. You get the point. If you just can't wait until you return, have a trusted friend or neighbor check your mail. By the time you read this, however, snail-mail may be a thing of the past. More and more schools are notifying applicants digitally, either by e-mail or posting decisions on password-protected web pages.

Request an Early Notification Only When Absolutely Necessary

There will be those rare occasions when it is absolutely necessary to ask for a decision from a school prior to their traditional notification date. In almost all cases, it will involve money or an athletic letter of intent. We say that because the most common case might involve an athletic scholarship.

Many schools will have a process in place to address the athletic situation. Let's suppose an outstanding baseball player has an athletic scholarship offer from Virginia but has his heart set on Dartmouth. The Ivy League schools (and others that do not give athletic scholarships) have developed a process to issue athlete-applicants a "likely" letter. It states that unless something changes dramatically between the date of the letter and the school's official notification date, that candidate will be admitted. In most cases, the coach of the school issuing the likely letter will be highly involved in this process and will be in touch with both the admission office and the applicant to ensure that the letter is mailed and that the applicant gets it.

Don't Celebrate Until Word Comes in Writing

Admissions is a complicated business, and you won't know for sure whether or not you'll be admitted until you receive official notification from the school.

Remember one important point. Only the admission office of that school can confirm that admission decision. And they will do it in writing. Promises, predictions, and verbal assurances from anyone else cannot be counted on. That coach who shares good news probably has the official OK, but wait until you hear it from the admission office before celebrating. That alumnus who loved you in your interview cannot guarantee you a spot. You should be able to trust your area admission officer who calls you to share the good news. But hold off on the full celebration until you get the written confirmation.

What to Do When Decisions Arrive

Sometime in March of your senior year—or earlier if you've applied early decision, early action, or under a rolling admission program—you're going to hear from most of the colleges you applied to. For most of you, there will be good news. And for some of you, there will be a real wealth of choices.

The old tradition of "fat letter/ thin letter" is gone. Open all your mail. In many cases, schools send that first decision in a thin envelope—even if it is good news. So don't blanch if you receive a thin envelope from Old Swami: it may contain your acceptance. Schools are sending out thin acceptance letters in order to save money on printing and postage. (And yes, they're saving a few trees too.) Instead of sending lots of printed forms and information, more and more colleges are directing kids they've admitted to special accepted-students websites.

Odds are you will get at least one rejection. It will be disappointing, but it is absolutely not the end of the world. It may not seem that way at first, but you will get over it. (One of us got so many rejections from various professional schools at Harvard that a personal note that said, "Stop applying already," was included in the last rejection. He got over it, and it didn't require a second mortgage to pay for therapy!) We discuss what to do about rejections later in this chapter.

What to Do with Your Acceptances

Congratulations and well done! You've finally been rewarded for all your hard work over the years. Now you have to make that big decision about where to attend college. Odds are, you've probably been accepted by more than one college. (And although you've probably been turned down by a few schools too, accentuate the positive!) You'll actually have very little time to decide, as May 1 comes up very quickly. So what should you do?

Do More Research

Talk to people. Even if you're absolutely sure that a given college is the place you want to attend, talk it out. You should do this not only to get other peoples' opinions, but also to hear yourself think and defend your reasons for wanting to attend a particular school. And if you're undecided, talking with others will help you clarify your own thoughts, ideas, and priorities.

Talk with undergraduates at the various colleges. Most schools today will set up an interactive website and phone system so you can speak with current students. Ask questions—see what they think. Even though they are working with the admission office, most will be honest with you. Who wants an unhappy student on campus? Check with your high school guidance office and find out which students from your school are at those colleges. What do they say? Are they enjoying their experience? What are they doing on campus?

Finally, revisit each school if you can. Most colleges will set up revisit days in April for admitted students. You'll get to meet some of your future classmates. The school will certainly put its best foot forward and do its best to convince you to matriculate at Old Swami. But use this opportunity to dig deeper: talk to students while you're there; sit in on a class in your future major; eat in the cafeteria; and sleep in a dorm. This visit may reinforce what you remember, or it could leave you with a completely different impression. Remember that what was important to you during that first rush of college visits—oh so long ago—may be different by April of your senior year.

Take time during your revisits to really compare courses in the programs you're interested in at the various colleges you're considering. Check out the career development office. Or the department's success in placing its graduates in graduate or professional school. Those four years will go by much faster than you can believe right now. Don't be oblivious to the school's location or social environment, but remember your primary objective for going to college: getting that great education.

A Random Walk

The revisit can be an opportunity to find out the nature of a school you may not have sensed during a first visit. I remember a fascinating young man named Alex who was visiting Brown from Michigan. Alex was a slam-dunk admit at every school where he applied. So on this eastern road trip in April, Alex was visiting Harvard and Yale as well as Brown. Alex stopped by my office before leaving campus—Michigan was my geographic territory at the time. He mentioned that he had wandered into a neuroscience lab and bumped into a professor who just happened to be there working. They wound up chatting for two hours. I asked Alex if he happened to learn the professor's name. "Leon Cooper," he said. I smiled and told Alex he had just spent two hours talking with a Nobel Prize winner—who loved to teach the freshmen intro class at Brown. I think you can guess where Alex went to college.

—MM

Parties and social life may seem important, but put them into perspective. On balance, go for the better education over the more appealing social scene.

Should You Commit Before May 1?

Most colleges require a commitment decision about whether you're going to matriculate—and a deposit— by May 1. Yes, you have to decide. And yes, it is a big decision. But no, your future is not hanging in the balance. If you make the "wrong decision"—choose a school that doesn't turn out to be a good fit—there are lots of ways to fix it in the future. So buck up and make a decision.

Years ago—the experience your parents may remember and think is still operative today—there was much more disparity in the admission world about response deadlines. Students and families often felt pressure to put down deposits or reply earlier than the traditional May 1 deposit date. Most colleges today adhere to the Candidates Reply Date Agreement or the bylaws of the NACAC (National Association of College Admission

Counselors). Both of these prohibit schools from placing early pressure on you to accept their offer of admission.

The most pressing reason today to commit prior to May 1 involves on-campus housing. Occasionally—and only occasionally—sending in your deposit early entitles you to a better choice of housing. If you are not ready to accept your place at a particular school, we suggest you do a few things.

First, let your high school counselor know as soon as possible. Even for issues of housing, schools are not supposed to do this under the spirit of the CRDA and NACAC bylaws. Your counselor can inquire whether this pressure is actually being applied or perhaps you are interpreting something incorrectly.

Second, if indeed the school does require such a deposit, have your school guidance counselor find out if you can get an extension. They should explain your situation, saying that you haven't yet heard from other colleges and want to make an informed choice. In most cases, the school should give you some more time.

Finally, if the school will not give you more time to respond, you have a choice. It's not really different from what we suggest you do if you end up on a waitlist (later in this chapter). You can send in the deposit, knowing you may lose it if you are admitted and enroll elsewhere. This is perfectly normal operating procedure. The college admitting you will already have factored in a certain number of no-shows among its "firm" enrollees. Alternatively, if you cannot afford the deposit for financial reasons, try to see if they might waive the deposit. That contact you made way back when in the financial aid office might help you with this.

Make Your Own Decision—After Listening to Your Parents

Remember when you arrived on campus last summer for that first admission interview and your mother told the receptionist that "WE" had arrived for "OUR" interview? Like it or not, there is a lot of family investment in the college process. We wish that there was some easy way to diffuse the demands and unspoken expectations of parents. If you are lucky, yours support whatever decision you make about your college education. Then again, your father or mother may be convinced that Princeton (or some other college) is the only place for you. And if you don't get admitted there, you're a failure. Or perhaps you are admitted, and Mom or Dad insist that you attend and threaten to cut you off financially if you go elsewhere. That's almost worse.

Unfortunately some parents are more concerned about what your college choice might say about them than with what it will do for you. By mid-April, parents will be swapping admission decisions at the office. By the weekend, they'll be discussing it with friends at their country club. The more places Junior is admitted to and the higher the caliber, the more prestige accrues to the proud parent. These comparisons are a part of our society. Often the offenders have no idea how difficult it is today to get into some schools and just how traumatic the whole process is. It's bad enough that you have to get over your own disappointment at being denied your first-choice school. You shouldn't have to deal with your parents' disappointment as well.

Another problem is that parents often know less about colleges and the admission process today. Their notions about selective schools may be based on impressions made 20 or 30 years ago—at a time when many selective schools were just going coed, with little interest in minority or international diversity. Here are a few suggestions for dealing with parents:

Sit down with them and talk. For one thing, they will be supporting you financially and emotionally, and they may help you define your own ideas if you're confused. At the very least, they will understand that you value their opinion and listened to what they had to say. If you then choose your college over theirs, they will hopefully feel that you involved them in your decision.

Carefully examine your own reasons for wanting to go to a certain college. Do they truly make sense? If they do, that might help convince your parents. Just organize your thoughts before you talk.

Get your ammunition together for your arguments. If you want to attend a private college over a state school because you believe you'll get a better education there, try to find some way to prove it—perhaps by digging up statistics on admission to graduate schools, long-term income data, student-faculty ratios, etc.

Be sure you're making the decision for the right reason. Choose the school you really want rather than choosing one just because it is in opposition to your parents' wishes. Most alumni kids have distinct opinions about their parents' schools. They tend to have either very positive or very negative feelings about Mom's or Dad's college—generally in direct proportion to the degree of the parent's enthusiasm and their respect for the parent. We've run into students who wouldn't dream of going to a parent's alma mater—just because they heard about it all their lives and were completely bored with the idea of it. But in some cases, it was far and away the best place they had been admitted to. Then again, there are others who blindly accepted their parents' choice as their own. Make the decision yours.

If you're excited about a place and your parents are not, consider whether they might become more enthusiastic after a visit there. While on campus, see if you can arrange for them to meet with an admission officer or faculty member.

Don't Forget to Send in a Deposit

Remember that you must send in a deposit to one of your admit schools by May 1 —even if you are confident you may come off the waitlist at another college (see "What to Do If You're on a Waitlist" on the opposite page). The only exception might be if you are granted an extension while a financial aid appeal is being reviewed. It is normal procedure to protect a place for yourself. In most cases, however, you will lose that deposit if you come off the waitlist at a school you prefer. And, unfortunately, you can't control your position on their waitlist—that is, how the schools make their selections. You may even lose a second deposit if you've been waitlisted at more than one

Only One Deposit!

Several years ago, one of our students decided to put down two deposits on May 1 because he couldn't make up his mind between the two schools. He mistakenly sent the wrong check to each school. Officials at both colleges then called each other and realized what the student had done. What he really did was jeopardize his place at both schools. Fortunately, one was more forgiving. So remember: send only one deposit on May 1.

school—and keep "trading up" waiting for your first-choice school.

In other words, you absolutely want to reserve a place at your safety by depositing by the May 1 deadline. You might hear from your second-choice waitlist school on May 10 and have only 48 hours to decide. So you send in a second deposit but are still waiting to hear from your first-choice waitlist. They then tell you on May 20, and you have 48 hours to tell that school your decision. (You've already sent in two deposits.) Understandably this puts families of lesser financial means at a disadvantage, but it is the way of the world. Your choice—but you're not getting those earlier deposits back.

There's even a thing called **summer melt.** Some "committed" kids choose not to attend a particular school as late as June. As a result, some colleges still go to their waitlist as late as July and will ask you if you still have interest in attending Old Swami.

What to Do If You're on a Waitlist

Getting on the waitlist can be good news. You're not quite admitted (yet), but you haven't been rejected. Second, many colleges use the waitlist as part of their enrollment strategy. Their projections include anticipated yield and an expectation that they will take some kids from the waitlist. That's a real departure from years past, when the waitlist was a "political" tool allowing kids and high schools to "save face." (That is still the case for a small number of kids who wind up on the waitlist.) So if you're on a waitlist, find out how the waitlist works at each school—and do it quickly. The bad news, however, is that more schools are putting more kids on their waitlists. And it's quite possible that a strong, but not outstanding, student could end up on several waitlists.

The biggest problem with a waitlist is that it is largely out of your control. Seldom does a school use it until after May 1. That's when colleges have seen their enrollment numbers because deposits are due. Remember when we discussed yield earlier in this book? This is where yield comes into play. (Occasionally, a savvy enrollment manager might see that the school's matriculation numbers are running behind projections. In such a situation, the admissions office might turn to the waitlist before May 1.) The bottom line is that colleges need to fill beds and classrooms, and the waitlist is a great way to complete the class.

Each school approaches the waitlist differently. For some schools, it is a great way to shape a class that might be short on males versus females, or engineers versus liberal arts majors. It might be a way to balance numbers for students of color or missing geographic areas. Several years ago, Mike heard that Duke might be going to their waitlist. And indeed they did: they were looking for engineers from Texas. Most schools won't be that specific, but you get the picture.

The way in which schools choose from their wait-lists varies. In the old days, colleges might need 50 students to round out the class, so they would send letters to 50 kids on the wait-list. They would then see how many kids from that first wave agreed to matriculate. Then the school would send out a second smaller wave to fill the remaining spots. That ap-proach is much rarer today because schools seek to tighten their yield on a case-by-case basis. Don't be surprised if you receive a telephone call from the college asking you for an immediate decision—or one by the next day. Unlike the NACAC rules that apply to the May 1 response/deposit date, there are no set rules apply-ing to how colleges must treat their waitlists.

Tell Them You're Interested!

You can enhance the likelihood of getting off the waitlist and into Old Swami by telling the school you're interested—really interested! Every school will send kids on the waitlist a response card or e-mail link to confirm your interest to stay on their wait-list. But you have to take that next step. *Respond quickly!* And send a follow-up letter to reaffirm your interest and say that the school remains your top choice. Schools want to gauge interest and the probability of your enrolling. You might also offer to come visit the school and meet with someone. But the bottom line is that you must let them know your interest.

In 2010, for the first time, NACAC conducted a survey of their membership and asked colleges how they built their waitlist—what criteria did they use? Fifty-six percent of the schools said they developed a list based on academic credentials, 45% by student interest in the college, 33% based on a student's commit-ment to attend if admitted, and 27% based on ability to pay. Obviously many students fell into several of these categories. And finally, the good news: 51% said they had accepted more students off of the waitlist than previous years.

Two notes of caution. First, many schools—even need-blind and some of the wealthier colleges—often have no financial aid for students they take off the waitlist. A full-pay waitlist applicant will often have a distinct advantage over someone with financial need. Second, determine how genuine your waitlist position is. Occasionally a school might give what is called a "courtesy waitlist" to an alumni family or to a strong-academic student with character flaws. The latter waitlist is used when it would be difficult to explain rejecting the kid. But people in the office know that student will never come off the waitlist.

Getting a rejection letter is never a pleasant experience. If you're lucky, you will be accepted everywhere you applied. But if you've followed our advice in this book, there is a good chance that you'll get rejected somewhere. After all, we've encouraged you to include a few reaches among your target schools, and they're going to be tough to get into—despite impressive resumes and smart strategies.

Let's assume you have opened all your letters, e-mails, and admissions websites. Chances are you have a rejection or two. (Or maybe more if you applied to a lot of reaches.) We know being rejected is difficult. But if you keep the following points in mind, you can make it easier for yourself and others around you.

No admission decision should lower your self-esteem. You're not a failure because you didn't get into a particular college. As we keep saying, admission into a particular school is determined by who the college wants that year and, more accurately, who applies that year. The point is that no admission decision is a perfectly objective one, as you'll see in our case studies in Appendix A. In most cases, there are just too many quali-fied students like you for the number of spaces available, and someone can't make it. Unfortunately, that could be you at some schools. If you were realistic about your application strategy, you were probably very qualified.

First, remember that the school isn't rejecting you. It is denying you a place based on those 20 documents in your

Dealing with Other Students' Acceptances

The reality is that some students who you think are less deserving than you may get into schools you had hoped for. And you may be upset when your friends get admitted to schools with bigger names and you only get into your lesser-name safeties. You may feel additional pain because you haven't been able to rejoice in your friends' successes. Don't—envy is a natural human emotion and what's done is done. Your task now is to try not to resent others or be angry at yourself, but rather to concentrate on making the best selection from the choices given to you.

At several New England boarding schools, there is a tradition in some dorms (particularly boys') to build a "wall of shame" full of the letters of rejection received by members of the house. It is a kind of public reaction to those decisions and a tradition of how they deal with others' rejections as opposed to admits. Perhaps it's their way to let off a little steam or just one of those boarding school traditions.

And remember, too, not to try to second guess why one student may have made it and you didn't. That will only make things worse. As you should have learned from this book, there are many reasons a student may be admitted. They might have been packaged in a way that you weren't aware of. You probably know if they are a recruited athlete but are less likely to know of legacy or any other special status or interest. So stop thinking about it—it's not worth the energy.

file and perhaps one or two meetings with you. That's not a foolproof way of making this important decision, but that is the way it is done. There is nothing wrong with you because they said no to your application. And they were not saying no to you personally—just to their image of you as compared to the images of others who applied.

Second, you are not going to be dogged forever by not going to a given college. Most employment counselors agree that a degree from a more prestigious college may make a difference in getting a first job or have some effect on graduate school admission. But ultimately, it's your performance in college that counts. A MacCauley honors graduate from New York City's CUNY system will do better in most cases than a B student from a more prestigious school when applying to graduate programs (and they will have saved a lot of money as an undergraduate too). And once you're on the job, it won't matter much where you went to school. Being a Cornell or Princeton graduate won't mean anything if you're not doing the job.

Third, you may be blowing the differences between two colleges out of proportion. Obviously, some schools will have more name recognition than others. But as we have tried to point out, this sometimes does not relate to reality. Think about fit and where you can be happy. When it comes down to the top 30 or 40 schools in the country, the differences are really not that great.

Fourth, there's nothing to be gained by complaining or whining. It does you absolutely no good to say, "I wish I was at X College." Or, "If I were at X College, everything would be fine." Like most of your freshmen peers, until your first semester is over and you've settled in and gained confidence that you can succeed and be happy there, you still might be complaining. Wherever you go, make the best of it. There's nothing sadder than a group of freshmen commiserating that they wish they were elsewhere. By senior year, you'll probably never want to leave.

And finally, you can get a great education at every school if you want one. Seek out the right professors, develop the right circle of friends, apply yourself, and you can excel. Success has more to do with ambition, discipline, and direction than it does with where you go to school.

How to Appeal a Decision

You've sulked for a few days now, and you are convinced the school made a mistake rejecting you. They didn't get your latest SATs/ACTs, or your best teacher recommendation was missing. The computer screwed up, and they confused you with someone else. For whatever reason, you believe your decision should be reconsidered.

First of all, find out the school's policy for reconsidering their decision. Many schools will simply say "sorry, we don't do that." Decisions will not be changed unless an erroneous credential was sent in or an extremely positive credential was missing at the time of the decision. Even in these instances, selective colleges seldom reverse their decisions. In many cases, it might establish a dangerous precedent, and the odds are still stacked against you.

If you still want to request a review of your folder and this is something the college is willing to do, submit your request as politely as possible. Accentuate the positive—how much you love the school—and persuade them that a review of your credentials might bring another decision. Tell them you are willing to do almost anything to be admitted—enter midyear, spend a term abroad, or even take a gap year. If you have a factual rationale for the appeal, provide it: admission committees are much more likely to review their decision if there is a compelling reason to do so.

Keep in mind that you're doing this for your own sanity, and perhaps even some greater insight into the original decision. It is unlikely that you will be admitted after an appeal, even at a college publicizing such procedures. And the odds against you at a school that has no appeal process are astronomical. But at least if you request reconsideration, you will know that you've done everything you could do to be admitted. In our opinion, unless the procedure is encouraged by the college, you may be wasting your time and their time. But most importantly, end the process politely—who knows, you may try to transfer a year later, and they'll remember how nice you were even though you were disappointed by their decision.

What to Do If You're Not Admitted Anywhere

Ouch! You've applied to eight colleges and you get eight rejections. Of course, if you had carefully followed our suggestions, it's unlikely this would happen. But it has.

The first thing you'll need to do is get over the initial shock of rejection. We know that isn't easy. Our best advice is that, since you have no college to go to this coming fall, you should concentrate on securing a place on some college campus. Some families prefer to step back and say, "Whoa, what happened and why? And let's not rush into trying to get into some college Chris really doesn't want to go to." That is a discussion you and your parents need to have quickly. Because if you do want to go to college in the fall, now is the time to secure that spot.

Your second objective should be to discover why you were passed over by so many institutions. Were your sights set unrealistically high? Was there some part of your application that was unusually weak or unconvincing? How can you improve it on the next try?

To formulate a strategy for an 11th-hour application to a college that will accept you, or to plan a useful way to spend your time until you can re-apply, we suggest taking the following steps.

Enlist the help of your counselor. In many cases, your counselor may be as upset as you are, especially if your application strategy was developed together. She can contact admission officers at the colleges to which you applied and try to find out what aspects of your application were the weakest. By getting a fix on mistakes you may have made, you can remedy them when you apply to new schools.

We say "apply to new schools" because the reality is that there will be schools still looking for students to fill their class for the fall. They may not be Ivy League schools, but you might be surprised by who has openings. After May 1, NACAC will actually release a survey that shares many schools who might still take an application from you. (Access to that information is limited to your counselor.) So your counselor should be able to find some pretty good schools pretty fast that are still looking for students after a disappointing yield.

Once your counselor has found out about these schools, you need to get moving quickly. You can rest assured you are not the only student in the country in this predicament, and the schools want to fill their classes as quickly as possible too. Take one night to research, and then get started. If your odds look fairly good at a particular school, it can't hurt to have your counselor let them know it is your top choice and that you will attend if you are admitted.

Your other alternative is to look into local and state colleges, including junior colleges. Many of these tax-supported schools accept students until just before classes begin. Once again, have your counselor contact the schools that appeal to you.

We know that these may not seem like the most appealing alternatives, but you should view this fallback plan as just that: a fallback. You don't have to spend four years there, and you can later transfer to a different or better-known college as a sophomore or junior. This means, however, that you must take your studies at these schools as seriously as you would take them anywhere else. The bottom line is that in order to transfer, you'll need to present an impressive record of success in some challenging courses, and that may not be so easy given your disappointment at not being admitted elsewhere. To succeed, you need to set aside that short-term disappointment in favor of your long-term goal.

You might also consider postponing college for a year and use that time to regroup and prepare yourself for another round of applications the following fall, as discussed in the next section.

Postponing College for a Year

If you decide to postpone college for a year, there are two good ways to spend your time wisely. Either of them can help you become a stronger applicant, so choose the one that will serve you best.

The Gap Year

Though we place this idea after the section about not getting into colleges, the idea of a **gap year**—a year off from academics—is appealing to (and even right for) many students. Even if you've been admitted to some highly selective colleges, a gap year might make real sense. You've completed your senior year, and you're feeling just not ready or energized enough to dive into college life. Perhaps you want to jump into a political campaign in an election year, volunteer for a community service program either domestically or internationally, or just want some time off to reenergize.

It might surprise you to know that many deans at many top colleges think that's a great idea. The Amherst College website recently released a list of the fascinating things that students who had deferred for a year were doing with their time. Many colleges believe that students who take time for themselves will come back more focused and excited about college. Check to see what their policies are on this issue. In most cases, they just want to know how you're planning on using that time away. One rule, however: most schools will not allow a gap year if they took you off the waitlist. The reason they may have taken you was because several students they had previously accepted had decided to do this, and they need you to fill that bed.

For those of you who didn't get into any school—or any school you're excited about—a year off may be a chance to take that information your counselor learned about why you were denied and regroup. You get to think about other schools and reapply for the following fall. It may just be a matter of picking another group of schools. But it may be packaging yourself differently and spending time doing things in that year off which support that package and make you a more attractive candidate. Let's suppose you have a genuine interest in environmental issues. Then think of all the things you might do starting the summer after your senior year that demonstrates that interest.

The important issue here is to make good use of your time. The key issue a college considers in your taking time off is whether you have grown because of the experience. And if you are reapplying, schools may want to see evidence of that growth, whether through recommendations, interviews, your essay, supplementary materials, or a combination of those elements. If you decide to work to help pay for college, don't be afraid to say just that. You can also think about how a work experience might fit in with your future plans or your positioning as an applicant.

Whatever you do, we recommend that you keep a journal of your experiences—at least the more memorable ones. This may make a great essay when you reapply or great reading later in life—maybe even the makings of a book. As you work, think about what your job is doing for you— what you're learning, what you regret, what you might do

differently, and what is most fulfilling. If you can articulate the value of what you've done and have gotten something worthwhile from the experience, it should be time well spent.

The Postgraduate Year

Many private prep (and boarding) schools offer postgraduate (PG) years for students who have graduated high school but aren't yet ready or able to get into the college of their choice. Your postgraduate year thoughts might be influenced by whether or not you got into any college or whether you think you just need another year of school before college. It can often be for either academic or athletic reasons (or both). The reality of the postgraduate process, however, is that it is becoming ever more competitive at the top private preparatory schools. And you might need to think about this alternative sooner rather than later if you are interested in more selective schools like Andover or Exeter.

We recommend that if you are thinking about PG as an option you start the process early in your senior year. In fact, some people employ a dual-track strategy and apply to both colleges and PG programs. The timetable for PG is just about the same as applying to colleges. Prep schools require essays, transcripts, recommendations, and interviews. So the sooner you get started, the better.

We see two tracts for the postgraduate year. For weaker students, it might be a chance to further develop their academic skills, repeat a course, and improve their writing. You might focus on bringing up your standardized testing scores. For many students, the academic side of the PG year is to perhaps open up college options that might not have been available with your previous scores and grades.

For student-athletes who have been encouraged by a coach, it is an opportunity to further develop their athletic (and academic) skills. Often the idea is presented by a college coach with an implicit guarantee of admission to a particular school the following year. We caution you on this because few coaches have the power to make that guarantee. Or they may find a more desirable recruit in the meantime. If, however, you see the wisdom in the idea—you will probably get bigger, faster, and stronger and be a more attractive recruit—the PG year may make sense for you.

For many students, the PG year can be extremely helpful. A student who has been bored by a less-than-top-notch high school may come alive when challenged by demanding classes and good instructors. Students who may have had family problems may do better when they are allowed a year away from the distractions at home. Athletes enrolled in PG programs often improve their academic skills to the point where they can survive a highly demanding college environment. And a young or less mature student may be better "seasoned" after a transitional year at a prep school than he would be by leaping into his freshman year.

So is a PG year worth the time, money, and energy it requires? Unless you can get a scholarship at the prep school—which is unlikely unless you are a blue-chip athlete—the expense may be almost as great as a year of college. In many cases, evidence of increased academic prowess or seriousness of purpose can be demonstrated just as well by attending a local or community college for a year. In addition, the coursework you complete at the community college will usually count for college credit—whereas the PG coursework will not. But remember: if you're a student-athlete, you hold on to that year of college eligibility by going the PG route.

If you fall into that group of students who didn't get into a PG program (or a college) anywhere, relax. Just like on the college side, there may not be spaces left at Andover, Deerfield, or Exeter. But there will be plenty of prep schools with spaces left for a late applicant.

Transferring to a Different College

Although the focus of this book is on the freshmen admission process, the reality is that many students will think about transferring from their first college to another one after just a semester or two. Much of what we've written for the first-year applicant will apply to the transfer. Colleges will still want transcripts from both your college and your high school—so avoid senioritis! Plus, you still have to write essays and secure recommendations.

The transfer college will also want to know what you'll bring to their school and often why you want to leave your current college. Think of valid reasons—majors not offered at the old school or sports programs or activities at the new one. Most colleges are not excited about bringing an unhappy student to their campus who might be just as unhappy there. Stress the good things about the new school and not the bad things about your current situation.

Too many students may want to transfer for the wrong reasons. They may attribute their own lack of discipline to an unexciting academic environment or boring professors. Some students think their emotional problems result from the social life or pressures of academic life at their current school and think a change of environment will change all that. There are all kinds of illusions that you can sustain when you're unhappy.

There are basically two good reasons for transferring. The first has to do with academics and the second with social or extracurricular life. Each is legitimate in its own right. But before you consider transferring, consider whether your motive is solid enough to justify the amount of time and energy you'll have to devote to the effort. It's applying to college all over again, and then some.

What Colleges Look for in Transfer Applicants

The most significant difference between freshmen and transfer admission is that transfer applicants are selected to a much greater extent on the basis of their academic record. (Freshmen applicants are evaluated more on their potential.) The reason for this is obvious: you're presenting a record of college work that can be evaluated and scrutinized. The admission committee can only make an educated guess about how well a freshman applicant will do if admitted, but with the transfer applicant, a report of college-level work already exists. Why admit someone with poor grades? So, the transfer admission committee concentrates on your record. SATs/ACTs and high school GPAs become less important in transfer admission. Many schools have a minimum college GPA that they require before even considering your transfer application.

The type of transfer applicants who are most appealing to admission committees are those who have a distinct and compelling reason for wanting to leave the college they currently attend and transfer to another. Those at single-sex schools may want the more open environment of coeducation. Those at specialized schools (art schools, conservatories, technical colleges, or service academies) may want a broader range of courses and students. The reverse may also be true—the liberal arts student may want the specialization of an art school or engineering program. Or there are those who want a major that isn't offered at their college or an extracurricular endeavor that isn't appreciated or supported at their present campus.

Of course, if you are applying for transfer, you have the advantage of knowing what college is like. You'll know what to look for in the campuses that interest you. And you can evaluate them dispassionately, without the starry-eyed enthusiasm of a typical high school senior. That doesn't mean, however, that you should neglect your research before you begin the application process.

The Randomness of Transfer Numbers

It's usually more difficult to predict the degree of selectivity for transfers at each college than it was when you were applying as a high school senior. At most schools, the number of freshmen applicants and the size of the freshmen class remain stable or planned from year to year. While you may not be able to ascertain who will get in, you can at least say that one out of so many applicants will be admitted. Transfer applicant pools, on the other hand, are far more volatile. The composition of the applicant group can differ from year to year, and the yield will vary accordingly.

More importantly, transfer openings are calculated each year on the basis of attrition, which can vary from year to year. One semester, a much larger group of students may fail out, transfer, take a leave, or study abroad than the previous term or year. And the administration may choose to expand or shrink the overall size of the student body via the transfer pool. That means that for one term a school may be looking to fill 100 transfer slots; the next, it may need only 15. A good enrollment manager, however, knows that beds need to be filled and paid for, which also means there is usually limited aid for transfer students too.

Conventional wisdom has it that it is easier to be accepted as a transfer if one applies for the spring, or even summer term if offered, than the traditional fall date. While this may be true in some instances, no college accepts exactly the same number of transfers for each term: the number depends on the unpredictable factors discussed earlier.

Therefore, if you would like to transfer to a particular school, you will have to plan carefully and perhaps be flexible as to when you start. You might consider using the same approach we discussed for coming out of high school, with reaches, cores, and safeties. But your strategy may have to be even more intricate since it is much harder to predict numbers and selectivity at many schools.

If there seems to be little consistency in freshmen application procedures, there is almost none where transfer admission is concerned. Some schools only accept transfers for the fall. Others admit them for every semester or quarter, even for summer term. A few will only accept sophomore or junior transfers. Some will consider applications from anyone who has completed a semester of college work. Others are only interested in those who have finished at least one full year at a college.

There is one requirement common to virtually every institution, however. After transferring in, you will be expected to complete two full years in residence at that school. That requirement exists to ensure that every graduate receiving the college's degree will carry its intellectual and social stamp.

And, finally, remember that transfer policies, numbers, and requirements will change from year to year. Never rely on outdated catalogs for deadlines and policies. If you're not sure or the published information isn't clear, call the admission office and ask.

Your Actual Transfer Application

You should pay the same attention to detail for your transfer application as you did for your application when you applied from high school. Find out the deadlines and obtain the required forms. Your application strategy should be carefully thought out. Here are a few guidelines to remember.

Current College Contact

Contact a dean or counselor at your present college. Most colleges appoint a dean to assist students interested in transferring to another institution. You should treat this person like your high school guidance counselor: work with them so they will work with you. If you befriended someone in admission, you might ask that person for advice too. Though they may not want to see you go, most counselors realize that their school may not be right for everyone. Remember too that just about any college you transfer to will require a "letter of good standing" from a dean stating that you are leaving that school on good terms and not for academic or disciplinary reasons.

Recommendations

It is essential that you secure recommendations from your college instructors. If you have enrolled in only large lecture classes and wouldn't even recognize your professor (and vice versa) at close range, ask the graduate assistant (or proctor, tutor, fellow, or whatever their title) who knew you to write the recommendation. Colleges will not take you very seriously as a transfer applicant if you cannot produce an evaluation of your college work from your instructors. And never submit

Two Generations of Transfers

Who said transferring isn't genetic? Not only did I meet Paulo when we were both transfer students to Brown—Paulo from RISD, me from the Naval Academy at Annapolis—but both my sons are transfer students. Peter, my older son, originally attended Bennington College after graduating high school. Bennington is a tiny (700 students) liberal arts college in Vermont. He loved it but, candidly, didn't have the self-discipline, and his freshman grades reflected it. He took a year off and interned for a first-rate documentary producer.

He then moved to Los Angles and enrolled in Santa Monica College, a first-rate community college—while working part-time at the Beverly Hills Hotel. After two years at SMC, Peter had a 3.9 GPA and applied to the University of Southern California. (USC had been his first choice when applying from high school, but he didn't get in.) USC accepted him—based on his proving his academic ability at SMC.

Peter is now finishing up with a solid academic record, having played on their intercollegiate squash team, and a wealth of contacts and experiences that he only appreciated after taking time off and attending a community college. And Jacob, his younger brother, just told us he wants to take time off from Arizona State and probably wants to transfer too.

—SC

recommendations from your high school teachers—that's now ancient history.

Always give your recommendation forms to the instructor who knows you best. Follow our suggestion about substantive comments: It's far better to get a detailed, insightful comment from a graduate assistant than a general endorsement from a Nobel Prize–winning lecturer who scarcely knows your name or the quality of your work. If, however, by some small chance she does indeed know you and appreciate your work, you have a killer recommendation.

The Essay

The same rules apply here that applied to your high school essays. Above all, avoid being tedious and repetitive. If the essay topic is open ended, it may be wise to explain why you want to transfer. Some schools will even ask that directly. If you can work the essay into a useful positioning, as we suggested in your earlier applications, do so. But keep in mind that your essay, positioning, and packaging will have less of an effect on your chances for transfer admission than they did when you were in high school. (The possible exception is the recruited transfer athlete.)

Extracurricular Activities

The important issue here is not how busy you were in high school. Rather, it is how active you were on campus and the degree to which your talents and experience will benefit the campus where you'd like to enroll. If you are applying to a school with higher academic standards and more rigorous classes, you must make a case for your ability to continue pursuing your activities in a more challenging environment. And, as with freshmen admission, you need to be aware of just what picture you are presenting. How are you positioning yourself and packaging the information about you?

Interviews and Campus Visits

Much of what we've said earlier about interviewing and visits in this book applies to your transfer application too. In many offices, there will be a transfer officer who will interview and answer questions for prospective applicants. The crucial difference is that in a transfer interview the conversation will focus to a large extent on your experiences at your present college and your desire to leave. When addressing these issues, avoid being too negative, and point out the positive benefits of your future school. Explain what you hope to get out of the new college that you don't presently have. The interviewer may be listening for signs that you are a malcontent. Avoid that trap! Colleges don't want students who may become equally unhappy wherever they go. It's essential that your reasons to transfer sound thoughtful and sincere.

A Final Word on Transferring

Transferring requires patience and flexibility. In most cases, application deadlines are in late spring for fall entrance and late fall for winter entrance. You will hear later than when you did in high school, and often not until the freshmen class is settled. You may not hear from the admission office until days or even hours before the start of classes. Because the transfer selection process tends to be much less formalized than the freshman procedure, decisions aren't made as predictably.

This ad hoc approach may work in your favor if you can be flexible, since it tends to hold lesser qualified candidates out for consideration until the last moment. Admission will be contingent on the number of spaces that become available as undergraduates choose not to return for that semester. If you haven't heard about your transfer application, you should assume that no news is good news. And pressing them for a decision may only hurt your chances. We know you may lose your deposit elsewhere or you may have to make plans to move halfway across the continent at the last minute. But there is really nothing you can do but wait if you really want that school.

A

Case Studies

We created some case studies to give you a feel for what various admission folks think of a particular applicant. First, we present basic application information for three students applying to fictional Fairbrook University. Then six admission officers from very good, private colleges evaluate each of them using the criteria for admission of their particular college.

To get the most out of this appendix, put yourself in the role of admission officer and evaluate the candidacy of each student. Ask your parents to role play as admission officers as well. But don't peek at the "answers" until you've actually played admission officer. Then read the "official" responses. Doing this exercise will enable you to evaluate your own application with a keener eye.

The Three Applicants

Makele Pauline Johnson
New Canaan High School
New Canaan, Connecticut

STANDING AND SCORES
Class Standing: 87/320
SAT Scores: 700cr/760w/550mr
(May, Jr. Yr.)
Subject Test Scores:
680 Spanish
580 Math Level IIC

HIGH SCHOOL PROFILE
Type of School/Accreditation: Public School, accredited by New England Association of Schools and Colleges.
Enrollment: 1350 in grades 9–12
Curriculum: College prep. and comprehensive. Graduation requirements are: 4 years English, 3 years Mathematics, 2 years Social Studies, (includes 1 year U.S. History), 2 years Science, 2 years Foreign Language, 2 years Physical Education, and 1 year Health.
AP courses offered in: Biology, Calculus, chemistry, English, French, History (U.S.), Latin, and Spanish.
Standardized Tests: Middle 50% of SAT scores; Reading 520–670, Math 530–680, Writing 540–650
12 National Merit Semifinalists and 15 Letters of Commendation
2 National Achievement Semifinalists and 1 Commendation
College Matriculation: 85% to four-year institutions. Approximately 1/3 of these attend the U of Connecticut. Among the private colleges and universities which have attracted New Canaan students in the greatest numbers over the last four years are: American, Amherst, Boston

College, Boston U, Brown, Bryn Mawr, Colby, Connecticut College, Cornell, Drew, Fairbrook, Franklin & Marshall, Georgetown, Hamilton, Lehigh, MIT, New York U, Penn, Princeton, Westgate, and Yale.

GRADES

9th Grade

English	A
Geometry	C+
Spanish II	B
Chemistry	B–
World Cultures	A
Band (1/2 unit)	A
Health (1/2 unit)	A

10th Grade

English (Honors)	A
Algebra II (Honors)	C
Spanish III	B–
Biology (Honors)	B
AP U.S. History	B
Band (1/2 unit)	A
Drivers Ed. (1/2 unit)	A

11th Grade

English (Honors)	A
PreCalculus (Honors)	C
Spanish IV (Honors)	C+
AP Chemistry	C–
Sociology	B
Journalism	A

12th Grade

AP English	A
AP Spanish V	B-
AP Biology	B-
AP Calculus (AB)	C-
Physics	C+
Journalism	A

PARENTS

Father: William; Financial analyst, Johnson, Lincoln & Beck
BA, Columbia University; MBA, NYU
Mother: Lucinda; Boutique owner, Flights of Fancy
BA, NYU

SIBLINGS

None

ACTIVITIES

School Newspaper (soph., jr., sr.)
Class President (sr.)
Volleyball Team (fr., soph., jr., sr.)
Field Hockey (soph., jr., sr.)
Softball (jr., sr.)
Tutor - Writing Center (soph., jr., sr.)

WORK

Summers 2003–05
Johnson, Lincoln & Beck
Office Assistant
35 hrs. per week

Weekends
Babysitting
4 hrs. per week

AWARDS

Honorable Mention, Young Poets of Connecticut Contest 2004
First Prize, Young Poets of Connecticut Contest 2005

DEGREE PROGRAM

Undecided

CAREER GOAL

Undecided

COUNSELOR REPORT

Makele does so much! It is unbelievable how many irons she has in the fire at one time. Somehow she gets it all done and still has time for a social life (she is one of the most popular girls in the class!) and time for her family.

Makele is a natural leader. Being chosen captain of the volleyball team, editor of the school paper, and senior class president in this school is no small feat. I can't tell you how great a loss her graduation will be to New Canaan. She seems to run it.

There is no doubt that this young woman will do well in college. Someone will probably want to elect her president by the time she leaves. Makele has struggled with some causes once in a while but always managed to keep the proper perspective and get the job done. Her English teachers even remark that she shows sparks of brilliance in writing when she has time to prepare well. I give her my strongest recommendation to your school!

In comparison to other students, I rate her as follows: Academic achievement: Excellent (top 10%); Extra-curricular accomplishments: Outstanding (top 5%); Personal qualities and character: Outstanding (top 5%); Creativity: No basis. Recommend this student: Strongly.

ESSAY

I never had a roommate before, particularly one that I had to watch die. In the way that one watches a flower blossoming in time-lapse photography, I watched her in reverse. Learning to cope with a damning diagnosis and an even more unbearable prog-nosis was a problem I hoped I'd never have to face. In the process, I learned what love is and what dying is not.

Although one might say she was only an aunt, she had come to mean so much more to me. In better days, we joked about her being on loan to me as a sister since my mother already had two of her own. She was the classic Auntie Mame in my life: the one to whom I told my secrets and the one who would listen, no matter how trivial they seemed. As a child, I looked up to her. As I grew older, I confided in her.

She had no family of her own and lived alone in Boston. When she grew ill, her visits became more frequent. They grew from weeks to months and then years, partly because her doctors were in New York but mostly because she needed a family's love. We became roommates. At first it was great fun. I had a live-in sister, one with whom there was no jealousy or petty sibling rivalry. During the two years she slept beside me, we offered more of ourselves to each other than ever before, hoping we might turn each other's despair around.

Then, everything changed and gradually our roles were reversed. She was ill with cancer and for the first time needed me more that [sic] I needed her. I hated playing grownup to her condition, but I learned more from that experience than I possibly could have if things remained the same. If we were to help her live until she died, we would have to become a "care unit" replacing the sterile hospital which had failed her so. We reconstructed her life as she wanted it—not as we were advised—no hired nurses in white for her. It was not so long ago that I felt the same about spinach, but I understood how necessary it was that she try. I did whatever was required to get that

stuff down: a little teasing, sometimes cajoling, firmness when necessary, and at times understanding. Often I disposed of the juice before my mother caught on. We were in cahoots, my aunt and I, as it must have been many years ago when I was a child. Now it was I who was covering up for her, listening to her stories, fetching, feeding, always remembering her dignity and careful not to let her see how clearly our roles had reversed—or so I thought.

Normalcy was what she needed most in her life now; in fact, she insisted on it. She needed laughter; lightheartedness and a total absence of morbidity. It was not always easy for me to meet those needs, but somehow it never seemed difficult for her. There were times when she could make me believe that nothing was wrong at all.

Gradually her pain increased, and her cancer laced its way into our lives. It hurt to see her hurt. I wanted to become the child again and blink my eyes, in some fairy-tale fashion, to replace that image with her former, healthy face. There were times when I was relieved to see her in the hospital because it freed me from the pain she brought to my life. It had come to be a pain that was as much mine as it was hers. Our love and attention was not enough to relieve it. Even her M.A.S.H. re-runs could not take the place of the morphine she was now dependent on.

There were moments when I wanted to complain: the alarm clock rang twice in the middle of each night, reminding her that her pain needed controlling with medication. There was no medication for me; my pain continued. I had to disconnect my phone each night at nine (a blessing for my mother) and more often than not, I had to complete my homework in the living room. How could I complain remembering that even in this pain, she typed my term papers and waited as anxiously as I for my grade? How is it possible that with all that pain, she still eagerly read my essays and laughed at my daily escapades? Her patience and interest never diminished. She took pride in my every move. And, how is it possible that she (not for one moment) abandons her sense of humor?

There were times when we all identified with her illness and referred to her diagnosis as our diagnosis, her prognosis

ours. So complete was that identification that when I once described remarkably similar symptoms I was having, she said, "Go get your own disease." She was happiest when she could turn situations like this (and our unhappiness) around to laughter, and I was obligated to let her do it.

It may seem insensitive to say hers was a happy end: I don't know what describes it better. She's had an abundance of laughter in her lifetime and was determined to end on that same note. She did everything to protect me from her torment, and if terror was part of her end, she kept that hidden as well. She brought humor into her illness: love and laughter into our home. That was her style. When she was wheeled into the operating room, the stretcher stopped at the nurse's station, which resembled a large glass-enclosed booth. My aunt, in extreme pain and under heavy sedation, managed to prop herself up on one elbow, look up at the booth and say, "I'll take two tickets to *Chorus Line,* please." She taught me not to fear the inevitable. We enjoyed even moments like this as if there would be a never-ending supply of them. Her humor was her only way of shielding me from the grim reality of her plight, protecting me, just as she always had. I wondered if we ever really reversed roles at all, and I prayed that I helped her to die the way she wanted to.

Obviously, this was a tragedy in our close family, but it was not a tragic death, no morbid sideshows for her. It was a dignified and loving end. It was her sense of humor that carried us through our roughest times. It was her last gesture as my aunt: the only one she had left to give.

All my aunt wanted was to see me graduate. She died just before my senior year began. As "poet of the family" I was honored to write her epitaph. They were the hardest few words I'd ever had to write.

RECOMMENDATION
English Teacher

I am writing on behalf of Makele Johnson, who was my student in the ninth grade and again last year in Junior Honors English. She was an exceptional student, one of the best I have taught in my fifteen-year career. She reads and responds to literature with the kind of care and insight one seldom sees in a high-schooler, and her own writing is elegant and powerful, if not always controlled. Although her analytical and expository papers were excellent, she did her best work on more creative and open-ended assignments. Her year-end journal, for example, was superb, and she wrote some dazzlingly clever imitations of Maya Angelou and Toni Morrison. Toward the end of the year, she asked me to read some of her poetry. I agree to such requests with a certain amount of dread, for as you know, most high school literary efforts are painfully unsophisticated and it's often difficult to make a critical appraisal without bruising the adolescent ego behind the work. What a pleasant surprise, then, to discover that Makele's poems are remarkably good—well-crafted, subtle, imaginative, and evocative. I think she has real promise. She is willing to take risks with her writing, just as she is willing to take risks with her literary interpretations.

I first taught Makele as a ninth grader; her ready smile and zest for living earned her many friends and my affection. It has been gratifying to watch her mature over the last few years. Her involvement in student government bespeaks that level of maturity, as well as the support and respect of her peers. Additionally, her accomplishments at school not only demonstrate her talents but the extensive network of relationships she had developed as Editor of the newspaper, captain of our volleyball team, and a spirited leader of her class.

It must be quite clear by now that I like Makele. She is the kind of student who keeps a teacher and a class on their toes, and her unabashed love of literature and language makes her an especially satisfying student. She will respond well to a first-rate college education, and I think she has earned it. I am happy to recommend her to you.

INTERVIEW REPORT

Poised, articulate, and clearly focused on her goals, Makele was a pleasure to chat with. Our mutual interest in literature gave us much to discuss the afternoon she came to my office. She is well read, but clearly prefers contemporary novels and those that focus on the struggles of minorities and women. In fact Makele had just finished the *Color of Water* and had such impressive insight about both the author

and the protagonist, his mother, that I have since purchased the book and now I am in the process of my own journey through the pages. Makele is bright and dynamic— charismatic really.

She is clearly a leader in school and has long-term goals about contributing to social change. My guess is that she is quite a star at New Canaan and she would be a good addition to the upcoming freshman class.

On a final note, I can't help but share that my committee had quite a tough time getting this interview to take place. In truth, I was not supposed to interview Makele at all, but the person I assigned her to was quite frustrated by a series of unreturned calls from Makele and/or her family. I also did not get a call back after my first message to Makele, and so I had to contact Ms. Lovelace, the counselor at New Canaan, to see if she could be helpful. I immediately got a call back from Makele with a brief apology.

Having met Makele, my instinct is to recommend acceptance particularly if she is a *highly* competitive academic candidate If she can back up her personal charisma with academic performance, she might be worth the fight. However, if there are other tentative issues, she may be better served at another institution. Perhaps, she really is not as interested in us as we would like her to be. This is a tough one.

Robert Michael Brandeis

St. Xavier High School
Tucson, Arizona

STANDING AND SCORES

Class Standing: 14/182
SAT Scores: 650cr/690w/650mr
(October, Jr. Yr.)
Subject Test Scores:
620 Spanish
700 Math Level IC

HIGH SCHOOL PROFILE

Type of School/Accreditation: Coed Episcopal day school; accredited by Southwestern Association of Schools and Colleges.
Enrollment: 800 in grades 9–12
Curriculum: College preparatory and comprehensive. Graduation requirements are: 4 years English, 3 years Mathematics, 2 years Social Studies,3 years Foreign Language (the third year can be waived in special cases), 2 years Lab Science, 1 1/2 years Theology.
Honors courses in English, History, and Mathematics.
AP courses in Calculus, Biology,

Spanish, European History, U.S. History and Chemistry.
Standardized Tests: Middle 50% of SAT scores; Reading 550–690, Math 580–720, Writing 530–680
1 National Merit Semifinalist, 2 Letters of Commendation
College Matriculation: 70% to four-year colleges, 20% to two-year colleges.
Class of 2010 attends: U of North Dakota, North Dakota State U, U of Mary, Beloit College, Carleton College, Fairbrook U, U of Notre Dame, Loyola U Chicago, Northwestern U, Washington U, Marquette U, Georgetown.

GRADES

9th Grade, 1st Semester

English I	A–
Deductive Geometry	A
P.E. Boys	P
Conceptual Physics	B+
Spanish II	A
Intro to Religion	A–
Computer	A

9th Grade, 2nd Semester

English I	A
Deductive Geometry	A
Classical Civilizations	A–
P.E. Boys	P
Spanish II	A–
Introduction to Scripture	A
Computer Illustration	A

10th Grade - 1st Semester

English II	A–
World History	A
Algebra II H	A–
P.E. Boys	P
Biology	A
World Religions	A
Spanish III	B

10th Grade - 2nd Semester

English II	A
World History	A–
Algebra II H	A–
P.E. Boys	P
Biology	A
World Religions	A
Spanish III	B+

10th Grade - Summer

Ceramics	A

11th Grade - 1st Semester

English III H	A–
US History H	A–
Precalculus H	B+
Chemistry	A
AP Spanish Language	A–
Bible as Literature	A

11th Grade - 2nd Semester

English III H	A–
US History H	A
Precalculus H	A–
Chemistry	A
AP Spanish Language	A
Ethics	A

PARENTS

Father: Richard; CEO, Strategic Associates
BS, Fairbrook University
Mother: Roberta; Community Volunteer
BS, University of Arizona

SIBLINGS

Jonathan, 13
Laura, 10

ACTIVITIES

Soccer (fr., soph)
Lacrosse (fr., soph)
Volunteer Docent, Sonora Desert Museum (jr., sr.)

WORK

Summer 2005
Strategic Associates
Warehouse Stocker
30 hrs. per week

Summer 2006
Sonora Desert Museum
Zoology Assistant
35 hrs. per week

AWARDS

Academic Honor Roll, grades 9–12
2nd Place, 10th Grade Division, Arizona Science Fair

DEGREE PROGRAM

Biological Science

CAREER GOAL

Zoologist

ESSAY

During junior high school two friends of mine and I spent a good deal of our weekend mornings and vacation days scrambling around the foothills of the Catalina Mountains, a small chain just north of Tucson which had always seemed remote and mystical to me when I was younger. Bicycles and a sense of adventure propelled us out the semi-paved streets of town into the desert and finally to a dry river bed at the foot of the Catalina's. We locked our bikes to a palo verde tree trunk and took old boy scout knapsacks full of canned food as high up as we dared toward the first set of outcroppings. It was about a forty-five minute climb, made all the more uncomfortable by the sharp digs of the cans into out [sic] backs.

Once under the rock formations, which looked so different up close—shapeless and diffuse compared to their distinct outlines from down below—we built a little fire out of dead cactus branches, opened a can of franks and beans, cooked it and ate with great satisfaction. Then we buried the remaining cans under small rock piles and felt absolutely sure that we could recover them when we needed to on a later trip. The word "cache" had a powerful grip on me then; it seemed to call back the essence of adventure stories I'd read, and I remember vividly the feeling of security and independence these forays gave me.

We usually spent some time trying to climb the rocks, but never really scaled one of them completely. The shady overhangs made great vantage points for looking down on Tucson. There was never anyone up there, so we were the unobserved observers, and we could make out many landmarks: the Catalina Theater, the dealership where my uncle works, churches, parks, and our subdivision. These trips included my first serious conversations on all kinds of topics, and we shared a lot of our "plans" (many of which were based on books we had read and were therefore usually full of strange escapades), in addition to typical matters of confusion and mystery. Occasionally we witnessed something spectacular, like a sudden rock slide or a pounding thunder storm in August.

I felt completely free, but not as though we were running away, even though a big part of the thrill was related to that notion, to escape and secrecy, and buried survival kits. I looked for my house from up on the mountain, and I think I loved the fact that I could look down on my life from such a distance and put it into some kind of perspective. My two friends went on to another high school, and I haven't been up on the Catalina's [sic] since ninth grade, but I have thought about it lately as I look ahead to college. I can see more similarities: I'll pack up and leave, I assume I will make good friends, and encounter unforgettable experiences. I also think that in moving on from one phase of my life I will be able to look back on it and understand it better from a new vantage point, like looking at my neighborhood from our mountain stronghold.

SCHOOL REPORT

Robert Brandeis is a young man who thrives on challenges. He sets high goals for himself and works until he feels he has achieved them. This level of perseverance is consistent throughout all of his endeavors, including woodworking with younger students and academics. Although a serious sports injury, followed by surgery, has prevented Robert from playing on the soccer and lacrosse teams of which he has been a valuable member at St. Xavier for two years, thanks to months of physical therapy and determination he has amazingly returned to his favorite sport—rock climbing. Robert is good-spirited, ready to tackle new challenges and finds rewards for his determined efforts.

A strong and independent student, Robert continues to choose more rigorous courses while expanding his technical skills. His teachers appreciate his consistent efforts as well as the new interpretations, insights, and inquiries he brings to class. His pre-calculus teacher, for instance, commends his "positive, cooperative, and patient participation in group efforts; and is happy to see him successfully taking risks in solving challenging problems."

The spiritual values of St. Xavier have had a positive affect on Robert's development. Through his religion classes, he has become more perceptive about the importance of community and the social and economic issues facing us today. As a result of his understanding, he has been a more active member of the school community and has participated in activities with younger children, serving as a good role model and guide.

Robert's pleasure in teaching younger students, with his love of science and the outdoors, have been enriched by his personal growth experiences. He has worked with young children as a counselor at a summer camp and volunteered at the Sonora Desert Museum working as an explainer for the mountain lion exhibit. He has organized a bike club at St. Xavier for other students who share interests in mountain biking and continues to participate on a ski racing team.

Perhaps the most influential experience in Robert's development was last summer in Mexico with the Amigos Program where he lived with a family in a small village and helped to improve community sanitation. There he also expanded his appreciation for other cultures and gained a new perspective on his immediate community and the United States. Robert recalls with delight and pride the experience of volunteering for a contest in his small Mexican town to stand at the foot of a greased pole, offering his shoulders for other men to stand on, creating a human pole to reach the prize at the top. With a smile, Robert recalls "the sense of camaraderie after climbing the pole overcame any sort of borders there might have been between the guys and me. It was truly a happy moment, because everyone clapped for me, and I felt happy because not only had I accomplished this major feat, but I was also accepted into the town as a person, not a gringo. These overwhelming emotions almost brought me to tears, but I did not cry for I was a Mexican person then, and we don't cry."

As you can see, Robert has developed his sensitivity to others. His enjoyment of learning and helping others learn and grow comes through his choice of activities.

RECOMMENDATION
English Teacher

The Shakespeare Course Robert Brandeis is taking now is my second term with him. Last spring in English III (Advanced Composition) Robert proved himself as a student eager to participate in discussion and willing to share ideas. Even when his thoughts were still in the formative stages, he was not afraid to take the risk of sharing them. He could at times be creative, at times analytical, but never glib or careless. This fall he seems even more mature, and he has developed a real interest in writing poetry, especially sonnets. Robert has been a good discussion leader. He did a fine job analyzing the text of Claudius's soliloquy in Hamlet, including a breakdown of the iambic meter as a reflection of Claudius's emotional disturbance.

Although he comes across as very confident, Robert characterizes himself as quite timid. Nevertheless, I think he is daring enough when it comes to intellectual risks, and very witty in his use of written language. I feel certain that he will find kindred spirits in college among both faculty and peers.

I consider Robert a kind and considerate young man, one who loves reading and writing as much as he seems to love the outdoors. He isn't one of those students who draws a great deal of attention to himself, who show how much they know by loud hallway arguments. He is an intellectual, and I am sure that he will flourish in college.

INTERVIEW REPORT

Robert Brandeis struck me as an interesting, intelligent young man with a clear interest in science, and a love of the outdoors. When I asked him which was his favorite class, he responded by telling me a great deal about his sophomore biology class, and how it had become more important to him in the wake of a sports injury which necessitated his dropping out of team sports, at least for a time. He said that because of that he had discovered an interest in outdoor activities—rock climbing, hiking, and so on—that these pursuits put science in a new light for him. He now loves exploring nature, observing animal and plant species, and working at a local natural habitat educational center.

My impression is that school work takes up most of Robert's time. He described himself as conscientious about homework, even in classes which are not his favorites. When I asked about activities, and his relationships with other students in his class, he had less to say; he doesn't seem to be a loner, but may be somewhat reserved.

I don't see Robert as a potential leader in college, but I do think he will handle the work very well, and his personality is certainly pleasant. He seems happy and well-adjusted. I would recommend him strongly on the basis of his academic interest and clear determination to succeed in college.

Kenneth Aldman

Priory School
Fargo, North Dakota

STANDING AND SCORES

Class Standing:
SAT Scores: 620cr/650w/600mr
(May, Jr. Yr.)
Subject Test Scores:
520 Spanish
590 Chemistry

HIGH SCHOOL PROFILE

Type of School/Accreditation:
Coed, Catholic Independent School,
accredited by Midwestern Association
of Schools and Colleges.
Enrollment: 660 in grades 9–12
Curriculum: College preparatory.
Graduation requirements are English 4
years, Math 3 years, Science 2 years,
U.S. History 1 year, Religion 1 year,
Foreign Language 2 years
A full range of AP courses are available.
Standardized Tests: Middle 50% of
SAT scores, Reading 480–970, Math
490–710, Writing 460–680
4 National Merit Semifinalists, 12 Letters
of Commendation
College Matriculation: 82% to four-year
colleges, 18% to two-year colleges.
Class of 2010 attends: U of Arizona,
Arizona State U, Loyola Marymount
U, U of San Francisco, U of
Colorado, Dartmouth, Stanford U, U
of Pennsylvania, Northwestern U of
Michigan, U.S. Air Force Academy and
Rice U.

GRADES

9th Grade, 1st Semester

English I	B
Deductive Geometry	B
P.E. Boys	P
Conceptual Physics	B
Spanish I	B
Inst Music: Adv. Improv.	A
Computer	B

9th Grade, 2nd Semester

English I	B
Deductive Geometry	B
P.E. Boys	P
Conceptual Physics	B
Spanish I	C
Inst Music: Jazz Improv.	A
Intro to Scripture	B

10th Grade - 1st Semester

English II	B
World History	B
Algebra II H	B
P.E. Boys	P
Biology	B
Spanish II	B
Inst Music: Adv. Jazz	A
Intro to Scripture	B

10th Grade - 2nd Semester

English III	B+
US History H	B
Precalculus H	B–
Chemistry	B–
Spanish III	B
Inst Music: Jazz Band	A

10th Grade - Summer

Drafting & Design	A–

11th Grade - 1st Semester

English III H	B+
US History H	B
Precalculus H	B–
Chemistry	B–

Spanish III	B
Inst Music: Jazz Band	A

11th Grade - 2nd Semester

English III H	B–
US History H	B+
Precalculus H	B–
Chemistry	C+
Spanish III	B
Inst Music: Jazz Band	A

PARENTS

Father: Edmund; Sales Manager,
Solar Technology
(No college)
Mother: Sarah; Loan Officer,
Bank of America
(No college)

SIBLINGS

James, 13
Evelyn, 10
Richard, 8

ACTIVITIES

JV/V Basketball (fr., soph., jr., sr.)
JV/V Baseball (fr., soph., jr., sr.)
JV Soccer (fr.)
Jazz Club (soph., jr., sr.)
Advanced Jazz Ensemble (jr., sr.)

WORK

Summer 2005
Foster's Ice Cream

Counter Sales
40 hrs. per week

Fall 2005 to Present
Junior year - Present
Police Athletic League
Youth League Referee
2 hrs. per week

Summer 2006
Circle Productions
Web Page Designer
24 hrs. per week

AWARDS

Bennington College Short Fiction Award
American High School Mathematics
Exam - top 20 in school
Great Plains Music Educators Award
for Solos
Skidmore Jazz Institute

DEGREE PROGRAM

Music or Computer Science

CAREER GOAL

Undecided

COUNSELOR REPORT

Ratings:
Academic Motivation: Excellent
Academic Growth Potential: Excellent
Academic Independence: Good
Self-discipline: Good
Creativity: Excellent
Emotional Maturity: Good
Concern for Others: Excellent
Leadership: Excellent
Summary Ratings:
Academic Promise: Good
Personal Qualities: Excellent
Community/extracurricular: Excellent
Overall: Excellent

ESSAY

Jazz has long been a part of
my life. It gives me confidence
and the ability to deal with
difficult moments. When my
grandfather died, I turned

to my saxophone and shared my grief with its brass body. Instead of crying, I played a haunting song of sorrow and grief. Music brings people together regardless of any differences they might have. The sax speaks a universal language that anyone can understand and it has become an extension of me. For all this, I am grateful to the Truman Middle School Jazz Band and to Mr. Ladd, my middle school music teacher, for introducing the wonderful world of jazz to me at the age of eleven.

I can remember sitting on a stiff unyielding plastic chair as I awaited my turn to audition for the Truman Middle School Jazz Band. Unconsciously, my fingers stroked the familiar keys of my instrument in anticipation. It was up to me and my trusty saxophone to pass this test. The enormous room, barred by two huge doors, engulfed me. My mind wandered back to old memories when I was a fourth grader and my brother was in the seventh grade. Reluctantly, I agreed to attend his middle school concert. I remember thinking, "What a waste of time."

Upon entering the concert hall, I had my first look at Truman Middle School. My first impression of the public school intimidated me. Its huge cement walls were unyielding and cold. Then I entered the warmly lit auditorium. It was a gigantic recital hall that could easily fit a thousand people, and it was packed. As the concert began, I slouched back into the wooden seat anticipating a comfortable nap. To the melodious notes of Bach and Mozart, I slowly gently drifted away.....Then.... boom!!.... crash!!... boom!! rat-tat-tat… crescendoed with the screams of hundreds of adolescent girls. The jazz band was swinging and hot, playing "Take the A Train." They were perfect. Before I knew it, the lights dimmed and a spotlight bathed a lone alto sax player in its sweet glow. It was an eighth grader, who is currently playing alto sax for the singer, Abby Lincoln. A chorus screamed out his name. To be like him, to have the audience screaming my name, to play in the Truman Jazz Band became my dream.

I aspired to be the best musician I could be. When I entered Truman Middle School, out of my class of five hundred, I was one of three sixth graders chosen to play in the Advanced Symphonic Band and Orchestra. I was one step away from my dream. My band director, Mr. Ladd, was a rather daunting looking man with a bald head and heavy brows. What he lacked in hair, he made up for in his love for music. At Truman, the "coolest thing" was not to be the baseball pitcher, or the basketball point guard, but to be a member of the elite jazz band.

As a seventh grader, I made the jazz band as a second tenor; and as an eighth grader, I became one of the key soloists. However, the thought of performing in front of a thousand screaming people frightened me. Being a member of an ensemble was one thing, but stepping out in to the spotlight to solo was another. I was a shy, quiet person who kept most of my emotions to myself. My personality was rather unusual, for my father's family was filled with exuberant and spontaneous jokers. I needed to incorporate this spontaneity and feeling for

life into my music and soloing. So on a cold evening in early December, I walked onto the stage for the winter concert and hesitantly steeled myself to play. I rose from my chair and walked into the spotlight. Mesmerized by the light casting down on me, I stood in front of my audience. My warm breath flowed through my body and my fingers caressed and felt every note. Feeling the warmth of light expire, I knew it was over and I felt almost sad, as if I had lost a new friend. That night, I overcame a fear and embraced it.

Now I am seventeen and a more experienced player. The audition room is packed with talented young musicians waiting to try out for the Disney All Star High School Jazz Band. Who will be the fortunate twenty this year? Then a voice rings out, "Kenneth Aldman." I leave my seat under the stares and side-glances of curious players. Stepping into another auditorium, I face the director. I clasp my sax to my mouth and start to blow, "In a Sentimental Mood," as she accompanies me on the piano. My mind drifts away interpreting the song in my own style. I quickly do a little sight reading and scale work. Lifting my sax case to my shoulder, I walk slowly down the hallway. I knew that I had played well, but I still wondered, "Was I good enough?"

For two years I had been disappointed with the inability to achieve one of my musical goals. I knew that some of the players were older and more accomplished than I was. Still, I remember the disappointment of receiving two prior "thin letters." When I look back, the frustration motivated me to work harder. I focused on the little aspects of my musicianship that I lacked. The answer came a week later in a letter from Disney. I was accepted!

The Disney Band was certainly an accomplishment and showed me that hard work and dedication pay off. However, even if I was rejected a third time, I would never lose my passion for jazz. When I walk on stage, sit in the living to practice, or just listen to music, the sounds of those notes enrapture me. After years of playing music, I have built a bond between my saxophone and jazz that is like my love for my family. My saxophone is my companion, my love, and my dearest friend.

SCHOOL REPORT

Kenneth Aldman is an exceptionally creative and imaginative student. He is very bright—both artistically and intellectually—as well as upbeat and sincere. Kenneth skillfully applies his talents to all of his activities, which range from music and creative writing to computer illustration. As a valuable member of this community, Kenneth has also been on the baseball, basketball, and soccer teams.

A musician since the age of five, Kenneth plays piano, clarinet, and saxophone with a passion I seldom see in students his age. He has won numerous musical awards and was invited to be one of fifty young musicians from around the country to participate in an intensive two-week study of jazz at the Skidmore Jazz Institute. He often plays in local jazz festivals and is the founder of our very first jazz club. Kenneth finds a great deal of satisfaction in sharing his love of music with others, donating his time to give jazz concerts and lectures for elementary and junior high school students throughout the city.

Kenneth's work experiences have given him the opportunity to experiment and improve his skills. He has cleverly incorporated his artistic and technical abilities working at Circle Productions as a web page designer. He found it very exciting to work in such a rapidly growing industry which nurtured creativity. Kenneth also worked in a laboratory at the North Dakota State University where he enjoyed the chance "to experience research, development, and scientific procedures in a lab setting rather than only theoretically in the classroom."

Kenneth's creative writing ability has been commended by his peers and teachers as well as recognized in the Mintekko Creative Arts Showcase, sponsored by Bennington College, in which he performed a jazz solo and short story reading. An articulate and enthusiastic student, Kenneth is an important contributor to class discussions. He doesn't mind taking a position different from that of his classmates and is eager to hear all sides of an issue before drawing his own conclusions. Kenneth stands by his beliefs and values, even if they are not considered "cool" by his peers, and he chooses to forge his own path in life. Kenneth says "after learning something, my mind will try to find different ways around it, getting it, and thinking about it. This is very helpful when trying to find the answer to problems."

While Kenneth has been diagnosed as learning disabled, he has kept up with a vigorous courseload with minimal accommodations. He has requested extended time in chemistry and math. We see him as clearly able to do college level work. I believe that whichever path Kenneth chooses to take, it will be original, interesting, and highly creative. During these past four years he has learned to integrate his gifts with an academic community, and the gifts that he will bring to any college will be valuable and unique.

RECOMMENDATION
Math Teacher

Kenneth Aldman is a personable, bright, athletically and musically gifted young man who brings a great deal of enthusiasm and social skill to whatever he does. As a student in my advanced math class, he has been a diligent worker, a completely trustworthy young man, one who, given a modicum of encouragement, will work diligently for anyone, always glad to pitch in, keeping everyone's spirits high. In fact, I would say that Kenneth keeps the focus from himself, generally speaking, and seems to be most himself when he is in a group.

In the math classroom, Kenneth takes to the small class, group-work style with real flair. In our Calculus class, he works very well with other students, and contributes to discussions thoughtfully and considerately. Though not a flashy student, he has a great determination: he will stay with a problem set or a write-up until he has it firmly in hand.

Kenneth communicates well with his teachers—candidly and effortlessly, whether seeking academic advice or simply chatting in the halls. In this sense, I think Kenneth has as a solid grasp of himself as a part of a community. As a matter of fact, Kenneth ran for student body office at the end of his junior ear. He was not elected, but I remember the reasonable, well-thought-out programs he presented in his "campaign," and the

good sense with which he approached the challenge.

Kenneth is an excellent musician, as I can attest having heard him play on numerous occasions here at Priory; I also know that he would like to play baseball in college, although he has a healthy sense of priorities on this topic. Perhaps his interest in sports has helped shape the team player that he is in other areas as well. But more importantly, especially because he is interested in a solid education, Kenneth is eager to find the right match intellectually. Energetic, personable, responsive to his teachers—I think Kenneth is a strong candidate, and one who will make the most of his college opportunities. He will certainly be constructively involved, and never give less than his best effort.

INTERVIEW REPORT

This morning I had an interesting interview with a young man from a nearby private high school. I knew going into the interview that he is an accomplished musician, that he is learning disabled, and that his academic record has been above average but not spectacular.

Our conversation got off to a good start, since I asked him initially about his experiences in music. He is clearly an impressive jazz saxophonist, with years of classes and private lessons, an array of awards in competitions, and, something I always admire, a sense of dedication to the program at his own school. His enthusiasm for music, and the maturity of his reflection and analysis of his own ability and motivation, were truly outstanding.

When I asked him about academic things, he was equally articulate—he described the difficulties he had experienced coming into high school, his assessment as a dyslexic student, and the renewed sense of commitment he felt when he began to improve academically as a result of basic accommodations and a greater understanding of his own learning strengths and weaknesses. I can see this turn-around, to some extent, in his academic record, and I felt that these experiences had added a great deal to the general sense of self knowledge and maturity that he manifests.

His sense of humor, candidate ability to discuss these issues, and his solid motivation impressed me considerably. I would recommend him enthusiastically, knowing that he will need certain accommodations in college, but I am confident that he will have the commitment to take full advantage of the opportunity and, though he may not lead his class academically, will certainly, in my opinion bring a great deal to our campus.

Case Study Reactions

Now that you've looked at the case studies—and tried to evaluate the candidacy of the three students to fictional Fairbrook University—you get some sense of how tough it is for admission officers to make these decisions. Each of these applicants had qualities that could make them attractive to a particular college in a particular year.

We asked six admission officers from very good, private colleges to evaluate these same candidates—using the criteria for admission of their particular college. We include six of them here, and you can find more reactions on our website www.zinch.com/casestudies. (We also invite you to post your comments.)

As you'll see, the criteria for admission differs from school to school—as does the process. Some of the admission officers' responses are briefer than others. But that certainly doesn't mean they gave any less attention to the prospective candidates. It does reflect the fact that most of these write-ups took place during the very busy late fall–early winter of 2010—when committees were evaluating early decision applicants. And thus we are particularly grateful to these harried professionals for taking the time and sharing their insights.

Brown University
by a Former Admission Officer

Makele

Makele may be the most frustrating of the three applicants. She's a no-need, African American girl, school president, editor of paper, and captain of volleyball. She should be a slam dunk at any school until you turn to the transcript. Though she has challenged herself, the junior-year grades are full of Cs, and senior fall is not much better. There is little said by the college counselor to explain this, though her English teacher writes a lovely recommendation, which is consistent with her strong standard-ized testing in that area. Her essay is nicely written, but I'm not sure what is tells the committee about her. The interview report adds another red flag that conveys either lack of interest in Fairbrook, disorganization, or rudeness.

Robert

Robert is a legacy and apply-ing ED—both big plusses. Arizona should have some geo appeal too. It appears he was a pretty good athlete, but a serious injury took him out of competitive athletics. He has channeled that energy into rock climbing and his interest in the desert and its wildlife, witnessed by his volunteer work. He has also transferred that energy into his academic work, with strong grades in excellent courses. He has solid scores for his interest in biology. He loves science and there is a real sensitivity and compassion that comes through about him in his recommendations. He gets strong school support. He has applied for financial aid but may not qualify for much in light of his parents' jobs.

Kenneth

Kenneth brings geographic diversity (North Dakota) and a real passion for jazz. It's obvious he loves music and it will remain a part of him in college, though he also has an interest in computer science. He has done AP and Honors-level work in several areas, and a case can be made for the fact that he has dealt well with a learning disability. His record has improved a bit over the years, but there are an awful lot of Bs in his record. His scores are okay, though a bit on the low side for Fairbrook in math given his interest in computer science. I suspect that with his GPA, he is below their norm too. He has an excellent interview report and good support from the school. He's a candidate for financial aid, and has held a job through school—a good thing.

Decision Time

Robert should be the top choice for admission at Fairbrook. As an ED legacy with the strongest record of the three, he is an easy admit. Though he doesn't bring that special talent to campus, he has his legacy hook and is just a good kid who reorganized his priorities after a tough sports injury. Kenneth would be my second choice—a waitlist if we need to use all three categories. Though his academic record isn't as strong as Robert's, he has overcome a diagnosed LD fairly well and has a real talent and passion with his jazz playing. And I suspect Fairbrook doesn't see many apps from Fargo. And finally, unless Fairbrook is desperate for students of color, I'd reject Makele. She needs to be sent a message that academics come first, and it's very disappointing that her counselor, at a school as high power as New Canaan, doesn't address this. She has had wonderful academic opportunities but fails to take advantage of them. And I personally would be offended by the interview report—it hints of arrogance and lack of interest from her.

Unfortunately, none of these three would have been compelling admits at Brown (if Brown was Fairbrook) unless Robert's father had been actively involved since graduation. I suspect not, and the application for financial aid suggests limited giving ability since his time in college.

Johns Hopkins University

by John Birney, Associate Director of Admission

At first glance, all three candidates have compelling attributes that many schools would like to enroll. These include leadership, contribution, legacy, diversity (in many forms), solid academic profiles, and interest in the school. Yet, as we look closer, each also possesses some areas of concern that need to be fully reviewed prior to an offer of admission being made.

Kenneth Aldman's file indicates that he is a first-generation student, in what could be described as an average course of study—based on the number of higher level academic classes in which he is enrolled. He is both an athlete and musician, and his essay clearly describes the impact that music has had on his life. He desires to study music or computer science. Should he decide on computer science, his lower grades in the math and science arena are troublesome.

Robert Brandies presents himself as the strongest academic applicant of the group. His demanding curriculum, strong GPA and class rank demonstrate that classroom achievement is his strong point. Unfortunately, Robert presents less of a case when it comes to extracurricular activities. His lack of involvement—and how that translates into involvement on a college campus—can be tough to overcome. However, Robert's legacy status could come into play.

Makele Johnson shows herself to be taking the strongest academic profile. However, her grade point average, and rank, are the lowest of the group. A consideration point here is what are more important, grades or rigor of curriculum? Makele, by a large margin, also has the strongest extracurricular involvement. Her positions of Editor, Class President, and Captain are certainly commendable. But did those positions (and the time they take) take away from her classroom performance?

Eventually, each admissions office has to make final decisions. From a Johns Hopkins point of view, we wouldn't admit any of these students. Here's a quick glimpse why. Kenneth's academic profile is not strong enough. Robert's lack of involvement is not encouraging. And Makele, for all of her strengths of involvement, leadership, and diversity, her low GPA is the culprit.

What type of student does Johns Hopkins desire? Take the leadership, involvement, diversity, and class selection from Makele, combine it with the classroom performance of Robert, add to that Kenneth's athletic abilities, musical prowess, and first-generation status—and we now have a most compelling applicant.

Muhlenberg College

by Alyssa Ellowitch, Associate Director of Admission

Makele
HIGH SCHOOL RECORD

- Makele's schedule is very strong. Starting in 10th grade, she really jumped right into honors and AP classes. She's taken five academic major subjects all four years, and her senior schedule is her most rigorous. These are all positive things, but unfortunately her grades have not been consistently strong.

- Makele has a bit of a downward trend junior year and seems to be doing better first quarter of senior year in a very hard schedule. I would like to see if her improved grades continue through the second quarter of senior year.

- Makele goes to a very good high school where 85% of students go to four-year colleges, so it's a competitive school and she's in a very competitive schedule.

- On a scale of 1–5, I would rate her as a 3 on quality and performance (with performance bringing her down a bit).

RECOMMENDATIONS

- Makele's recommendations are solid. Her teacher and her guidance counselor really like her, and I was impressed with the positive things they all had to say.

- Phrases that stood out include: "Makele is a natural leader," "shows sparks of brilliance in writing when she has time to prepare well," and "she is the kind of student who keeps a teacher and a class on their toes."

- Makele sounds like a force to be reckoned with. She has a lot of extracurricular energy that her recommendations talk a lot about, but it sounds like she also has trouble keeping her academic commitments as a priority.

- On a scale of 1–5, I would rate her recommendations as a 4. They are positive, but also honest and realistic.

PERSONAL QUALITIES

- Makele's extracurricular involvement is very strong. She has many leadership positions under her belt and has a nice diverse list of activities. I believe she would take a college campus by storm with her extracurricular and social energy. Makele's energy and leadership is very attractive for a small private college. We need students to come and keep programs running and provide leadership in different areas.

- Makele is diverse. She is a student of color, but she is also from Connecticut which, for us, is a geographic outreach area. Makele also indicates on her application that she does not intend to apply for financial aid, which is something worth noting. She won't cost the college anything and could help pay for other students to attend.

- One troublesome piece is the interview write-up. Makele's lack of interest in the interview process and lack of communication with staff trying to get in touch with her is troubling. Is she really interested in Fairbrook? Are we simply a safety school for her? Perhaps this isn't someone we want to invite into our tight-knit community if she doesn't really want to be here.

- On a scale of 1–5, I would rate her personal qualities as a 3+/4–. Her interview interaction brings her down.

TESTING

- 700cr 550m = 1250
- Her critical reading score builds profile, but her math score is at the low end of the admitted student range. It's obvious her strengths lie in English and writing, based on test scores and also on her high school record.
- On a scale of 1–5, I would rate her scores as a 4.

ESSAY

- Makele's essay was quite moving. It's long and more about her aunt than about Makele, but the writing is strong and the topic is quite personal.
- I like the fact that this is such a personal essay that deals with an emotional subject. The essay does tell us something about Makele that we wouldn't otherwise know about, which always makes for a great essay.
- On a scale of 1–5, I would rate her essay as a 4. I would like to read more about Makele and less about her aunt, but otherwise it's solid.

OVERALL

- Makele is a compelling applicant. She's an interesting young woman who's done a lot in high school.
- I worry about her academic performance. It looks like she may have overloaded herself academically and socially and, as a result, had trouble keeping up in school. This coupled with her troubling interview experience makes me believe that wait list is the right move here. If she is interested, we'll hear from her and this will give us an opportunity to see if her senior-year grades continue on an upward trend.

Robert

HIGH SCHOOL RECORD

- Robert has a very good class rank (top 8% of the class) and a very good schedule. His schedule has gotten more challenging over four years, and senior year is his toughest schedule yet. As his schedule has gotten more rigorous, his grades have stayed consistent in the A/A– range. Robert has taken at least four or five major subjects all four years.

- Robert attends a strong high school where 82% of students attend four-year colleges, and his guidance counselor says he is in the most demanding schedule. His schedule is tough at a good high school, so he is working hard for his As in Honors classes.

- On a scale of 1–5, I would rate his quality of program and performance as a 4+/5.

RECOMMENDATIONS

- Robert's recommendations are solid. It's a shame they aren't a little longer and more detailed, but we can't penalize him for that.

- His teachers and his guidance counselor rate him very highly. The phrases that stand out in his recommendations include: "thrives on challenges," "strong and independent student," and "he is daring enough when it comes to intellectual risks, and very witty in his use of written language."

- Robert made a great impression on his English teacher and guidance counselor. He sounds like a solid student and someone who will contribute to the classroom discussion and the intellectual environment at the college. For a small school like Fairbrook, he sounds like a great fit.

- On a scale of 1–5, I would rate his recommendations a 4.

PERSONAL QUALITIES

- Robert's personal qualities are not the strongest part of his application. The interview write-up is fine and certainly positive, but Robert sounds more like an introvert and someone who is the "silent thinker" type.

- He has made a positive impression on the adults at his high school, and it sounds like teachers really appreciate how deep, thoughtful, and engaged he is in the classroom experience.

- Robert doesn't have a lot of extracurricular energy or passion. His activities are on the thin side, but fortunately his recommendations shed a little more light on hobbies and activities he enjoys outside of school. He could have highlighted his passions more clearly in the application.

- Robert does build profile in two ways—he is from Arizona, and for a Pennsylvania school geographic diversity is always a positive! Also, in a letter he wrote to the admissions committee, his dad is an alumnus of the college. *And* he checked off the ED box on the common application, so if he's indeed an ED candidate—even better!

- On a scale of 1–5, I would rate his personal qualities a 3+.

TESTING

- 650cr 690m = 1340

- Robert is above the average range for admission in both critical reading and math. He builds SAT profile all-around.

- On a scale of 1–5, I would rate his scores a 5.

ESSAY

- Robert's essay is very personal and accomplishes what we hope the essay would accomplish—we learn something about him that we didn't know before.

- The writing is solid and the topic is interesting. On a scale of 1–5, I would give him a 4.

OVERALL

- As an ED male with an alumni connection, Robert is kind of a no brainer! He builds SAT profile, class rank profile, and has a 3.8 cumulative GPA. He's interviewed, so we know that there is sincere interest here (in addition to the ED commitment), I would admit.

Kenneth

HIGH SCHOOL RECORD

- Quality of high school schedule is solid. His schedule has gotten more rigorous over four years. His most challenging schedule is senior year, which is a good thing to see. Kenneth has taken at least four or five major subjects all four years of high school, which is also a plus.

- He's obviously not a strong science student, as his lowest grades are in Biology and Chemistry junior and senior year. He's a consistent B/B– student, and has stayed pretty consistent even as his course schedule has gotten more difficult.

- Kenneth goes to a solid high school where 70% go on to four-year colleges, so his curriculum is a strong college prep curriculum.
- On a scale of 1–5, I would rate his high school record, including both quality of program and performance, a 3+/4.

RECOMMENDATIONS

- Kenneth's recommendations are strong. The phrases that really stand out include: "important contributor to class discussions," "stands by his beliefs and values," "very bright, upbeat and sincere," and "brings a great deal of enthusiasm and social skill to whatever he does."
- He sounds like a self-advocate, which is very important for diagnosed LD students. He talks with teachers, puts a strong effort into his classroom work, and isn't afraid to put himself out there and take risks.
- On a scale of 1–5, I would rate his recommendations as a 4.

PERSONAL QUALITIES

- The interview write-up is positive. The interviewer believes that Kenneth has very strong personal qualities—sense of humor, candid, motivated, committed, and mature.
- He sounds like a very charismatic and personable young man. His dedication to music is admirable. Kenneth sounds like a young man who is mature and competent and ready for the challenges of college.

- On a side note, Kenneth also helps build our profile a bit as far as geographic diversity (he's from North Dakota and we're in Pennsylvania), and he adds diversity as a first-generation college student.
- On a scale of 1–5, I would rate his personal qualities a 4+.

TESTING

- 620cr 650m = 1270
- His scores are within our average range for admitted students. His critical reading score is actually above the average range, and math is at the high end of the range.

- On a scale of 1–5, I would rate his test scores as a 5.

ESSAY

- His essay is long. Choosing one experience and really focusing on that experience, the emotions associated with it, and the outcome would be a better plan for the essay. His writing is fine and the essay is clear. It is obvious that music is his passion, and I do commend him on writing about something he really cares about and is so connected to. This is definitely a personal essay.
- On a scale of 1–5, I would rate this essay a 3+.

OVERALL

- Kenneth is a solid candidate. I believe Fairbrook is a realistic option for him. He adds geographic diversity, his musical talent is a hook, and his SAT scores make him a qualified applicant. Kenneth did interview and express a sincere interest in attending Fairbrook, so that gives him big points in the application process. The one hesitation would be his high school record. I would like to see how well he's performing in a really tough senior schedule. If he can manage to keep his grades in the B range, or even bring some grades up, that would really strengthen his application. I would wait list for right now and see what senior grades are like.

Oberlin College
by a Former Admission Officer

We might look at these three differently from other schools. First of all, Kenneth could be quite appealing to our Conservatory of Music. He appears to be an excellent talent in music. With our dual degree program between the conservatory and the college, we could satisfy his dual interest in jazz and computer science. His audition and talent level would be the key for admission to the conservatory. Though his grades are slightly below the norm for the college, we might also take into consideration his learning disability and geographic diversity. We don't see many jazz saxophone-playing applicants from North Dakota.

Robert would certainly have some academic appeal to us. His scores are below our norms, but he has good grades in a strong curriculum at a school that sends over 80% of their students on to four-year colleges. This is probably not a school we see many applicants from, so we'd have to investigate the rigor of the curriculum at the school. He has made a nice adjustment after his sport injury, and his free spirit and rock climbing interest would fit well at Oberlin. He has applied for financial aid, which is something we might look at. The alumni interview report raises little reason to get excited about him, but he would get serious consideration in committee. He might, however, end up a waitlist for financial reasons.

Makele would frustrate us on the committee. You rarely see such wonderful leadership from a student of color at a strong high school in Connecticut not known for diversity. For her to be school president, captain of the volleyball team, editor of the paper, and a full-pay student of color would make us give her a serious second look despite the grades. She's taken good courses, and it's too bad the college counselor doesn't help explain why she has struggled in some of her classes. The interview report might raise a

red flag, but there might have been a good reason for the disconnect. Makele could end up as a waitlist for us, with the hope that senior grades might give us a reason to look at her again if we opened up spaces in May.

Tufts University

by David Kochman, Brooklyn Chair, Tufts Alumni Admissions Program (TAAP)

Makele Johnson is the star of the three, but has some red flags. I am sure that reasonable minds would differ on which of the three to admit. Some like me are "wowed" by her potential and are willing to overlook her inconsistent academic performance including several Cs, while I am sure that others will be unable to see beyond the Cs and pick one of the other two candidates who certainly are the safer choices, particularly Robert who has a stellar academic record and expressed the most profound interest by applying early decision as a legacy. I would pick Makele if I had only one student of the three to admit. My reasoning and a discussion of all three candidates follows.

Makele

Brilliant at English and writing and at best inconsistent otherwise, Makele poses the greatest challenge of the three to properly evaluate. A college has to want the student who runs her high school. She has won the "Extracurricular Triple Crown": Editor in Chief of the School Newspaper, President of the Senior Class, and Captain of a sport—volleyball—and this is not at a small school. She has about 350 classmates which makes it all the more outstanding that she has three leadership positions. She has to be extraordinarily talented, able to multitask and budget time, and have an amazing ability to work well with others while at the same time being both popular and a leader.

Her recommendations show that "she does it all," she is "charismatic," and academically, at least in English, she has "sparks of brilliance" and is among the finest students in an experienced teacher's career. Her personal essay was thoughtful, mature, and well written. Her inconsistent grades in a most demanding curriculum (with probably too many APs) show that she isn't perfect and frankly may have bitten off more than she could chew, but the academic ability is certainly there; and, as she matures and learns to pace herself, she likely will do just fine academically. Some may also be put off by her possible lack of interest in Fairbrook as evidenced by her not calling back the interviewer. I can't explain that, but I am willing to overlook the lack of returning phone calls as teenage immaturity that she will outgrow in college—just like her email handle of "volleygirl" was not mature and polished. Of the three, Makele has the potential to be a star on the college campus. She will be involved in many activities and likely will rise to a leadership position, plus her charisma and abilities will make her an asset in the classroom, adding to class discussions and overall campus intellectual life.

Robert

Robert is the safe choice of the three. He is obviously a talented and consistently excellent student. He has excellent grades in a rigorous curriculum. He is focused on biology and zoology and clearly has a demonstrated interest (somewhat short of passion in my view) for science and the outdoors. He has a strong sense of community and strikes me as a person with compassion for others, particularly as demonstrated by his experience in Mexico living with a family and helping improve community sanitation. To me, Robert has certain red flags. He is quiet and reserved and does not appear to be a potential leader. His involvement with extracurriculars seems relatively light when compared to the other two. He seems like a nice, smart young man who will do well in college, but I don't see him as the same type of active learner and potential participant in school life as Makele. He won't add nearly as much to the college class, based on his high school record. He does not seem to have the spark or passion.

Kenneth

Kenneth is a very good, but not excellent student who has overcome a learning disability to have a strong academic record, particularly in a rigorous demanding academic course load. His strengths are that he has been described as energetic and creative—two adjectives that will serve him well in college. Beyond being a valued member of the basketball and baseball teams, Kenneth also has a demonstrated passion for music/jazz and no doubt will continue with music on campus. Kenneth takes on a lot and does well with everything he does. I also was impressed by his persistence in repeatedly trying out for the Disney Band—other less dedicated high school–age musicians might have given up. Kenneth is a doer and a finisher as evidenced by his consistent participation in his sports and music throughout his high school career. Ken would make a nice choice for a college, but I don't see the same potential brilliance in Ken that I see in Makele.

The University of Chicago

by Sonia Arora, Assistant director of Admission

Makele

Makele attends a good public school in Connecticut. Her testing is strong; her critical reading score hits a high

700. That said, her academic performance has been spotty. She's ranked 87/320, outside of the top 20%. Makele's coursework is difficult (four AP classes this year alone), but she earned a string of Cs in both her junior and senior years. She shows signs of brilliance, apparently, when she has time to do her work. Other major commitments on campus, including leadership in publication, athletics, and student government, get in the way, though they are an important outlet for her. Makele has grown into quite the popular leader on campus and would pursue a lot of opportunities and have a big impact on our campus, too. English is her strong suit, and her 9th- and 11th-grade English teacher is extremely supportive. It's worth noting that her English teacher checked her down for disciplined work habits, and also that our interviewer had a difficult time making contact with Makele until an adult was involved. Perhaps she's not interested in being a student at Fairbrook? Overall, Makele is a weaker student who has trouble balancing her priorities. I would recommend that we look at her again later in the year to see if she's grown out of some of these problematic habits. She will have some good options for college, and we might want to take her in the end.

Robert

Bob is our rock-climber—biologist-zoologist legacy applicant. He attends an independent school in Arizona where he is in the top 10% of his class of 182. He's taking three AP classes this year and took 1 AP last year. Though he is checked down for extracurricular activities (he never really got involved in his high school community after he injured himself in athletics), he is supported by his school. I don't see him getting very involved in our community either, as he enjoys more solitary activities. Nature seems like a big part of his life—his personal statement was a nicely organized piece about being on a mountain and seeing his usual habitat from a different perspective. A thoughtful one, for sure. Bob's English teacher shows us an active student (he's no slouch) who almost mischaracterizes himself as timid. Bob is definitely interested in being at Fairbrook, and he's qualified to be here. He might not be a high-impact community member, but he will do fine academically. I'm worried that he will miss nature and feel a little isolated on campus. All said, however, we should consider him a strong candidate in the pool.

Kenneth

Kenneth attends a parochial school and will be the first in his family to go to college. His testing is solid and balanced. His four-year commitment to athletics is good; the fact that he started Jazz Band at his school shows his proclivity for leadership. I'm glad that he chose to write about the saxophone for his personal statement, highlighting his passion for music and growth as a performer. Kenneth is mostly a B student in a fairly rigorous curriculum, though not the most rigorous the school offers. His grades take a bit of a turn in eleventh grade; we even see a C in the second semester. The school supports him strongly, not enthusiastically, and Kenneth's college counselor discusses his musical abilities and interest in web page design more than his academic potential. The teacher rec (math) is warm and supportive, as is the interview report. Overall, however, I think Kenneth is going to read a little softer in our pool. The downward trend in his grades also concerns me.

Wesleyan University

by Jami Silver, Associate Dean
of Admission

I am not sure any of the students would be competitive for admission at Wesleyan; at least without seeing senior grades.

Makele

A very active student, but her grades decline as the rigor increases. Her essay/personal statement is less personal and more about her aunt and the kind of woman she was. There are some questions that are raised about her personal qualities and interest in our community, particularly due to the concerns of setting up the interview and her personal statement. While she is in a competitive academic program, her performance is not up to par.

Robert

A legacy kid who clearly wants to be on campus. He has solid grades and a strong academic profile yet seems like he would have little impact outside the classroom. He has shown that he has potential in new areas of interest, such as zoology, which helps support him as a contender at a residential community.

Kenneth

A strong first-generation kid who continues to overcome obstacles and challenges. He is an accomplished musician who shows signs of soaking up opportunities. He would need solid 12th-grade grades to be competitive, especially since that seems to be his toughest program. Strong personal qualities and seems like someone who is worth the risk.

B

Sample Essays

Most colleges require an essay to be submitted as part of the application. (A few very good, large state schools—like Arizona State—do not, but most do.) We wanted to bring you a selection of really good essays, essays that worked for the admission officers at several top colleges.

We've included essays written by successful applicants for the class of 2014—at a range of very selective colleges. The first group are from Tufts University and are what the Tufts admission folks refer to as "exceptional essays." The remaining essays were written by kids who got into Northwestern, the University of Michigan, Duke, and NYU.

An important note: These essays worked for these applicants and should not be copied, imitated, or aped in any way. Your essay should reflect you!

Exceptional Essays from Tufts Class of 2014

Tufts University, a terrific and very selective university just outside Boston, has given us permission to reproduce some really good—and successful—essays. They were written by students who applied to Tufts in 2009/2010.

Students *always* ask about the essay. Topic selection, length, style, message—there is so much to think about. We realize that it is not an easy process, to say the least. So it is our pleasure to share with you eight exceptional essays penned by members of the Tufts Class of 2014.

So why do we love these essays?

These pieces captured the distinct voices of these young men and women, and forged a powerful and affective human connection with their readers. They truly helped to set these students apart in our applicant pool. They compelled, magnetized, and fascinated us. They demonstrated creativity and illuminated curiosity.

We are infinitely proud of these students and the essays they wrote. We hope that these works will inspire you to find your unique voice as you craft your words and stories in the months to come.

—The Tufts University Admissions Officers

Christopher Drakeford

Yorktown Heights, NY
Yorktown High School

QUESTION:

"Kermit the Frog famously lamented, 'It's not easy being green.' Do you agree?"

"It's not easy being green." In today's world, green is everywhere from supermarkets to car showrooms. But to be honest, I had not given much thought to green until I was introduced to Ayr Rand and the Clover food truck, a green business on the campus of MIT. Through an internship at MIT's Community Innovator's Lab, a research center in the department of Urban Studies, I created and filmed a short documentary about the Clover truck.

Ayr, an MIT graduate, gave up a job on Wall Street to create his dream business, the Clover Food Truck. He found innovative ways to deal with the many obstacles that green businesses face, such as limited investment funds for green technologies, limited customer interest in green products, and customer unwillingness to pay a premium for the products. Clover actually did not promote the fact that it was green, but instead concentrated on building a base of regular customers by making great food. While many people might shy away from a menu stacked with vegan sandwiches, the truth is that the food was simply delicious. In fact, several customers we interviewed were not even aware of Clover's commitment to sustainability. Clover's prices were comparable to, if not better, than those of other local eateries. Ayr was able to maintain lower prices by purchasing his organic food from local suppliers, avoiding the cost of shipping food from further away.

Every aspect of Clover's operation was designed with sustainability in mind. The truck itself was built with many recycled materials, such as the counter made from a local red oak that fell during a storm. It was equipped with energy-efficient appliances, and the staff used less than 20 gallons of water a day in food preparation. In addition, the truck was fueled partially by biodiesel (french-fry oil).

As a person who had little prior knowledge about sustainability, I learned a great deal from Ayr and the Clover truck. I learned that sustainability has many faces, whether it is wind power and other alternate forms of energy, or the little green things we can do each day. I now find that I am much more conscious about habits such as recycling, switching to fluorescent lights and turning them off when not in use, and using less water. I spent very little time thinking about such things before my experience with Clover.

The daily lunchtime rush to the truck is evidence that Ayr has overcome the challenge of successfully establishing a green business. It is his philosophy that "businesses have a greater impact on society than anything." Businesses such as the Clover Truck can pave the way to a greener future. Our short "clover movie" can be found at http://techtv.mit.edu/videos/3760-the-clover-philosophy.

William H. Farris

South Chatham, MA
Chatham Jr./Sr. High School

QUESTION:
Common App Choices
" . . . who will blame him if he does homage to the beauty of the world?"
—Virginia Woolf,
To the Lighthouse

I never planned on going to college. Until junior year, I had a fixed vision of my future art school. It was the beacon shining at the end of my high school career, my light at the end of the tunnel. But the torrential, unpredictable, ever-changing currents and waves of high school had a different destination in mind. With a change of the tide, the end of my high school career metamorphosed. The result: myself as a future-English major, applying to some of the best schools in the country. The catalyst for this change was Virginia Woolf and her brief but expansively profound novel *To the Lighthouse*.

The only term I can use to try and define what happened

after reading *To the Lighthouse* is a "literary epiphany." Her acute sense of humanity and her ability to capture the human mind moved me. It was a type of enlightenment reminiscent of a Transcendentalist enraptured by nature. I knew the second I finished that book that I had, before then, been envisioning a future not meant for me. The idea of art school was now alien. Although Virginia Woolf died tragically decades before my birth, I feel like I had just met my best friend in the pages of *To the Lighthouse*. I could feel her personality, her psyche—her being—in every fiber of paper, telling me to study English. In fervor, I bought every Virginia Woolf novel I could find, poring over them like the sun beaming over a sandy beach.

Although I had abandoned art school, art never left my interest—I plan on pursuing art in college and after. Books just speak to me. It's the only way I can describe my reaction to books. They speak to me as if they were a psychologist and I was a patient—they have the same cathartic effect as a psychologist or a best friend. Books are my best friends. I love art, and I love creating art, but books will always be my passion. They are the art of art.

My life wouldn't be the same if I hadn't read something by Virginia Woolf. She started a chain reaction in me, and a chain reaction in what I was reading. Virginia Woolf cascaded into Toni Morrison, into Walt Whitman, into William Faulkner, and into my James Joyce—I'm writing my senior thesis paper on *Ulysses*, and it not only reaffirms my belief in books and the human nature of books, but highlights, underlines it, bolds it, and magnifies it. And I thank Virginia Woolf.

Thank you Virginia, for your writing. Thank you for your sincere commitment to writing in a truly human form. Thank you *To the Lighthouse*. Mostly, Virginia, thank you for navigating the last two years of my high school career—thank you, Virginia: thank you.

Melissa A. Ferrari

Winchester, VA
Phillips Academy

QUESTION:
Common App Choices

I carefully placed her torso and legs in a black trash bag to bring her to the sanctuary. Carrying her across campus with her head in my hand, I was conscious of the strange looks I was getting. Seeing the shape of her bony spine pushing through the thin trash bag, I could not shake the eerie feeling that I was carrying a corpse. The grey, empty woods felt very surreal as I stumbled through dense rhododendrons and traced the creek to an old stone bridge. I had to chase several hands and one of her legs down the creek but I finally succeeded in assembling her.

The Concept

For my studio art class, our assignment was to create an installation in the Andover Bird Sanctuary that would interact with its wooded environment. Conceptually, I was drawn to an idea that is explored in The Bhagavad-Gita: people should strive to attach themselves to a process rather to an outcome. I decided to create a sculpture out of wax because of the material's vulnerable, temporary nature. I envisioned a girl sitting cross-legged, thoughtfully looking into a creek as if she was searching for something. As I sketched, she evolved into a life-sized candle formed with a wax skin and a wick rising from her top vertebrae. The expired wick would highlight the physical impermanence of the wax girl. I would cast my friends' hands in wax and scatter the hands around the piece. These hands would represent shed vestiges of the girl's past, like exfoliated cicada shells.

The Process

Wax was a foreign medium to me and I had no idea how to craft a life size human form. But with growing excitement, I ordered fifty pounds of candle wax and a double boiler and acquired some old wire lath that had been rusting away in my art teacher's studio for ten years. Modeling my sculpture out of lath, I developed a method of applying the wax by scooping gel-like film off the boiled down wax and carefully layering it onto the wire. I sat in the dark art room for hours each night reheating and reworking the lines and curves of her spine and face. For the next month, the entire first floor of the art building smelled like Yankee Candle.

Despite my initial attempt to focus on the process of construction rather than the finished product, as the end of her creation neared, I realized that I had become very attached to my wax girl. She was a little creepy though; her eye sockets were hollow, and a jet black synthetic wig coated in dripping wax framed her harsh features. Her cold, ghostly skin had the intense fragrance of eucalyptus. I positioned her head at a strained, tilted angle. In this uncomfortable position, I almost expected her to shift her weight a little. She had a large presence in the crowded art room, and when other students walked in they jumped upon seeing the ghoulish white figure perched on the counter.

The Installation/Critique

I carried my wax girl out to a creek in the sanctuary and installed her at the water's edge. With my classmates standing on the opposite bank from us, I lit the wick and a tall flame leapt up from her spine. The class was both fascinated and perplexed by her. I stumbled, trying to explain what I had created.

The Travesty

When my critique was finished, our class walked through the woods discussing the other installations. An hour later, returning back to my sculpture I spotted two school security vans parked next to the creek. My heart dropped—oh god, what had I done? I knew the candle was extinguished . . . so nothing was on fire . . . right? What kind of trouble had I gotten myself into? Had they hurt her? I saw two uniformed officers, and I yelled repeatedly to them, "Can I help you?"

Is this yours?

Yes. Is there a problem?

What is it?

My art project. I'm in the senior studio art class. We're doing installations in the sanctuary and today was the critique . . . problem? My teacher is right up on the hil . . .

At first they looked grim; then the mustached officer burst out laughing. "This is great!" He explained that a group of freshmen girls had seen my piece from the path and called campus security sobbing and screaming that there was a lady in the water. There had also been multiple complaints from runners. Prank? Voodoo? . . . Dead body? The guard snapped a picture on his phone. "This is just great. Could you take it apart though? It's scaring the hell out of everyone."

Abdiel Garcia

Los Angeles, CA
Brentwood School

QUESTION:
Are we alone?

We are alone in the realm of space-time. We are new to the notion that we are not alone in the universe and that we are not the most significant planet to the galaxy or the solar system. Within our own planet, we are dispersed by the width of the oceans and the humid thickness of deserts. In my own city, buildings tower over-stressed pedestrians and ill-tempered drivers, and the life inside those building walls is further broken down into the isolation that accumulates inside a topless cubicle. The night composes half of our time on Earth, and we spend most of it on our own. We dwell in dreams, completely unaware of the world outside our heads. During the day, we spend the day working for our families and ourselves. Many work in their own isolated space for concentration. The day ends and the next one begins. A routine is established. The end comes for us all, and it is in those final moments that we brace ourselves for what may lie ahead, and we acknowledge that we are alone. All cosmic creations remain after one person is gone, and the rest of humanity does, too.

Our world functions in respect to the laws of physics, as do all the other planets and stars and meteors. In our routines, we become disconnected at times from each other. Yet, from overlooking the universe, the things we do have no great significance. There is no one out there to please. There is no one to save or no one to save us. We are alone for eternity, or until the sun disposes of us. For centuries men have studied the skies and pondered what lies out there. Such an interest we have in life forms outside our planet! It excites many to read alarming news of potential life forms in other planets, but discovering a plant in Mars does not change the fact that we are alone. We do not accept plants as members of the domain of rational beings. Discovering plants or dirt or water only feeds our imaginations, but it does not have any importance. The universe is what it is, regardless of what we know about it. We are not meant to discover the secrets of the universe, and we must learn to live in limited knowledge. As far as we know, there is nothing out there, and we should be satisfied to know that there are another six billion creatures like us who can benefit more from our assistance to one another than our worries about being a lone planet. Being alone can be appreciated. We should be thankful that we were given excess beauty, wonders, and space for our planet. In terms of our social lives, we have the

Hazal Kansu

Istanbul, Turkey
Robert College

QUESTION:

Common App Choices

power to choose whether or not we want to be alone.

I have the kind of curiosity that keeps bugging me whenever I glimpse something that I don't know much about. I'm obsessed with my friends' "Favorite Music" on Facebook; I make lists of the artists and songs I don't know and then listen to them all to figure out which ones I need in my library. I can't get enough of edgy artists. When I first became obsessed with Dali's paintings, I nagged my friend's grandfather, a professor, until he got us into the university's library so that we could research what ants, crooks, etc. symbolize in his paintings. A project I was preparing for Art History is about Goya's sketches, and for a while that's all I looked at. Then came photographers. This time it was my photography teacher who guided me through different photographers and their styles; after I've explored Sebastiao Salgado's documentary works, I found the courage to pick up my camera and take such photos in rural Turkey. Another interest of mine surfaced after I visited the Einstein exhibition. I've never been a physics lover, but thereafter I simply had to learn more about how his mind worked. I visited the exhibition several times and read a bunch of books that explain his ideas to laymen.

While my obsessions may be many, they're not shallow. I'm not as curious now about Dali as I once was, but that's because I've developed a solid core of knowledge about him, making it time to move on to something new. I figure that, in life, we'll get the chance to become an expert on one or two things. That's already exciting, but equally exciting is the chance to learn enough about many things that you can have a great conversation with an expert—and learn a whole bunch more—when you come across one. So beware experts at Tufts: I may be knocking on your door!

Michael D. Marks

Bethesda, MD
Sidwell Friends School

QUESTION:
Common App Choices

My favorite book has no author. It has no chapters and little text. Some would say this book has no plot and no characters, but I know otherwise. This book actually reflects the physical and political history of our world, covers hundreds of nations, thousands of ethnic groups, and billions of people.

This book is the 1987 *Rand McNally Universal World Atlas,* a tall green volume with a worn cover and loose binding. I am enamored of almost all atlases and even individual maps, but what makes this particular atlas so special is the impact it had on me as a young child. I vividly remember discovering it for the first time on a bookshelf in our house. When I opened it, I discovered pages upon pages of maps—maps of every region and country in the world and every U.S. state and Canadian province.

I was entranced. I spent hours pouring over the pages of the atlas that first day. I wanted know more about where I fit in the world.

As my interest in geography grew, I amassed a collection of atlases and other books related to geography. My other favorite was a world factbook that had a small dossier on each country. I remember discovering, much to my surprise, that various country borders shown in the 1998 factbook were different from the ones in my 1987 atlas. Germany was no longer divided, Czechoslovakia no longer united, and a tiny country called Eritrea had popped up on what used to be Ethiopia's coastline. My curiosity about these changes led me to begin reading history books, and I soon learned the two fields complemented each other well. When I read about the American Civil War, I often would open my atlas to the map of Virginia. And when our family visited Gettysburg, Antietam, and other Civil War battlefields, I intensely studied the maps of these battles.

I also began to notice how geography shaped current world events. Every four years, I tracked the presidential electoral votes on a map of my own, and every two years I made lists of the key congressional districts and Senate seats. I started following the progress of the American campaigns in Afghanistan and Iraq in my atlas. To find out more about world events, I began to voraciously read *The Washington Post, The New York Times,* and *The Economist.* My interest in geography also stimulated my interest in languages. After discovering that so many places had Spanish as their native tongue, I decided learning the language was a necessity. And when I read about the increasing economic and political power of China in *The Economist,* I realized that knowledge of Mandarin Chinese would be a valuable skill in our globalizing world, so I endeavored to learn Mandarin as well.

Ever since I was very young, I loved reading. I have read many powerful and influential books (fiction and non-fiction) that have helped shaped the way I look at the world, but none had been more important than my first atlas. I still return to it regularly and imagine I always will.

Alexander Polyakov

Norwalk, CT
St. Luke's School

QUESTION:
Common App Choices

"That's Alex. He's from Russia." This is the way in which I'm usually introduced to people (and if it's not, I can always be sure someone will find a way to work it into the subsequent conversation). While it's a great conversation starter, I've always been baffled as to the significance of my "being from Russia." To me, it's never been worthy of "introduction icebreaker." I don't feel that it's affected me on a level deeper than inspiring the occasional joke about my being a Communist or eating borscht.

Contrary to (what I presume to be) the belief of these people who introduce me in such a manner, my family and I do not participate in profoundly Russian ethnic activities. I would provide examples, but I honestly don't even know what they would

be. We speak Russian at home, but out of convenience, and not a sense of cultural preservation. Most of our dinners consist of either pasta with red sauce, or steak (and occasionally, McDonald's), not borscht, beets or bear meat. I know next to nothing about Russian literature, art, cinema, or music. Most importantly, however, I don't feel any sort of affinity for other Russians. My Russian heritage really only betrays itself in my father's thick accent, and in my mother's tendency to use broken English when she sends me text messages. And even then, it's stranger that she sends me texts than it is that they're in broken English. It seems that I've fully assimilated into the American way of life.

And yet, when asked my nationality, I hesitate.

My family came to America in 1997, when I was five years old. After a month of being here, I was enrolled in the local public school's kindergarten class (not knowing a word of English in kindergarten is a traumatizing experience for a five year old). I was forced to abandon five years of cultural conditioning, and start over in a foreign country. For me, doing so at five meant that I hadn't yet come to fully feel a sense of Russian identity. More importantly, it meant that I was too old to foster the foundations of a sense of American identity. From the very beginning, I felt as an outsider. We still spoke Russian at home, and hadn't yet adapted to this new country. Because I got my start with an out-of-place mindset, I've grown up with it. What's resulted from my transplantation is confusion. I don't see myself as Russian any longer, a fact about which I'm ashamed. I don't see myself as American, either, whatever that may be. Most of the time, I feel like an outsider looking in, regarding both of my nationalities. Sometimes, there are jokes on Russian TV shows that I don't understand, simply because they're things that only people who've grown up in the country would get. Other times, my inherited sense of Soviet pragmatism doesn't quite fit in with the accepted American idealism, and I find myself at odds with those around me. I feel a sense of displacement: I have nothing to look back to, since I've abandoned one undeveloped identity, and yet I haven't really had a full chance to embrace the other. Yes, I have a bit of both, but not enough of either to feel a sense of national identity.

More than confusion, though, this experience has left me with a heightened sense of objectivity. Because there's so little attachment, I find myself able to see through the perspectives of both nationalities. My Russian pragmatism works well with my American idealism; in a way, they balance each other out. Being between two distinct sensibilities has given me the advantage of understanding both of them, without being dominated by either. Convictions and beliefs are, to an extent, governed by nationality. I have the fortune of being able to formulate mine by drawing from two different pools. Though it still chafes (a little) to be introduced as "the boy from Russia," I've come to realize that I'm fortunate; not having the restriction of attachment to any one country is . . . liberating.

Meysam H. Rajani

Dar es Salaam, Tanzania
The International School
of Tanganyika

QUESTION:
Common App Choices

The True Potential of Mathematics

I stared at the top of the tree; curious and occupied, "Why are you staring at the tree?" My friend asked. My reply sounded strange, if not bizarre. "I'm trying to figure out the angle of elevation of that tree top from this point." That is my story; I try to relate everything I see to mathematics, be it the number of grains in my rice bowl, or the trajectory followed by my urine. I like to think that the millions of cells in my body have been conquered by numbers, the simple language of mathematics. I believe numbers lie at the core of everything, even in the fields that seem to be miles away from math such as the social sciences.

The universal existence of mathematics and its reputation as the least refutable science always intrigues me.

Yes, we humans have our differences; race, sex, religion, ethnicity, experiences, perspectives, opinions, and the list carries on infinitely, but we have one thing in common; the science of math. Nations do not fight wars because of disagreement over Pythagoras' theorem nor do they dispute over the fundamentals of Algebra. Globalization has forced us to dissolve our dissimilarities and live with them; the idea that these discrepancies can be ignored is absurd according to me. However, if we can all hold on to a string, a string so powerful that nobody dare refute its authority, we CAN overlook these disparities. I believe mathematics is that string that we are all searching for.

The frustrations of being in a developing world where problems are rarely tackled with logic have increased my passion for Mathematics. I often question why Tanzania, even with its great potential is one of the least developed countries in the world. Despite the great number of resources, many problems still exist in the country. Power cuts are one of the many aggravating things that occur here. Recently, a power rationing scheme attributed to maintenance and repair of power lines was publicized in the government gazette. These schemes have become more frequent currently. Halfway through working on a school paper, the electricity would cut off. The rationing schedule given in the paper was merely for decoration. The cuts were random, and even more frequent than what was published. When the electricity providers would be called, they would say, 'we are working on it,' which was translated into, 'you are not going to have power for the next 12 hours'. I wondered what it would be like, living in the outskirts of Dar-es-salaam, where they hardly got power throughout the year. I considered myself fortunate. The government's tax revenues amount to a couple of hundred million dollars every month; this fact coupled with the resources Tanzania boasts of made me think. I wondered why half of the nation would slip into darkness for almost half a day three times a week. Most people blamed it on the leaders of the country, claiming they are corrupt and not capable. However, the reality is much simpler. The people here lack skills in one of mathematics main aspects; logic.

Common sense would tell us, that Tanzania with all its gifts and capabilities is able to supply the entire country with electricity. It is sad to notice, that a big portion of the population is denied of something so essential, even though the solution to it is very simple. A mathematical revolution is what the nation requires, and I would be more than willing to be one of the propagators of this revolution.

Ten years from now, I see myself unraveling the secrets of life using the science of Mathematics. I see myself urinating at a different angle in order to reduce the corrosion of the ceramic. I see myself measuring human behavior through a formed equation or reducing poverty through careful calculations. Thinking in terms of numbers has been prevalent in my life. I intend to pursue this passion for mathematics through further studies. I dream of solving problems in areas secluded from mathematics. Yes, the idea of solving political or cultural problems through mathematical avenues may sound outrageous, but I have built an inclination, and a will that I believe shall take me a long way in this path.

Some Really Good Essay-Writing Advice

The following letter was written to a smart high school senior in response to his draft essay. The advice we offered him is probably applicable to 90% of the essays we've read over the years.

Pat,

This isn't bad at all. A couple of suggestions however.

Open it up "visually" by adding space between paragraphs. If it is too dense visually, it is harder to read and not at all appreciated by the reader. You want that admission officer reading your essay to be your advocate. You don't him/her saying, "Ugh!"

You, like 99% of the young people I come across—and 97% of older people—write LLOONNGGGG sentences. Don't!!! If you write a sentence that is more than 8 words, break it into two sentences. (I just made that number up, but you get the point.) When in doubt, break it up. When you're not in doubt, break it into two.

When I worked at Time magazine many years ago, they taught us an aphorism repeated to everyone who worked there. Henry Luce, Time's founder, said, "It is not what you put on the page that matters. It is what comes off the page into the reader's mind that counts."

Keep it simple and keep it visually open. An admission officer "might" be impressed that you can construct complex sentences correctly—although most people can't. But she will appreciate it more if you get your points across easily.

Don't make stupid errors! You did. Let someone—your mother—scrutinize every essay for typos. Typos, misspellings, improper homonyms are easy reasons to reject an applicant. Remember, virtually everyone applying is "qualified." Thus AOs are looking for reasons to reject someone. Don't give them a reason.

OK, on to the substantive part. I get it: you're the debate kid. That's good; you want to have a positioning. When they present you at the admissions meeting—and they do "present" each kid—the AO responsible for SmartKid High will say, "This is Pat Smith the kid from SmartKid who is . . . fill in the blank." Through your essays you help them fill in the blank. And through this topic you're positioned as the "debate kid."

Now I think you want to take it one step further: you want to make it a bit more memorable. Do that by giving one or two very specific examples—something they can remember. And preferably, something that makes them smile! We call it a "hook to hang their hat on." (You started to do it by describing yourself as having an Upper-West-Side Blue-state vision of the world . . . .)

Imagine how tedious it must be for an AO to read 50 earnest applications in one sitting. So you want to make yours easy to read and memorable (in a good way!).

Go back, do another draft. Open it up—either as I suggested or, preferably, as you feel comfortable doing it. And add one or two interesting, personal anecdotes.

Make it easy to read, and make it a pleasure to read.

Good luck!

Other Successful Essays

The Common App—and most colleges which don't use the Common App—ask applicants to write an essay of no fewer than 250 words. The topics for 2010–2011 are as follows:

- Evaluate a significant experience, achievement, risk you have taken, or ethical dilemma you have faced and its impact on you.

- Discuss some issue of personal, local, national, or international concern and its importance to you.

- Indicate a person who has had a significant influence on you, and describe that influence.

- Describe a character in fiction, a historical figure, or a creative work (as in art, music, science, etc.) that has had an influence on you, and explain that influence.

- A range of academic interests, personal perspectives, and life experiences adds much to the educational mix. Given your personal background, describe an experience that illustrates what you would bring to the diversity in a college community or an encounter that demonstrated the importance of diversity to you.

- Topic of your choice.

Many colleges request additional essays or ask that you address a particular topic.

Here are a few longer essays that helped contribute to the applicant's successful admission at some particularly selective schools. They were provided by our friends at A-List education, a New York–based tutoring and admissions counseling firm. You can learn more about them at www.alisteducation.com.

Northwestern University (Early Decision)

The song playing on my iPod was fading out, signaling it was time to choose another tune. I scrolled through my artists, and came upon an old song that my friends and I recorded a while ago. I pulled down the shade and momentarily thought back to when we recorded the track. The artificial atmosphere created by the cabin pressure had made my throat a bit dry and I looked around for a stewardess. Scanning the aisles, I suddenly felt my stomach rise into my chest and with a shudder I gripped the arm rest. The plane began to shake.

I caught my breath and assumed it was regular turbulence. Then the plane moved sharply to the left. I looked up at the cabin's television screen which was playing the movie *Hairspray*. Not in the mood. Besides, focusing on it was nearly impossible. I could sense anxiety wash over the passengers as the plane banked sharply yet again. A drop, followed by another roll to the right, unleashed a wave of screams—shrieks of pure terror. Not the, "Ahh, I'm on a rollercoaster and afraid but still having fun" scream, but the horrified "Am I going to die?" scream. The noises stopped, giving us a few seconds of calm to collect ourselves. I thought for a second I could actually feel my heart beating so hard it might break through my rib cage.

Another drop. No, a plummet: several seconds during which the suspended air craft dropped uncontrollably. I experienced the weightless feeling you get for a split second when landing, when the plane drops just a little bit, lifting you from your seat. Except now, it lasted for about 10 seconds, and we were three miles above the ground. Screams pierced the stiff air. My mother screamed. A noise unlike anything I had ever heard in my entire life. Just the thought of the genuine fear gripping my own mother still haunts me. The plane leveled out.

Fear and confusion filled the airplane, although there was a palpable sense of relief that we weren't yet crushed cadavers sinking towards the bottom of the Atlantic. I looked down and saw my hand gripping the arm rest. When did that happen? My knuckles were whiter than snow, and my veins stood out as if they might try to follow my beating heart right out of my body and off of that godforsaken plane. I looked over to my older brother.

He was silent, wearing a look of utter disbelief.

I took long, deep breaths in order to bring myself out of the fear-induced shock. My mother was sitting in front of me. I started stroking her hair to soothe her. She is tough by any measure, but I knew there was no way she could just shrug that one off. She looked over her left shoulder through the seatbacks. Her tear-drowned eyes looked back at me helplessly as she mouthed the words, "I love you."

"You're okay mom," I said in slow, measured tones. "We're okay."

I fell into my seatback, and couldn't move. I began to tear up as well. *Ding.* "Hello ladies and gentlemen." announced the captain from the cockpit. His voice was stern and serious, yet reassuring. "We're terribly sorry about that. We hit an updraft, a strong body of wind from a storm down below us. We've got everything under control and are out of the storm. We hope that no one got jostled around too much, and we're sending our staff around to make sure everyone is okay." Okay? He had to be kidding.

In truth, I didn't know how to feel—none of us did. I sheepishly admitted I was mad he had not given us some warning we were about to free fall for several thousand feet, but I was relieved that at least the wings still seemed to be attached and the engines still seemed to be working. I lifted up the cover to my window.

We were enveloped in stormy clouds. *It's not over,* I thought, and shoved the cover back down, as my heart began to race again.

The stewardess came around with a complementary tray of wine for the adult passengers. My father took a small plastic, single-serve cup of white wine. That's how I knew he was shaken up. He never drank white wine. He hates it. He clearly wasn't thinking straight, but his mind was on calming my mother down, who was still hysterically crying.

People started getting up out of their seats to use the bathroom, to walk around, or to check on family. I began to reflect on what had just happened.

They say that in the midst of a near-death experience, your life flashes before your eyes. Such was not the case with me. When I realized the nostalgic vignettes were not playing in my brain, *only then,* did I start to think of my life. I started to tear up a little again. What would happen if I died? Who would miss me? I began to think of random people. Not family, but other people: workers in my synagogue, my orthodontist, my doctor, my teachers. Would anybody remember me? My entire family would have been gone. I imagined the look on my relatives' faces as they opened the door to my apartment, speaking in hushed tones about the former inhabitants who had all died in a tragic plane crash. I could almost make out the chords of some clichéd cinematic dirge that would almost certainly be playing in the background.

I then began to think of who I would tell this story to and how I would tell it. Should I exaggerate, or be honest? I thought I was going to die, but in reality that was probably as likely as me winning the lottery. A smile crossed my lips. This experience could never be about what almost happened; it had to be about what I would do when my feet touched solid ground again and what I could actually make happen. At that moment, the script might have called for an inspirational denouement with a personal call to action to live my life to the fullest and save the world. But Hollywood isn't producing my life story, at least not yet.

I walked off the plane with my arms around my mother, humbly promising myself that the next time my life was supposed to be flashing before my eyes, I would see countless scenes of me doing what I love. For all of the triumphs and struggles I have had so far, thankfully, the rest of the script has not yet been written.

University of Michigan

I had been volunteering at Albert Einstein Medical Center for about three weeks and had grown comfortable with the environment. The doctors I worked for treated me with interest and respect and I was fortunate enough to listen in on many of their medical discussions. But for all that I was learning my greatest lesson came one afternoon when we returned from lunch to utter chaos: everything was in motion and everyone seemed to be running frantically through the emergency room.

Confused, I asked one of the doctors what was going on. All I could process were a barrage of red lights and a cacophony of shouts and commands. A patient had been robbed and suffered a gunshot wound to his brain. The doctor standing beside me, the man I had just seen finish a turkey club at lunch, was going to perform the surgery and attempt to save this man's life. It was surreal to witness the sudden transformation of a mundane reality into the most consequential scene of my young life.

I had never seen this doctor appear so uneasy. He was pale, sweating, and had a look on his face that could not mask his fear. I had always seen him as confident and self assured, but in that moment he was human—fragile and uncertain. I watched the doors to the OR swing closed behind him. As night approached, I went home to my family and friends, anxious but sure everything would work out.

I remember thinking at the time about moments in my life when I was forced to perform under pressure. Images of the ballet recital when I was eight and left the stage in tears floated through my mind. Somehow I found it hard to believe that my relatives still carried around any disappointment about the whole thing, considering I continued dancing long after and they got the chance to see

me perform probably more times than they could have ever wanted to. I thought about those figure skating competitions when all eyes were glued on me, but competition never scared me; in fact, it pushed me to do even better. My speeches for student government, important exams—nothing I had ever done could even come close to the kind of drama of that day.

When I returned the next morning, it was business as usual at the hospital. Naively I thought the doctor must have rescued the man from the brink of death, like they so often did on TV, but he didn't. The patient died on the operating table. I was stunned. I never even knew the patient and yet I felt like somehow I had failed him. It was ridiculous, although I couldn't help but think that here was some significant moment in my life and instead discovering a storybook ending, I found a cruel reality.

I walked aimlessly down the hallway until an elderly woman tapped me on the shoulder. "You remind me of my granddaughter." There it was, plain and simple. I had been pondering what exactly I had learned from an experience that was so obviously important, but seemed to offer no clear, understandable "lesson" for me. I first met the woman at the beginning of the summer in the nephrology unit, and we had spoken several times since. "All I want to do is see her graduate," she continued. The patient had opened up to me before, though I had never fully appreciated until right then exactly what she had been telling me.

Some lessons are learned in the classroom and some are not; some are easy to see and some are not. It took a dramatic moment in the ER to make me pay attention to a seemingly trivial moment in the hallway. I realized the big epiphany I was searching for was actually an illusion. What I had been doing all along in my life was more important than this dramatic life and death moment. Those performances and those speeches are what define me—as a student, as a daughter, as a grand-daughter. I am the sum of my experiences, not the girl in the background of someone else's final hours.

I honestly believed my college essay was supposed to be the story of some brilliant triumph, some larger than life moment when I could show off my skills or insight. I now recognize that life isn't really about those fleeting experiences; it is what we do before or after that makes us who we are. The memories we carry around may be small, but they are precious and, at just the right time, they can be exactly what we need to get us through the day.

Duke (Early Decision)

My sister collects snow globes, my cousin collects stickers and my mom collects buffalo nickels. But not me. I collect things that make me giggle, wonder, and even cringe. I collect words. *Pumpernickel. Poikilotherm. Infrastructure.* Whether stealing from a cereal box, my favorite cartoon, or even the news, I grasp onto words that let my mind wrap around fresh sounds: the silkiness of the word tranquil, the crunch of the word crisp, the romance of the word *laundromat.* My shelves may be empty, my stickers books bare, my pockets light, but my head bubbles with crazy combinations of vowels and consonants. Some people simply assemble words into sentences and paragraphs, but my love of words has defined much of my life's journey and helps me further appreciate the world we live in.

I began my most recent word collecting adventure on the bustling streets of a Beijing hutong. The moment I stepped out of the comfortable climate controlled van into the teeming alleyways of this traditional Chinese neighborhood, I was assaulted by blaring bicycle horns and staccato mandarin chatter. *Zuo ba. Xie ni. Zai jian.* The sweltering heat of the Chinese summer and the lack of affordable air-conditioning forces Hutong residents to live their lives outside, visible and audible to anyone who wanders through. As I made my way down the street for the first time, avoiding the growling stray dogs and sizzling woks, I watched shirtless old men crouching in the alleys, screaming at each other over an aggressive game of chess and vendors barking out prices on everything from ancient tea pots to dentures. Navigating the crush of the crowd, I tried to listen to every voice that bombarded me from what seemed to be every direction at once. *Bao zi. Luo ma. Bing hong cha.* My collection grew by the second.

Later that night, as we walked back through the grittiness of the hutong, the smog above us turned dark, and drops began to fall. In a matter of seconds, the clouds unleashed a downpour and we raced through the alley trying to make it back to our hostel before we had to swim there. But, as soon as the rain had reached ankle level, it was obvious that the storm drains had overflowed and our walking path became the sewage's path as well. So on this first night in China, our weary group of students trudged through a filthy soup in the heart of Beijing.

Overcome by dirt and exhaustion, we happily collapsed onto the dingy sofas back at the home of our host mother. She welcomed us with a warm smile, freshly brewed green tea, and the familiar greeting, *"Ni hao ma?"* At first, I was too busy greedily downing my tea to offer any kind of answer. Then, as I tried to arrange the right words in my head, I paused. It was strange, because this wasn't a new phrase to me; in fact, it was the first thing I was ever asked in Chinese, how are you? And from my first days in class I had been captivated by the sound of the answers: *hen hao, bu hao or ma ma hu hu.* But in that moment, these three phrases that were once so simple, seemed to take on greater meaning. I looked through the window into the hutong where I'd be living for the next few weeks, at my host's smiling eyes, and down at the brown goo streaming through the perforated holes of my sneakers. Although I was muddy and tired, I wouldn't have wanted to be standing there any other way: ready to take on the challenges that lay ahead, excited to be living in this world which seemed so alien to me, and surprisingly okay with getting dirty.

That night I added the question to my ever-growing collection of words; words that were now about so much more than just sounds. They were about what sprouted from them: the differences in culture I was able to observe, the experiences I learned from and the relationships I formed along the way. They are my souvenirs, memories I can carry with me wherever I go.

I have often been told that so much of life is fleeting, yet I still catch myself smiling every time I say *pumpernickel.* Perhaps what I've been told is true, and the reason I really, deeply love collecting words is that on some level I believe they have the power to connect me with a world outside myself—even if that world offers nothing grander than a sincere, "How are you?"

NYU (Early Decision)

I like watching reruns of *The Wonder Years*. I like taking pictures with foreboding subway-dwellers. I like smelling the pages of a new book. I like walking aimlessly along Riverside Drive with my friends in search of some inevitably disappointing house party. I like a good flick. I like chicken parmesan. I like cruising about the Internet for interesting, gimmicky, YouTube-esque videos. But most of all, I like listening to outdated, cheesy music that would be grounds for execution by way of guillotine among my contemporaries.

For a while, I was satisfied with all these idiosyncratic tidbits of self-definition; that is until college application time reared its ugly head. I knew the day would come eventually, but it always seemed so distant to me. "This can't be real," I thought. "College is for 'big kids.'" Despite my hesitations, though, the admissions process was here and there was no stopping her.

After I recovered from the initial shock, I went straight to the drawing boards. What do colleges want to know about me? How can I make myself stand out? Then, as if imbued with the all-knowing powers of a divine spirit, the answer struck me like a blow to the face: I could write about that life altering trip I took to that impoverished, third-world country last summer. "Brilliant!" I concluded. "They'll think I'm some sort of magnanimous crusader!" There was just one teensy-weensy drawback: I have never been to an impoverished, third world country. Oh well, on to the next idea. How about I write an evocative piece on my toil with adversity? I'll seem sensitive without seeming vulnerable, poignant without seeming sentimental. This is great; I think I'm finally making substantial headway. Pulitzer, here I come! Alas, there's trouble in paradise after all. I have never faced true adversity. Sure, I've had my fair share of ebbs and flows, but don't we all? My problems are not severe enough to merit a page's worth of writing.

All hope was rapidly waning. Writer's block had seized me by the throat. Bereft of even a halfway decent idea, I decided to call it a night. But, ironically enough, it was at that precise moment when inspiration finally struck. I had something of an epiphany: I am not defined by the trips I take; I am not defined by hardships I've overcome. Neither my character nor my value can be reduced or adequately illustrated by a single event. Instead, I am a fusion of all my little penchants. I am that guy who watches reruns of *The Wonder Years;* I am that guy with bad taste in music (and so on and so forth). Of course, as I get older, I plan on making my mark, but for now, I am completely content with my humble, adolescent life. Bear in mind that I am only 17 years old. It would be shameful to take myself too seriously. Nothing I've done or seen is important enough to warrant further elaboration. In sum, then, I am a mere shopping list.

Index

A

academic hook, 171–172. *See also* hook
academic index (AI), 195–197
academic major, changing, 92
acceptance(s). *See also* gap year; transferring to different college; waitlist
  additional research on school(s), 241–247
  committing before May 1, 243–244
  consulting with parents, 244–246
  dealing with other students', 250
  revisiting campus(es), 242
  sending a deposit, 246–247
ACT. *See* SAT/ACT
activity hook, 172–174
admission committee, 179
admission constituencies, 46–52
admission decisions. *See also* decisions, awaiting
  acceptances, 241–246, 251
  alternative plans, 258–264
  appealing, 252
  arrival of, 240–241
  awaiting gracefully, 237–240
  committing by May 1, 243–244
  consulting with parents, 244–246
  continuing research, 241–247
  improving odds/chances, 5
  rejections, 253–254
  sending deposit, 246–247
  waitlist, 247–251
admission officer(s)
  establishing personal relationship with, 182
  factors considered in rejecting applications, 4
  general discussion, 42–45
  insights into review process, 68–75
  objectives for visiting high schools, 67–68

  using social media in admission process, 45, 75
admissions
  categorizing applicants, 58–63
  competition among students, 66–67
  considerations for admitting students, 58–66
  financial aid and, 228–230
  front loading of, 129
  myths regarding, 3–10
  review process, 67–75
  statistics, interpreting, 7–8
  statistics for popular colleges, 41
  yield, 52–55
advanced placement (AP) class, 22–24
affirmative action programs, 46, 60, 63
Agriculture and Life Sciences School, Cornell, 160
AI (academic index), 195–197
AIAW (Association for Intercollegiate Athletics for Women), 203
Alfred University, admission officers' objectives, 68
A-List Education tutoring firm, 34
alumni
  as admission constituency, 47–48
  as resource for researching colleges, 90
alumni interview, 103
American University, learning disability support, 32
Amherst College, 41, 68–69, 196, 255
AP (advanced placement) class, 22–24
appealing rejection, 252
applicants
  attracting, 12
  categorizing, 58–63
  first-generation, 60, 168
  legacy, 48, 59, 168–170
  myth about qualification, 8

early decision statistics, 130–131
high school course completion
   expectations, 19
policy for legacy applicants, 169
public relations, 50
Buckley Amendment, 183

C

campus-based scholarship, 227
Campus Pride, 96
campus tour, 44, 98, 101–102,
   263–264. *See also* visiting colleges
case studies
   applicants, 266–286
   extracurricular hook, 174
   college reactions to applicants,
      286–302
categorizing applicants, 58–63
checklist, positioning and packaging,
   181
choosing college. *See also* visiting
   colleges
   accounting for possible change
      in academic major, 92
   arts, 94
   climate, 94
   community, 93–94
   competitive attitude, 93
   compiling list, 80–82
   cost, 92
   distance from home, 93
   distribution requirements, 92
   family involvement, 79
   final list, 118
   grades and test scores, 79–80
   Greek life, 94
   internships, 94
   location, 93
   music, 94
   options for studying abroad, 94
   overview, 78–79
   political orientation, 94
   ranking colleges, 108–115
   ranking yourself, 116–117
   researching schools, 82–91
   sexual orientation, 94
   sports, 95
   theater, 94
Cicero, 146

Classical High School, 62
coaches. *See also* athletic recruiting
   as admission constituency, 47
   role in admissions decision, 64
Colgate College 130–131
college advisor, 136–137
College Board, 220
College Division schools. *See* Division
   II (College Division) schools
College Essay Organizer, 145
college evaluation worksheet,
   110–115
College of the Atlantic, 39
college newspaper, 90
College Prowler, 38, 83
College Scholarship Service (CSS)
   Profile, 216–217
college(s)
   admission constituencies, 45–51
   appealing to student's
      preferences, 15
   as businesses, 15
   as political institutions, 16
   gatekeepers, 42–44
   guides, 38–40, 84
   personality, 13
   "selective," 38
   selectivity of, 40–41
   what they don't want you to
      know, 11–16
Colorado College, 102
Columbia University, 41, 130–131,
   146, 160
Common App (Common
   Application)
   extracurricular activities,
      151–152, 174
   overview, 158–159
   supplemental essay, 148
   video essay, 147
   view on score choice, 28
community, factor in choosing
   college, 93–94
community service, 65, 156–157
competition
   among colleges, 12, 14
   among student applicants, 66–67
   financial aid, 217
   strategy for dealing with, 6–7

"value proposition" of college, 7
Ivy League colleges
    athlete recruitment process,
        193–194
    athletic recruiting, 195–197
    defined, 39
    "feeder" schools for, 61–62
    role of athletic staff in admissions
        decisions, 47
    SAT writing sample, 27

J

job experience, value of, 152–157
Johns Hopkins University, 71,
    289–290
Juniata College, 71
junior colleges, late admittance, 254

K

Kaplan, 33, 45
Kenyon College, 130–131

L

Lafayette College, 71–72, 130–131
Lawrenceville preparatory school,
    61–62
leadership skills
    emphasizing, 151–152
    as factor in admissions decision,
        65–66
learning disabilities (LDs)
    extended time for SAT/ACT, 31
    factor in testing environment, 31
    finding supportive colleges, 83
    revealing, 32–33
legacy applicant, 48, 54, 59, 168–170
letter of interest, 133
letters of reference, 5
liberal arts colleges, 14
lifers, admission directors, 42–43
"likely letter," 240
loans. *See also* financial aid
    parent PLUS, 226
    private, 226

state education, 226
student, 224–226
locals, applicants identified as, 62

M

Macalester College, 72
major, changing, 92
Marist College, 32
marketing
    college, 14
    using financial aid as tool, 54–55
master list, 79, 82
matching services, scholarships, 227
mean scores, SAT scores compared
    to, 124–125
merit scholarships, 190, 214
Michigan State University, 64
Middlebury College, 196
midyear school report, 132, 235–236
military work-study programs,
    222–223
minorities, 63, 167–168
misrepresentation, avoiding, 175
MIT (Massachusetts Institute of
    Technology), 133
Moses Brown preparatory school,
    61–62
Muhlenberg College, 72–73, 102,
    290–296
myths of college admissions
    admission statistics, 7–8
    extracurriculars, the more the
        better, 3–4
    importance of well-rounded
        student, 3
    improving chances of acceptance,
        5
    improving odds/chances of
        acceptance, 5
    letters of reference, 5
    over-emphasis on preparatory
        schools, 8
    overloading admission office, 6
    recommendations, 5
    rejection factors, 4
    talent, 4
    too much competition, 6–7